The College and Community Development

Julian Martin Laub

The Praeger Special Studies program—utilizing the most modern and efficient book production techniques and a selective worldwide distribution network—makes available to the academic, government, and business communities significant, timely research in U.S. and international economic, social, and political development.

The College and Community Development

A Socioeconomic Analysis for Urban and Regional Growth

Praeger Publishers   New York   Washington   London

PRAEGER SPECIAL STUDIES IN U.S. ECONOMIC AND SOCIAL DEVELOPMENT

PRAEGER PUBLISHERS
111 Fourth Avenue, New York, N.Y. 10003, U.S.A.
5, Cromwell Place, London S.W.7, England

Published in the United States of America in 1972
by Praeger Publishers, Inc.

Library of Congress Catalog Card Number: 75-166397

Printed in the United States of America

This work was developed under a contract/grant
with the U.S. Office of Education, Department of
Health, Education and Welfare. However, the opinions
expressed herein do not necessarily reflect the
position or policy of that Agency, and no official
endorsement should be inferred.

For Naomi and Beth

Colleges established in urban and rural areas can aid in community and regional development. The purpose of this study is twofold: first, to describe the social and economic impact of the college on various communities and, second, to predict institution-related inputs that are basic to this impact. This analysis can assist the city and regional planner in making decisions on institutional location, expansion, and programming. Further, it can also aid in research and development work on social indicators, social-area analysis, and community-simulation models. Perhaps most important, it can help indicate the social and economic investment needed to transform a community to a desired level.

Important factors in community development include increases in retail trade, property values, family income, educational levels, and social interaction. The college presence can strongly affect these factors, based on five major inputs: These are professional and auxiliary staff, local and nonlocal students, college purchases, physical factors such as buildings, and visitors and miscellaneous agents.

Economic impact of the college basically depends on the proportion of staff and students living in the college community and the proportion of their expenditures made through local vendors. Social impact depends on the extent of staff and student interaction with local residents and institutions. Some proportion of the college input fails to enter the community and, instead, spills out to the region. Spillout varies for different localities, and although it may be inconsequential or beneficial for the region, it detracts from benefits obtained by the college community and may lessen its ability to support institution-related services.

The high input of social and human capital
augers change. As a group, professional staff is
generally above average in community-service potential and less conservative than other residents in
the community. Its influence on school-district
policy and local government can be substantial, especially in the small locality with a sizable community college. With planned impact, its effect on
the urban district can be considerable. Through university extension work and informal groups, college
and university faculties and students have engaged
in development of disadvantaged communities. They
have joined in a multiplicity of actions to assist
in extracurricular education and training programs,
to aid ghetto groups, and to affect a broad number of
solutions to local problems. They have also engaged
in activities counter to the views of some local fac-
tions. These considerations should be evaluated in
college and community planning.

Locational analysis of social and economic input
combined with the predictive techniques demonstrated
in this study can be useful in coordinating educational planning with area development and public-in-
vestment decisions. A wide number of computer-stored
items can be examined in impact analysis. The use
of spillout accounting can give a more accurate pic-
ture of the impact of the institution.

ACKNOWLEDGMENTS

This study was made possible through a grant from the U.S. Office of Education and the Division of Higher Education Facilities Planning of the New York State Education Department.

I am especially indebted to Professor Kermit C. Parsons, Chairman of the Department of City and Regional Planning, who inspired this work, and to Professors Parker Marden, Joan R. Egner, Wayne Thompson, Barclay G. Jones, and Allan G. Feldt who offered many helpful suggestions. However, I alone am responsible for any error or limitation in the study.

Many other individuals offered assistance in various phases of the research. These include President Kenneth E. Young, Dr. Clarence H. Bagley, Director of Institutional Planning, and Gene Krause, Director of the Computer Center at the State University of New York College at Cortland; President Leland Miles and Charles H. Schultz, Assistant to the President at Alfred University; President David H. Huntington and Orville Johnston, Assistant to the President at the State University of New York, Alfred Agricultural and Technical College, at Alfred; President Albert T. Skinner at Auburn Community College; and President Rhea M. Eckel, Dean Malcolm H. Forbes, and Peter A. Anderson at Cazenovia College; Dr. William Fuller and Dr. Robert H. McCambridge of the New York State Education Department, Division of Higher Education Facilities Planning, suggested various approaches and supplied data relative to higher education in New York State. Professor Harold Carpener, Head of the Department of Rural Sociology at the State University of New York Agricultural College at Cornell University, aided in administrative matters. A list of resource persons is included at the end of this study.

CONTENTS

APPENDIXES

LIST OF TABLES

xv

LIST OF ILLUSTRATIONS

The College and Community Development

1

THE COLLEGE
AND
THE
COLLEGE
COMMUNITY

In college planning and location, especially at
the two-year college level, decisionmaking has fo-
cused on county, two-county, and community benefit.
Although the region and state are considered the ul-
timate client, the latter is definitely subordinated
in making the final location decision. Recent wran-
gles over location in Sullivan County, Kings County,
Tompkins County, Mercer County, and other areas pre-
cisely indicate how the field for decision tapers
down to focus the argument between two or three communities and then to location within one of these
communities.[1]

In seeking to extend the benefits of the two-
year college, big-city ghetto areas, small towns,
and developing regions are frequently considered as
possible locations for the institution. Communities
have actively lobbied for the placement of state university colleges in their locality. The actual benefit derived by the community and its environs is in
question, and this study is directed toward determining the degree to which a locality benefits when
a college is so located.

PURPOSE OF THE STUDY

The purpose of this study is twofold: first, to describe the social and economic impact of the college on urban and rural communities and second, to predict institution-related inputs that are basic to this impact.

This analysis can assist the educational planner in making decisions on institutional location, expansion, and programming. It can aid the town planner in forecasting housing, commercial, and related needs.[2] It can also aid in planning the deliberate input of economic, social, and human capital into an area.[3]

In conjunction with the above purposes, the variation of input and impact with community size (population) will be explored. Of primary interest is whether the city and small town can retain a goodly portion of the stream of benefits generated by the college presence.

COLLEGE IMPACT ON A LOCALITY

When a college is located in a village or city, the input of jobs, students, college purchases, and other economic and social factors has important impact on the locality. Social and economic benefits depend, in large degree, on what proportion of the input stays in the community, at least in the first round of transactions. Benefits may rapidly diffuse to localities outside the college community and help develop surrounding areas. From the regional or state point of view, this may be a good thing. From the more parochial viewpoint of the local residents, especially business and real estate components, the first-round loss of benefits in substantial amount may defeat an important original goal, that of economic development, for the community.

One writer has stressed the importance of economic considerations from the viewpoint of a potential college-town's hosts:

> The economic value of a community college
> was evident from the beginning. . . .
> There was sentiment that the college would
> be "good for the county" economically, but
> probably this sentiment was at least
> matched if not overwhelmed in many cases
> [by the sentiment] that it would be "good
> for the town."[4]

Economic development is a highly important factor in
the potential college community's consideration, although most often its strongest reasons for establishing a new college center on a sincere desire to
bring advanced education and cultural activities to
the locality.

A full inventory of college impact on a locality
would include a multiplicity of items related to social, economic, and political factors and would involve land use, transportation, environmental health,
and other considerations. This study is only concerned with the college impact on selected factors
in community development: (a) economic factors such
as retail sales, property values, taxes, labor-force
size, family-income levels, and demand for town services; (b) sociological factors such as educational
levels, housing quality, degree of social interaction,
and social attitudes; and (e) political factors such
as those affecting local government, school-district
administration, political attitudes, and community
action.

STATE PLANNING FOR
HIGHER EDUCATION

In most states, governmental planning for higher
education is centralized at the state level. State
agencies affect decisions on disbursement of funds,
enrollment, staff size, college location, expansion,
and long-range planning for public colleges, as well
as on state financial and other aid for private institutions. Consequently, the decisions of the state

agency bear upon the community and region as well as
on educational development.

Many states are expanding their facilities for
higher education by establishment or extension of a
system of state colleges. The primary intent of
these programs of expansion is to broaden the acces-
sibility of higher education to state residents and
to aid economic and social development of urban and
rural areas by a beneficial output of the educational
plant. The latter is aimed at deriving direct and
indirect economic and social benefits for the community as well as for the student.

In some states, large investments in higher educational facilities already have been made. California, New York, and Pennsylvania have matured and
extensive systems; Connecticut, Massachusetts, and
many other states more recently have engaged heavily
in this area of investment.[5]

In the New York State University system, community colleges and technical colleges have been established in over thirty rural and urban locations, and
new colleges are in the planning stage. The goal of
the State University of New York (SUNY) has been to
have a two-year college within commuting distance of
95 percent of the state's population by 1970.[6] Typical of the colleges placed in relatively rural areas
are those in Chautauguc, Cayuga, Sullivan, and Allegany counties.[7] Colleges recently established in
metropolitan areas include Schenectady, Onandaga
(Syracuse), and Kingsboro (Brooklyn) community colleges. Private colleges have also developed and expanded in response to increased enrollment needs.

The above-indicated programs can result in problems of deep concern for urban and rural area development.[8] These problems include the need to estimate
potential social and economic benefits and burdens
yielded to specific areas in which colleges have been
located and in which future colleges are planned.
On the darker side, so-called town-and-gown conflict
can occur.[9] Even substantial state university investment can be economically ineffective or weak in

community development, and there is the possibility that a college ineffectively located can tend to be a liability for the community. This is especially so when problems of land use, sociocultural differences, and requirements for town services are weighed against the college's potential as an income generator and as an educational and cultural factor.

This study must initially acknowledge that education is the primary task of the college or university. However, from a broader point of view, the college can be a key factor in city, rural, or regional development.[10] When a college is located in a community, input to the area includes social, economic, political, psychological, and physical factors transmitted through the presence of staff, students, and college activities. These factors can be thought of as units of economic, political, social, and human capital that may either enrich or detract from an area and that alter its basic characteristics and operation.

FUNDAMENTAL FACTORS IN INPUT, SPILLOUT, AND IMPACT OF THE COLLEGE POPULATION

The residential distribution patterns of staff members and students are fundamental in assessing the college's potential effect on social and economic development in an area. The degree of input to a locality, the proportion of leakage, and the amount of interaction of staff, students, and community residents are important modifiers in determing the degree of change or potential for change generated by the presence of a college. In sum, the amount of college community and regional change and development depends on initial and operational inputs and their interaction in the area considered.

Consequently, to study impact on a location due to the presence of a college, it is first necessary to study the population input and its characteristics, activity, and location. Second, it is necessary to relate this study to such key factors in social and

economic growth and community development as family
income, property values, commercial development, attitudes, and educational levels.

A village, city, or region presents a tableau
of characteristics dependent on population distribution, activity, and land use. This tableau changes
with time. The isolated and relatively inactive village may remain either stable or may show decline.
The large city ferments in rapid change with inmigration of people and their activity. Interaction within
a village, city, or region causes change as well as
in- or outmigration.

This study is first concerned with the initial
input due to the injection of public and private institutions into an area. Next, it is concerned with
the impact or internal reaction and interaction of
the injected matrix with the previously existing tableau. A key point is that if we wish to focus growth
and development within a limited area either to
create a strong point, to create change, or for other
reasons of policy, it is necessary to determine the
actual input of people, dollars, and other social and
economic factors to that area. In seeking to estimate actual input to a locality by the college, it
is necessary to evaluate the amount of leakage of
the basic effort. An important consideration is determination of the proportion of college components
that either never enter the locality in order to provide benefits (or costs) and the amount that spills
out after entering the locality's boundaries.

FORMAT FOR THE STUDY

Chart 1 is a guide to the format of this study.
Input and leakage of economic or social units are
depicted by use of a flow chart for college components. In the diagram, I represents a unit of input
deposited within the boundaries of a locality, and S
is a unit externally incurred owing to leakage or
spillout.[11] Economic inputs of a similar nature,
such as flow of funds into a locality, can be summed.[12]
Social units are generally not additive unless they

CHART 1

Flow Chart: Distribution of Social, Economic, and
Physical Factors Related to College Input

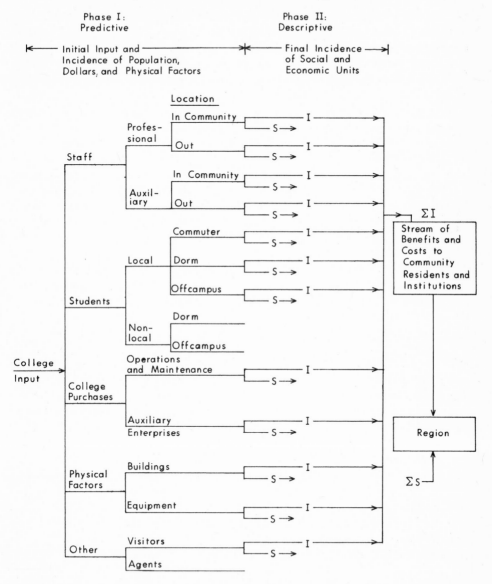

(I) = Units of input to the community.
(S) = Units of spillout to the external world.

can be assigned an agreed-upon dollar value or other
quantitative evaluation in a given category.

As indicated in the flow chart, the study basically is divided into two phases. The first phase
considers predictive factors involving input of college staff and students to the college community or
other locations. The second phase is descriptive
and analyzes the interaction of the college population
in regard to selected social and economic factors
operating within the community.

Another important factor to consider in evaluating impact of the institution is the location of
purchases made by the college acting as a corporate
unit. In some instances, this incidence can be predicted, and it then becomes possible to forecast the
impact of college purchasing on the local and regional economy.

Physical factors shown in the flow chart are
generally fixed by an arbitrary decision to expand
or not to expand and are not analyzed in this study
The impact of visitors, and other agents, is also
omitted.

As shown in Chart 1, a stream of social and
economic benefits and costs (I) enter the college
town along with the input of population, dollars,
and facilities. This has impact on the community and
causes local and regional change and development.
When units of spillout (S) occur, they have a direct
impact on the area surrounding the locality. It is
important to estimate the extent of spillout in determining the actual impact of the instrument of
change--in this study, an institution.[13] We also
wish to determine whether spillout varies with community size (population) and location.

Spillout results in cost or benefit to a locality. For example, the movement of retail trade
or of the wealthier segments of the population to
locations outside a community is most often detri-
mental to the locality sustaining this loss, but it
is beneficial to the receiving area. On the other

hand, increased demand for town services by an increased population can also burden a city. Spillout
may not be a direct problem from the regional point
of view (and may often benefit the region), but it
can yield a heavy burden at the county, town, or
village level and even severely hamper the large
city.[14] Eventually, regional effects become evident.

This study will examine the variation of spillout with community size and location in predicting
factors affecting community change and development.
A prime concern is the potential of the public and
private college as an instrument for planned input
of social and economic factors into a community. A
device for prediction of the levels and effects of
this input is sought along with a demonstration and
explanation of spillout of college staff, dollars,
and other social factors.

Study Limitations

A complete outline for examination of this the-
sis would consider the gamut of college and college
community characteristics and the incidence of social
and economic factors involved. To explore this fully
would require extensive investigation beyond the
scope of this effort; this study makes a partial at-
tack on the problem with special concern for predictive elements and presents a methodology for further
analysis.

The localities studied are necessarily a fraction of the total panoply of college communities in
New York State. They cannot offer exact models for
educational and town planners. However, they can
provide insight into social and economic interaction
and problems found in the college community. Colleges in both urban and rural settings were considered. Although the intent is to apply this research
to college-community analysis in the large and small
city, the smaller cities (Auburn, Cortland, Poughkeepsie, etc.) and rural towns (Alfred, Cazenovia,
Geneseo, etc.) were selected for study because these
offered better boundary conditions and sharper analysis of locational factors in population, dollar

flow, and other socioeconomic input. The study's
techniques can be applied to impact analysis of a
college in the Bedford-Stuyvesant area of Brooklyn
as well as to that of Buffalo University in the Am-
herst area near Buffalo, and to Stony Brook on Long
Island. The impact of the expanding (existing) college as well as that of the relatively new college
is considered.

For a study and prediction of staff residential
spillout, thirty-nine college communities were examined for New York State. Size minimums were necessarily imposed on the colleges studies in order to
obtain data exhibiting significant impact and to
analyze a stabilized situation. The colleges examined
had from 400 to 5,000 undergraduate students enrolled
in 1964.[15] They were located in communities with
1960 populations above 1,000 and ranged on up to agglomerations near the 80,000 level.[16] Techniques and
methods used in making this study are described in
detail in Appendix A.

The Hypotheses

As indicated above, this study is divided into
two phases. The first considers the input of the
college population, dollars, and other elements into
the college community and surrounding region. The
second considers interaction of these elements with
local counterparts.

Area change and the impact of benefits on a college community and its environs depend in good measure on the input and interaction of the college
staff, the proportion of local students attending and
commuting to the college, and the point of impact of
college purchases. Concurrent with this view and
relative to the colleges selected for study, the following hypotheses were examined in Phase I:

Hypothesis I. The proportion of professional
staff residing in a college community is a function
of college-community size (population).

Hypothesis II. The proportion of auxiliary staff residing in a college community is a function of college-community size.

Hypothesis III. The number of local students enrolled at a college is a function of college community size.

Hypothesis IV. The proportion of local students commuting to a college from a sector outside the college town is a function of the radial distance from that sector to the college.

Hypothesis V. Major cities within the region of a college attract its purchasing dollar in accordance with a gravity model.

In Phase II of this study, data obtained at specific colleges were analyzed to determine significant socioeconomic factors relating to the analysis of Phase I. Basic input and spillout determinations made in Phase I were elaborated on, as was the potential of the college as an instrument of change in community and regional development. A variety of factors that increase the burden and benefit for a locality were given consideration.

HISTORICAL FACTORS IN NEW YORK STATE HIGHER EDUCATION

Shortly after World War II, it became apparent that great expansion would be needed for the system of colleges in New York State. Higher education had been predominantly a private effort. In 1948, the state supported thirty-two colleges, schools, and institutes of higher education, but enrollment was only about 30 percent of the state's total, including the public colleges in New York City. If New York were to meet its growing needs in higher education, a larger measure of state and local governmental participation was needed. A commission was appointed to investigate the situation. It recommended a program of greatly expanded operations and establishment of the State University as a corporate entity.[17]

Population factors relative to the college-age group had an important influence on the growth of the higher education system. Between 1940 and 1950, the eighteen-to-twenty-one-year age group dropped from 923,000 to 788,000. It decreased again between 1950 and 1955 and reached a low of just under 700,000. A turnabout occurred between 1955 and 1960, and by 1965, the college-age group rose to above 7 million.[18]

However, college enrollments do not depend solely on the size of the college-age group. Social factors exert a high influence. During 1940-55, although the college-age group decreased substantially, enrollment increased from 195,000 to 325,000. Returning war veterans and societal changes that required more college training had created a new enrollment pattern.

The above situation applied to both public and private colleges in New York State. At State University colleges, enrollment especially increased after 1960. The State University's fifty-nine different campuses, including community colleges, enrolled 138,027 full-time students and 82,968 part-time students in the fall of 1967. In the following year, the State University's projected full-time enrollment rose to 164,081, with a part-time projected enrollment of 98,383. This represented an increase over 1967 of 18.9 percent and 19.6 percent, respectively, in these categories.[19]

The rapid growth of the State University can also be seen in the increasing operational budgets of selected colleges in New York State. Table 1.1 indicates that appropriations approximately tripled between 1950 and 1960. It is important to note that the amounts allocated for personal service in these budgets were about 85 percent of the total.[20] A major component in economic impact of the college is salaries and wages to staff. By 1968, recommended budget appropriations were over five times those recommended in 1960, and several of the liberal arts colleges had budgets above the $8-million mark.

Many public and private colleges in New York State are located outside metropolitan areas. Because

TABLE 1.1

Operational Budget of Selected Colleges in New York State
(recommended appropriations)

| | 1949-50 | | | | | 1959-60 | | | | | 1968-69 |
| | Personal Service[a] | | Other Maintenance and Operation[b] | | Grand Total[c] | Personal Service[a] | | Other Maintenance and Operation[b] | | Grand Total[c] | Grand Total |
	($)	(%)	($)	(%)	($)	($)	(%)	($)	(%)	($)	($)
Brockport	392,952	84.0	70,567	15.1	467,519	1,151,347	85.7	165,200	12.3	1,341,547	8,125,400
Cortland	493,780	84.6	85,398	14.7	582,513	1,545,521	88.8	193,300	11.1	1,738,821	7,698,078
Geneseo	358,102	85.4	61,560	14.7	419,662	1,060,664	85.8	139,700	11.6	1,200,364	7,167,961
New Paltz	404,267	85.4	68,921	14.5	473,688	1,210,168	87.2	178,350	12.8	1,388,518	9,517,900
Alfred Ag. & Tech.	264,550	87.4	38,250	12.6	302,800	698,432	85.9	114,500	14.1	812,932	4,294,000

a personal service includes administration, instruction, maintenance, and temporary service.

b other maintenance and operation includes traveling and automotive expense, general office supplies and expense, printing and advertising, communication, fuel, light, power, water, household, laundry and refrigerating supplies and expense, medical, surgical and laboratory supplies and expense, farm and garden supplies and expense, special supplies and expense, repairs, and rentals.

c Grand totals for 1949-50 and 1959-60 may include miscellaneous payments for services and expenses such as closed-circuit television. These payments are not listed under personal service or other maintenance and operation categories.

Source: State of New York, The Executive Budget, Volume 1, 1949-50, 1959-60, and 1968-69 (Albany: State of New York, 1949, 1959, and 1968).

large proportions of college faculty and students at
these colleges are initially from metropolitan centers, a high input of social and economic benefits
accrues to the hinterland.

INPUT OF POPULATION TO AN AREA

Formal investigations of social and economic impact of the college on the community are few in number, and most researchers in this area have utilized
studies and techniques from related fields in seeking
to assemble a pertinent body of literature.[21] However, in analyzing the effect of the college on community and area growth and development, our approach
is to initially determine population input as a fundamental factor in impact and then to examine the
degree of interaction or activity of the population
as a modifying factor. We also seek predictive elements for this input.

One writer dramatically describes the impact of
population input to an area at the beginning of his
text:

> A birth occurs. The need for an additional
> hospital worker becomes urgent. A southern
> field hand and his family migrate to New
> York. Income of the New York region rises.
> Gross regional product as well as household
> expenditures and government outlays in New
> York edge up.[22]

Birth and inmigration are two primary sources of population increase for an area. The latter, especially,
is a familiar situation in the college community, and
it is particularly so during a period of increased
enrollment in higher education. Primary sources of
inmigration are new staff at the expanding college
and the large body of transient students.

The literature generally predicts total staff
employed at a college via student-faculty ratios or
other enrollment-based relationships.[23] However,
analysis of the impact of college-staff inmigration

to the college community has been largely ignored.
An empirical model for estimating population increase
in a locality as a result of a defense-plant installation has been developed.[24] The model depends on a
knowledge of the number of direct personnel needed
at the plant and the size of the town involved. However, its application to the collegiate institution
is limited.

Researchers have found that population input to
a locality in response to industrial and other development does not always follow a pattern. This is
especially the case in predominantly rural areas.

> We expect to find a strong urban center with
> tributary rural, suburban, and satellite
> settlements in the hinterland. We look in
> vain for this pattern. . . . Although many
> of the manufacturing activities are located
> in urban centers, these centers are not
> large enough in size really to support them.
> The labor force . . . has to be recruited
> from a larger region . . . ratios, such as
> one worker in an industry of this kind,
> would eventually result in eight additional
> people being added to the population . . .
> do not seem to apply in this region at all.[25]

The labor force is supplied from scattered locations
in the region, and commutes to the new employment
center.

This is often the case with defense plants: A
large proportion of employees commute to their jobs,
and the pay checks that leave the area reduce the
economic advantage that would otherwise accrue to
local retail businesses and other economic enterprises in the community. When analysis is made, high
spillout rates for employee-residence location are
evident.[26]

Relative to student input, several investigators
have attempted to predict college-student enrollment
by state and by county with good results. John R.
Stewart worked on enrollment at Princeton and Harvard,

by states, and he found that the number of undergraduates coming from an area was approximately proportional to its population and inversely proportional
to its distance from the college.[27]

Other investigators have also used a gravity
model in predicting student enrollment. Harold Mc-
Connell studied enrollment at the county level; he
used total population and population weighted by per
capita income in the numerator and distance squared
in the denominator. With enrollment as the dependent
variable, regression equations were obtained, with
R-squared values of 0.82 and 0.84. Enrollment was
overpredicted for those counties closer to other large
colleges and for those most distant from the home
base; it was underpredicted for counties with highest
population and per capita income.[28]

Herbert G. Kariel also worked at the county level
and studied student enrollment and tested population
size and highway distance to the estimated population
center of the county.[29] Others have used a gravity
model with a time-distance-cost variable in the denominator and empirically derived exponents for distance to obtain better prediction of student enrollment. Still others have applied weights to population
and distance or added other relevant variables to
form a regression equation. Additional methods have
also been used to predict student enrollment at colleges. They are generally based on high school and
population projections, college-age population, and
regional trends in enrollment.[30]

SOCIOECONOMIC IMPACT OF
THE COLLEGE POPULATION

The impact of staff and students on the college
community can be divided into benefit and burden columns; these can be subdivided into economic, social,
and cultural categories.

A few investigations have been made of the direct
financial impact of the college on its community and
region. These involve determination of the amount of

institutional input to the area's flow of funds and include an analysis of college income and disbursements as well as student and staff expenditures.

Student purchases have been found difficult to measure; although students living in a college dormitory or at home indicate some regularity in outlays, data on students living in private facilities show great variation.[31] A survey in Bridgeport, Connecticut, indicated that durable items were generally purchased at home or outside the college area, and local expenditures were made for food, cigarettes, gasoline, telephone calls, and other items. In Bridgeport, about 70 percent of the full-time students were drawn from outside the region. Thus, higher education is an important source of employment and income for the area and functions as a so-called export industry.

Impact studies at Cornell University concluded that this institution generated over $100 million in income in Tompkins County through payrolls, college purchasing, student rentals, state aid, local taxes, construction, student spending, and other categories. In another study in New York State, Roy Gerard investigated the economic impact of Le Moyne College on the Syracuse community; this included an analysis of staff, student, and college expenditures.[32]

At a theoretical and practical level, an input-output approach to analysis of college expenditures was used to determine the extent of the University of Colorado's impact on Boulder, Denver, and the State of Colorado. The multiplier derived by Ernest R. Bonner indicated that for every $1.00 spent by the university, $1.37 worth of sales resulted in the Boulder area. The multiplier was based on a summation of direct, indirect, and induced expenditures. A regression equation was also developed to show the relationship between enrollment and annual operating expenditures, and these were indirectly related to sectoral employment.[33] Werner Z. Hirsch and Burton A. Weisbrod analyzed the direct and indirect benefits and costs of public education for a school district. In addition to direct costs featured in the usual

educational budget, indirect costs cited included the
following: (a) costs for community, county, and district services, (b) expenses for students and parents,
and (c) earnings foregone by students while at college.   Among the benefits cited were the following:
(a) the incremental productivity and disposable income of students and their parents, (b) increased
money inflow into the county, (c) tax reduction and
service improvement for nonstudent families resulting
from the graduating student's increased income, (d)
increased literacy and more effective citizenry, and
(e) increased income for interacting area inhabitants
and firms.[34]

On the other hand, the economic burden of the
college presence on the town is most often evident
in its use of community services, in traffic conges-
tion and parking, and in tax exemption.   Other dis-
advantages to the town may result from campus expansion and heavy demands on local housing.

Although universities often provide their own
police, fire, and refuse-disposal services, some
overflow frequently falls on the locality.   To com-
pound the problems involved, college communities may
experience a decrease in their taxable property along
with an increase in nontaxable property, especially
when universities seek to expand in locations where
there is insufficient land to provide for community
needs.   Furthermore, insufficient dormitory facilities
may cause neighborhood decay, and poor housing for
students and other community residents subsequently
increases the need for town services.[35]   These and
other burdens become greater as universities and
their college population grow.

In a broader perspective, studies have indicated
that every increment of 1,000 residents necessitates
additions of 4.8 elementary, and 3.6 high school,
rooms, 100,000 gallons of water, 1.8 policemen, 1.5
new firemen, and 8.8 acres of land for schools and
recreation areas.[36]   These needs multiply as the
graduate, undergraduate, and staff population grows,
and the college community must be able to supply these
needed services and functions that develop when a

college is newly implanted or expanded. It can only
do this with a sound financial base that expands with
the college.

Lloyd L. Hogan identified three primary measures
of the fiscal ability of local governments.[37] These
are based on per capita values of personal income,
property values, retail sales, and related modifiers.[38]
These measures are highly dependent on population and
labor-force characteristics as well as commercial development. When a college staff composed of professional and auxiliary personnel with salary levels
above those generally prevailing in the typical rural
area is injected into a town through the college instrument, the area obtains greater fiscal ability
along with the added burden. However, the amount of
additional fiscal ability depends on the actual input of staff to the community and its contribution
to the locality's tax revenues and economic health.

Analysis of the economic impact of a college on
a community indicates only part of the total benefits
accrued.[39] It is necessary also to consider social
and political factors, especially when institutions
of higher education are involved. Reliable social
indexes can assist in this broader analysis, and
their utilization is described in subsequent chapters.

REGIONAL PLANNING

In evaluating the impact of the college on the
community, it is also important to consider regional
implications. In effect, the college has impact on
the community, and the community has impact on the
region. Conversely, regional development affects
the community and the college. Existing regional and
urban theory presents some insight into the relationship between college impact and community size (population) and also offers guidance for the planning
of college location with a view toward city and regional benefit.

John Friedmann has assigned a major creative
role to the university in regional development. For

maximization of its benefit, the institution should
be located at a regional growth point selected for
activation.[40] Friedmann favors the concentration of
large public infrastructure investments in the bigger
cities. A cost-benefit analysis should be made, and
the investment's relationship to other projects and
programs should be carefully considered.[41]

The city is a device for organizing economic
life, and its efficiency in the collecting, processing, and distributing function determines the vi-
tality of the region. Incidence of economic growth
generally varies with distance from the central city.
However, for regional development, it is important
to activate new core regions and corridors of growth
and to draw population from poor and undeveloped districts.[42]

The small college can serve the rural area and
the city that is in a position to take advantage of
its impact. Placement of a college in a locality can
help attract additional central services and amenities and can draw industry and tertiary activity.
The college can help diversify the community, increase
social interaction, and offer a strong center or
focal point.

In evaluating the small town as a place for public investment, caution is advised by some, optimism
generated by others, and judgment delayed by a third
group of theorists and researchers. First, the low
economic multiplier of the small town lessens the
local impact of the investment dollar. Second, the
economic uncertainty and instability of small towns
cause concern. There are no clear-cut answers as to
their future, and, for many years, writers have predicted the decline or demise of the small town. These
predictions have been based on technological changes
in farming and transportation and the increased concentration of activities and population in large centers. More recently, industry has been moving into
rural areas, and a cautious optimism has developed.[43]
Demographers in the U.S. Department of Agriculture
have indicated that the twentieth-century flow of
population from rural areas to the cities has leveled
off and is at a low point.[44]

Wilbur R. Thompson stated that with the development of the highway system and the widespread ownership of automobiles small- and medium-sized urban
areas tend to interrelate in a loose network. By en-
gaging in complementary functions, a grouping of
towns and small cities may attain the critical size
in development needed to preserve the collective
existence of the member localities. A college or
university may play an important part in this informal
federation by providing additional educational, cultural, and social factors and in generating recreational amenities.[45]

If location factors are favorable, economic
growth will readily take place, but where natural
economic advantages are low, economic-development
programs have only limited success.[46] The small college that acts alone and is without appreciable commercial and industrial development to complement its
activities cannot be expected to economically and
socially transform an area. On the other hand, adding a college to the existing infrastructure of a
large town may yield more efficient use of that infrastructure in addition to attracting new industry
and services.

NOTES

1. Pierre Clavel, "The Genesis of the Planning
Process: Experts and Citizen Boards" (unpublished
Ph.D. dissertation, Cornell University, 1966), pp.
70-100; see also The Ithaca Journal, January 4-March
6, 1969; Dennis A. Rondinelli, "Establishing a Com-
munity College: The Public Decision Process, A Case
Study" (unpublished paper, City and Regional Planning
Department, Cornell University, 1966), pp. 33-39;
also The New York Times, January 21-April 21, 1964.
The locations cited are in New York State and New
Jersey.

2. Coordination between urban and educational
planners is especially important in community development. Governmental planning agencies have great
power to shape the development of areas under their

jurisdiction.   However, tools are needed to effectuate
social and economic change.   The college is one such
tool, and this study is an evaluation of the educational institution as an instrument in urban and regional development.   The development of rural areas
with potential is discussed in Edgar M. Hoover, The
Location of Economic Activity (New York: McGraw
Hill, 1963), pp. 196-200 and 241-50.   Of interest in
planning for urban development is John Friedmann,
"The Strategy of Deliberate Urbanization," Journal
of the American Institute of Planners, XXXIV, 6 (November, 1968).   The utilization of the educational
institution in planned community change is described
in Dorothy D. Bourne and James R. Bourne, Thirty
Years of Change in Puerto Rico, A Case Study of Ten
Selected Rural Areas (New York: Frederick A. Praeger,
1966), pp. 218-65.   Social, economic, and political
implications in state planning for a community are
concisely described in Ada Louise Huxtable, "The
State Office Building Dilemma," The New York Times,
Section 2, Architecture, November 2, 1969.

3.   Human resources have been referred to as a
form of capital by many economists, including Adam
Smith, H. von Thunen, and, more recently, by Irving
Fisher and Theodore Schultz.   See Theodore Schultz,
"Investment in Human Capital," The American Economic
Review, LI (March, 1961), pp. 2-17.   See also Gary S.
Becker, "Underinvestment in College Education," The
American Economic Review, L (May, 1960), pp. 346-54;
and Gary S. Becker, Human Capital (New York: Colum-
bia University Press, 1964), p. 50.

4.   Clavel, op. cit., pp. 70-72.   In a broad
view, Talcott Parsons discusses input-output inter-
changes between societal levels and subsystems, with
special reference to the area of education; see Parsons, "General Theory in Sociology," in Robert K.
Merton, Leonard Broom, and Leonard S. Cottrell, Jr.,
eds., Sociology Today, Problems and Prospects (New
York: Harper and Row, 1959), pp. 3-37.

5.   "The Campus Boom: A New College a Week,"
Newsweek (February 20, 1967), pp. 65-73.   Expansion
of higher education in relation to manpower needs is

discussed in Frederick Harbison and Charles A. Myers, Education, Manpower, and Economic Growth, Strategies in Human Resource Development (New York: McGraw Hill, 1964), pp. 195-96. See also Herbert S. Parnes, Forecasting Educational Needs for Educational and Social Development (Paris: Organization for Economic Cooperation and Development, 1962); Fritz Machlup, The Production and Distribution of Knowledge in the United States (Princeton: Princeton University Press, 1962); and A. H. Halsey, Jean Floud, and C. Arnold Anderson, eds., Education, Economy, and Society (New York: Free Press of Glencoe, 1962), pp. 15-52.

6. New York State Division of the Budget, "The Executive Budget, Fiscal Year April 1, 1968 to March 31, 1969," submitted by Nelson A. Rockefeller, Governor (Albany: New York State Division of the Budget, 1968), p. 980.

7. State University of New York, The Regents Tentative Statewide Plan for the Expansion and Development of Higher Education, 1964 (Albany: State Education Department, 1965), p. 4.

8. Vincent J. Moore, Buffalo-Amherst Urban Impact Study Design (Albany: New York State Office of Planning Coordination, 1968), pp. 13-15.

9. Kermit C. Parsons, "Universities and Cities: The Terms of Truce Between Them," Journal of Higher Education, XXXIV (April, 1963), pp. 205-16. See also Delbert C. Miller, "Town and Gown: The Power Structure of a University Town," American Journal of Sociology, LXVIII, 4 (January, 1963), pp. 432-43; Peter H. Rossi and Robert A. Dentler, The Politics of Urban Renewal (New York: Free Press of Glencoe, 1961). See Wilbert E. Moore, The Impact of Industry, "Modernization of Traditional Societies Series" (Englewood Cliffs, N.J.: Prentice Hall, Inc., 1965), pp. 89-90. Moore points out that changes in social structure have wide ramifications: Rural areas lose their rural character; isolation and self-sufficiency of the village is steadily eroded; no amount of

nostalgic regret is likely to preserve or restore
the qualities of rural life if economic growth per-
sists and proceeds; the old order is soon transformed.
The broad impact of the campus on national and local
political and social life is demonstrated especially
in the peace movement; see The New York Times, November 16, 1969.

10. A major creative role in the development of
downward transitional areas can be played by the university, especially in the area of research and planning. See William H. Starbuck, "Evaluation and
Prospectus: School of Business Administration,
Clarion State College" (Ithaca, N.Y.: Cornell University, 1968), pp. 17-34. (Mimeographed.) See also
John Friedmann, Regional Development Policy, A Case
Study of Venezuela (Cambridge: Massachusetts Institute of Technology Press, 1966), pp. 95-101.

11. To describe leakage of economic and social
factors to areas outside a locality's political
boundaries we will use the term spillout. The terms
spillout and spillover, as used in this study, relate
to their use by Burton A. Weisbrod, External Benefits
of Public Education (Princeton, N.J.: Industrial
Relations Section, Princeton University, Research Report Series No. 105, 1964), pp. 1-8. See also Werner
Z. Hirsch, Elbert W. Segelhorst, and Morton J. Marcus,
Spillover of Public Education Costs and Benefits (Los
Angeles: University of California, Institute of
Government and Public Affairs, 1964), p. 175. Also
see Roland N. McKean, Efficiency in Government
Through Systems Analysis (New York: John Wiley and
Sons, Inc., 1958), pp. 134-36; he uses the term spillover in describing neighborhood effect, "impacts of
actions by some decisionmaking units on the activities
of others, impacts that are not directly felt by the
first group. . . . Thus, the cost of doing the family
laundry is increased as smoke-producing factories expand their operation." Weisbrod uses the term spillover to describe "geographically externalized benefits . . . which accrue to persons outside a district." Spillout of benefits are beneficial to those
outside the district and represent a loss to those
inside the district.

12.   Michael K. Mischaikow and Thaddeus H. Spratlen, "A Regional Impact Model for Measuring the Flow-
of-Funds and Income Effect Generated by Institutions
of Higher Learning," Annals of Regional Science, I
(December, 1967), pp. 196-212. Mischaikow and Spratlen have developed a model for measuring the economic
impact of a college on its locality and on the external world. Their model can be applied to evaluate
total inflow and outflow of funds owing to the college
presence. Categories in the model are the external
sector (D), the local sector (L), visitors (V), the
capital sector (K), auxiliary enterprises (A), faculty
and staff (F), the student body (S), and the institution (C). The interaction of these sectors is indicated, and equations are set up to identify the
flow of funds (E) between the sectors. For example,
outflow of funds (Q) from the local sector (L) is
indicated by

$$Q_l = \Sigma E_l \text{ or}$$

$$Q_l = E_{l_c} + E_{l_s} + E_{l_f}$$

The first lower-case letter shows the source or
disbursing sector, and the second indicates the re-
cipient of the outlay. For example, E_{l_c} indicates
outlay of the local sector to the college. This can
occur as a return on services rendered, rentals, or
through other transactions. Flow of funds (Y) to
the local sector is indicated by

$$Y_l = \Sigma E_l \text{ or}$$

$$Y_l = E_{c_l} + E_{f_l} + E_{a_l} + E_{k_l} + E_{v_l}$$

where, for example, E_{c_l} indicates the outlay of the
college to the local sector. In similar manner, a
series of other equations are indicated for each
sector's inflow and outflow of funds. One of our
major interests is flow of funds to the local sector
and to outside the local sector from the college's
components or sectors.

13.   Many other instruments are available to governmental agencies for effecting change. Examples include low-cost housing, recreational areas, and armed-forces bases; financial instruments include government contracts, federal and state aid, and taxation. The college matrix is treated in this discussion as one component in the total community. Its impact adds to that of others, as it interacts with other components.

14.   Raymond Vernon, The Changing Economic Function of the Central City (New York: Committee for Economic Development, 1959), pp. 40-62.

15.   State Education Department, Division of Higher Education, Going to College in New York State (Albany: University of the State of New York, 1965), pp. 112-45. Cornell University was not included in this study because it is remote and alone in its size characteristic.

16.   U.S. Bureau of the Census, U.S. Census of Population: 1960, Volume I, Characteristics of the Population, Part 34, New York (Washington, D.C.: U.S. Government Printing Office, 1963).

17.   State of New York, Report of the Temporary Commission on the Need for a State University (Albany: Williams Press, Inc., 1948), pp. 7-20.

18.   State University of New York, The Master Plan (Albany: State University of New York, 1960).

19.   New York State Division of the Budget, op. cit., p. 429.

20.   Community colleges have operated on a somewhat different budget arrangement. The State University reports that personal-service expenditures for twenty-eight community colleges ranged between 58 percent and 82 percent of their total budgets, and many of the colleges operated in the 65-75-percent range. See New York State Division of the Budget, "Community Colleges, Budget Analysis 1965-1966" (unpublished report; Albany: State University

of New York, 1966). The community college derives
much of its income from local sources; other colleges
in the state system obtain the greater proportion of
their funds from nonlocal sources, and these funds
are funneled into the area through the state university system. Private colleges operating on similar
budget rations and funds from student tuition and
other sources again attract money to the area. Because private colleges generally draw more students
from outside the community and from outside the state
than do the public colleges, the former act to increase local funds in greater degree.

21. Ernest R. Bonner, "The Economic Impact of
a University on Its Local Community," Journal of the
American Institute of Planners, XXXIV (September,
1968), pp. 339-43.

22. Walter Isard, Methods of Regional Analysis:
An Introduction to Regional Science (Cambridge:
Massachusetts Institute of Technology Press, 1960),
p. 1.

23. New York State Division of the Budget, op.
cit., pp. 446-48. See also Bonner, op. cit.

24. Clark N. Crain, A Prediction Model for Popu-
lation Impact by Military Installations, Part II,
Operations Analysis Standby Unit, University of Den-
ver (Springfield, Va.: U.S. Department of Commerce,
Clearinghouse for Federal Scientific and Technical
Information, Sills Building, 1959), pp. 3-10.

25. Barclay G. Jones and Jon T. Lang, Studies
in Regional Development: Population, Activities,
and Incomes in Chenango, Delaware, and Otsego Counties (Ithaca: Cornell University, New York State
College of Agriculture, 1965), pp. 120-21. See also
Wilbert E. Moore, op. cit., pp. 76-80.

26. Gerald Breese, comp., The Impact of Large
Installations on Nearby Areas, prepared by the Bureau
of Urban Research, Princeton University (Port Hueneme,
Calif.: U.S. Naval Civil Engineering Laboratory,
1965), pp. 240-41 and 256. The Breese compilation

indicates the impact of additional population on income, employment, housing, schools, utilities, and other municipal services as well as on community attitudes, tax rates, and other problems.

27.   John R. Stewart, "The 'Gravitation' or Geographical Power of a College," Bulletin of the American Association of University Professors, XXVII (1941), pp. 70-75. The gravity model is derived by analogy from Newton's formulas for mass-distance relationships. When applied to population, this model can take the following form:

$$I_{ij} = G \frac{P_i P_j}{D_{ij}^b}$$

Where: I_{ij} = the total number of units resulting from the interaction between factors at points i and j,

P_i and P_j = population at areas i and j, respectively

D_{ij} = distance between area i and area j

G = a constant of proportionality

b = an exponent, most often varying between values of 1 and 2

A broad discussion of the gravity model occurs in Isard, op. cit., pp. 496-533, with applications describing population interaction and the spatial distribution of human activities. The gravity model is used in analysis of telephone calls, express shipments, money flows, market potential, social participation, and other phenomena.

28.   Harold McConnell, "Spatial Variability of College Enrollment as a Function of Migration Potential," The Professional Geographer, XVII (1965), pp. 29-37.

29.   Herbert G. Kariel, "Student Enrollment and Spatial Interaction," Annals of Regional Science,

II, 2 (December, 1968), pp. 114-25.

30.   Kermit C. Parsons, "The Potential Demand for
Higher Education in the Chemung Valley Region to
1985" (report to the Executive Committee of the Che-
mung Valley Study of Higher Education, Ithaca, N.Y.:
March 11, 1968).   (Mimeographed.)   See also Ronald
B. Thompson, Enrollment Projections for Higher Educa-
tion 1961-1978, American Association of Collegiate
Registrars and Admissions Officers (Washington, D.C.:
American Council on Education, 1961); Michael Brick,
The Need for Higher Education Facilities in the Mo-
hawk Valley (New York: Teachers College, Columbia
University, 1965); F. Stuart Chapin, Jr., Urban Land
Use Planning (Urbana, Ill.:   University of Illinois
Press, 1965), pp. 196-216 and 444-48; and Isard,
op. cit., pp. 5-79 offer detailed discussions on
population projection, migration estimation, and
school enrollment.

31.   Frances S. Doody, The Immediate Economic Impact of Higher Education in New England (Boston:
Bureau of Business Research, Boston University, 1961);
Ralph G. Wells, ed., The Economic Value of Educational Institutions to New England, New England Council Education Study (Boston: Bureau of Business Research, Boston University, College of Business
Administration, 1951).

32.   John L. Kraushaar, "How Much of an Asset Is
a College?" College and University Business, XXXVI, 2
(February, 1964), pp. 43-45; and Ithaca Journal,
April 9, 1969.   See also Roy Gerard, Impact I, Economic Impact of Le Moyne College on the Syracuse,
New York Community (Syracuse: Le Moyne College,
1962); Warren J. Winstead, "The Economic Impact of
a New University upon Its Community," Investment
Dealers Digest (November 17, 1967), pp. 51-52, discusses the new trends for the cluster of research
parks and educational institutions.   For an examination of the importance of export-type industries to
an area, see Charles M. Tiebout, The Community Economic Base Study (New York: Committee for Economic
Development, 1962), pp. 27-55.

33. Bonner, op. cit. The annual operating expenditure of the university, 0, is related to the
FTE enrollment, E, at the university by the following
regression equation:

$$0 = -28,835,581 + 3,453 \text{ E}$$

An increase of one FTE student yields an increase of
$3,453 in operating expenditures in accordance with
this equation. For a more detailed description of
input-output techniques, see Isard, op. cit., pp.
309-74. For basic multiplier theory, see Tiebout,
op. cit., pp. 57-61.

34. Hirsch, Segelkorst, and Marcus, op. cit.,
pp. 24-30; and Werner Z. Hirsch, Decision Tools for
Education (Los Angeles: Institute of Government and
Public Affairs, 1964), pp. 6-9. See also Weisbrod,
op. cit., p. 104. The literature on cost-benefit
analysis is rather extensive and demonstrates impact
of public investment at various governmental levels.
Some basic sources are: Otto Eckstein, Water Resource
Development: The Economics of Project Evaluation
(Cambridge, Mass.: Harvard University Press, 1958);
Robert H. Haveman, Water Resource Investment and the
Public Interest (Nashville, Tenn.: Vanderbilt Uni-
versity Press, 1965); Nathaniel Lichfield, Cost-
Benefit Analysis in Urban Redevelopment (Berkeley:
University of California, Institute of Business and
Economic Research, 1962); David Novick, Program Bud-
geting, Program Analysis and the Federal Budget, a
Rand Corporation study (Washington, D.C.: U.S. Gov-
ernment Printing Office, 1965), in which a section
on educational program budgeting at the national level
especially is pertinent, pp. 131-54; Arthur Maass,
"Benefit-Cost Analysis: Its Relevance to Public In-
vestment Decisions," Quarterly Journal of Economics,
XXC, 2 (May, 1966), pp. 208-26.

35. Spencer M. Hurtt, "The Impact of Institutional Growth on Urban Land Use," Urban Land (January,
1968), pp. 3-10. The author indicates that 40 percent of Boston's assessed property is tax exempt,
but he also indicates that there is hardly a community
that has not benefited more from its institutions

than it has lost in taxes: "In most situations,
proper land use adjacent to an institution will increase in value rather than decrease."

36. These data apply to metropolitan residents
and were obtained through the World Health Organization and an article in Graduate School of Public Affairs, State University of New York, Metropolitan
and Area Problems: News and Digest, VII, 5 (Albany:
State University of New York, 1964), p. 7. Hospital
beds needed is over 10 beds per 1,000 population in
some areas of the United States. Fred D. Lindsey,
What New Industrial Jobs Mean to a Community (Washington, D.C.: Economic Research Department, Chamber
of Commerce of the United States, 1965) indicates
that 100 new factory workers bring the following to
a community: 359 more people, 100 more households,
91 more school children, 65 more employed in non-
manufacturing, 3 more retail establishments, $331,000
more retail sales per year, 97 more passenger cars
registered, $710,000 more personal income per year,
and $229,000 more in bank deposits. See also John
Fischer, "Survival U: Prospectus for a Really Relevant University," "The Easy Chair," Harper's Maga-
zine (September, 1969), pp. 12-22.

37. Lloyd L. Hogan, Measurement of the Ability
of Local Governments to Finance Local Public Services (Albany: Bureau of Educational Finance Research, State Education Department, University of
the State of New York, 1967), pp. 21-26, 64-66 and
94-95. Hogan found that the three measures of fiscal
ability were all higher for counties in Standard
Metropolitan Statistical Area. He concluded, in
general, that cities possess greater abilities to support all functions. But high taxes are not necessarily associated with relatively high ability, nor
are low taxes necessarily related to low ability.

38. Costs and benefits of a central business
district have been evaluated in Raymond J. Green,
The Impact of the Central Business District on the
Municipal Budget (Washington, D.C.: Urban Land Institute, 1962), pp. 175-95.

39.   Stefan H. Robock, "A Socio-Economic Evaluation of the TVA Experiment," John R. Moore (ed.),
The Economic Impact of TVA (Knoxville: University
of Tennessee Press, 1967), pp. 105-20.   Irving A.
Fowler, Local Industrial Structures, Economic Power,
and Community Welfare, Thirty Small New York State
Cities, 1930-1950 (Totowa, N.J.:   Bedminister Press,
1964), pp. 77-202, evaluated the impact of industry
on the social welfare of the community.   Yehezkel
Dror, Public Policymaking Reexamined (San Francisco:
Chandler Publishing Company, 1968), pp. 129-216, in
a broader approach, advised that optimal public policymaking combines economic rationality with extra-
rational processes.

40.   Friedmann, Regional Development Policy,
loc. cit.   The effect of a small college in the state
university system is briefly discussed in Barclay G.
Jones, Richard L. Ragatz, and Phaichitr Uathavikul,
Regional Analysis for Economic Development: A Demonstration Study of Schoharie County (Ithaca, N.Y.:
Cornell University Center for Housing and Environmental Studies, Division of Urban Studies, 1964),
pp. 119-37.

41.   Friedmann, Regional Development Policy, op.
cit., p. 213.   See also John R. P. Friedmann, The
Spatial Structure of Economic Development in the
Tennessee Valley, A Study of Regional Planning (Chicago: University of Chicago Press, 1955), pp. 131-
33.   The importance of the educational institution
is also indicated by John H. Thompson, ed., Geography
of New York State (Syracuse: Syracuse University
Press, 1966), pp. 320-29; and by Harvey S. Perloff
and Vera W. Dodds, "How a Region Grows, Area Development in the U.S. Economy," Supplementary Paper No.
17 (New York: Committee for Economic Development,
1963), pp. 144-45.

42.   See Appalachian Regional Commission, A Regional Investment Plan for the Appalachian Region of
New York State (Albany: Appalachian Regional Commission, State of New York, 1967), pp. 22-24.   The
Appalachian Regional Commission has identified a
number of urban complexes or growth centers in rural

areas of New York State. These include one or more
urban places and nonurban territory with a direct
economic relationship to the central urban places
and are not limited by political boundaries.

43. Gustav E. Larson, Can Our Small Towns Survive? (Washington, D.C.: U.S. Department of Agriculture, Resource Development Aid, July, 1960); Wilbur
Zelinsky, "Changes in Geographical Patterns of Rural
Population in the United States, 1790-1960," The Geographic Review, LII, 1962, pp. 492-524. Zelinsky
analyzes growth and decline of rural areas in the
United States. Edmund de S. Brunner and T. Lynn
Smith, "Village Growth and Decline, 1930-1940," Rural
Sociology, IX, 1944, pp. 103-15. Brunner and Smith
conclude that most of the larger small towns indicate
satisfactory growth rates. See also Adna N. Weber,
The Growth of Cities in the Nineteenth Century (Ithaca, N.Y.: Cornell University Press, 1963), pp.
446-75.

44. The New York Times, March 23, 1969. The
statement was made by Calvin L. Beale, Chief Demog-
rapher of the U.S. Department of Agriculture. Professor Edward Lutz, School of Agriculture, Cornell
University, has indicated that rural counties are
now gaining population at a greater rate than urban
counties.

45. Wilbur R. Thompson, A Preface to Urban Economics (Baltimore: Johns Hopkins Press, 1968), pp.
20-35. Thompson discusses the "urban size ratchet"
that insures the existence and growth of an urban
area after a minimum point of development has been
reached. He describes the Chapel Hill-Durham-Raleigh
triangle in North Carolina, which encloses 250,000
people in an area. See also Robert E. Dickinson,
City, Region, and Regionalism (New York: Oxford University Press, 1947), and F. Stuart Chapin, Jr. and
Shirley F. Weiss, eds., Urban Growth Dynamics: In a
Regional Cluster of Cities (New York: John Wiley and
Sons, Inc., 1962).

46. Committee for Economic Development, Community
Economic Development Efforts, Five Case Studies (New
York: Frederick A. Praeger, 1966), pp. 19-20.

2

**STUDY OF
SELECTED
COLLEGE COMMUNITIES:
ALFRED VILLAGE
AND
THE CITY OF CORTLAND**

This study began with an investigation of the
impact of the State University colleges in the Village of Alfred and in the City of Cortland.   These
localities are very different in population, size,
economic characteristics, and physical setting.
Their disparities were used to obtain survey data
that clearly exhibit variation in impact and spillout.
A better understanding of these variations was then
achieved by adding additional colleges to the study.

ALFRED TECHNICAL COLLEGE
AND ITS COLLEGE TOWN

Alfred Village is the home of Alfred Technical
College, New York State Ceramics College, and Alfred
University.[1] It is a college town in the full sense
of the word, with a permanent population of about
1,700 people who are closely associated with the colleges.   Its coed student population of over 3,000 is
undergraduate except for about 250 students in
Alfred University's Graduate School.   Alfred Village,
located in Allegany County in southwestern New York,
is nestled in the foothills of the Allegheny

Mountains. It is the home of the Davis Memorial
Carillon, and Glidden Galleries, and bears some re-
nown in art and pottery primarily in relation to the
College of Ceramics. The small town has a mix of
faculty and students, both local and foreign in origin, and its initially rural culture has been invested
with a cosmopolitan flavor and a scholarly, artistic
mien.

Alfred is 70 miles south of Rochester, 90 miles
southeast of Buffalo, 70 miles west of Elmira, and
15 miles from the Pennsylvania border. In its narrow valley, it is somewhat isolated although easily
accessible north-south via nearby U.S. Highway 15,
and east-west via State Route 17. The City of Hornell,
about 20 minutes away by motor, is served by the
Erie Lackawanna Railroad and a chartered air service.
Chautauqua, Corning, and the Finger Lakes are within
easy reach. The Alfred Agricultural and Technical
College was formerly housed in several of the buildings now part of the Alfred University complex. But
by 1968 a completely new campus had been built for
the two-year college. Dormitories were provided for
a great majority of its students in State University
buildings and in property owned by the Benevolent
Association, an auxiliary enterprise.[2] Curriculums
are offered in agriculture, business, engineering,
and health technologies. Total full-time enrollments
for 1950, 1960, and 1967 were 739, 1,375, and 1,991,
respectively.[3]

As indicated previously (Table 1.1), the Alfred
Technical College annual budget increased from
$302,800 in 1949-50 to $4.29 million in 1968-69.
Close to 85 percent of this expenditure is for pro-
fessional- and auxiliary-staff salaries, and in 1968,
the average annual salary for faculty was $10,668;
maintenance-staff salaries averaged $5,598 (as shown
in Appendix Table G.1). In 1960, persons employed
in educational services comprised 41 percent of the
town's employed labor force and helped raise economic
levels in the area.

The country around Alfred Village is generally
characterized by forestland, agricultural cropland,

and pastureland, as shown in Map 1. Alfred University
is at the center of town and occupies several buildings in the very small commercial area. The new campus of the State University Agricultural and Technical
College lies to the west, just outside the business
center, on an adequate site with a sloping terrain.
Steep slopes standing close to the center of the village impose a Y shape and tend to limit residential
and commercial construction. New housing has developed south along Elm Valley Road up Jericho Hill, and
west toward Moland Hill Road. Also, the lower slopes
of Pine Hill, south of the university, have been
developed, and attractive housing overlooks the valley. There is little new construction within village
limits (as shown in Appendix Table G.2). In 1964,
a peak year, the value of new construction was
$306,100, but its more common value has been close
to the $100,000 annual level.

Although the full-time instructional staff at
Alfred Technical College increased from 82 in 1960
to 173 in 1967, and the colleges expanded their administrative and auxiliary staffs over this period, construction in the village did not match the needs of
newcomers.[4] Suitable lots and homes in Alfred Village have become expensive and scarce. Therefore,
many new faculty have settled in nearby Almond and
other villages.

Distribution of the places of residence of staff
at Alfred Technical College is displayed by village
in Table 2.1. If Alfred Village is considered by
itself, only 41.5 percent of the professional staff
and 14.2 percent of the auxiliary staff live within
its boundaries; for the total staff, this figure is
25.2 percent. However, when one considers administrative and social factors, housing in the Alfred
area is perhaps more properly observed as an agglomeration, that is, at the town level. This suggests
the combination of data on Alfred and Alfred Station
and includes the housing on Jericho Hill, in Tinkertown, and elsewhere just outside the village boundary.
Thus combined, the percent of professional and auxiliary staff living in the town comes to 60 and 26.4
percent, respectively.

MAP 1

Topographical Map of Alfred Village

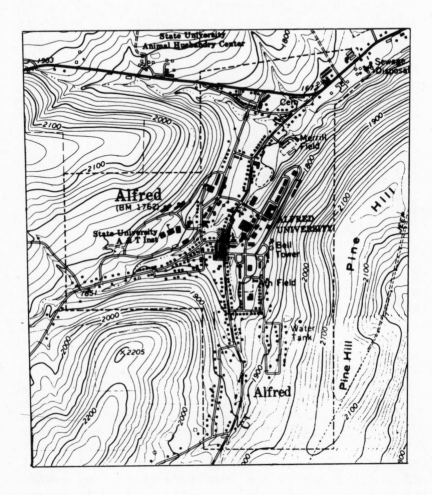

Note: Most retail trade in the village occurs in the shaded area. The village boundary is indicated by the line of dashes.

Source: U.S. Geological Survey, Washington, D.C., Map of Alfred, 1964, and based on field study and information from the Center for Air Photo Studies, Cornell University, Ithaca, New York, "New York State Land Use Study," July, 1968 (files of the Center).

TABLE 2.1

Places of Residence and Incidence of Estimated Payroll for Staff at the State University of New York, Alfred Agricultural and Technical College, 1967

City or Village	Number and Percent of Staff Residing at the Indicated Location				Estimated Payroll to Residents at the Indicated Location	
	Professional Staff		Auxiliary Staff		Profes-sional Staff ($)	Auxiliary Staff ($)
	Number	Percent	Number	Percent		
Alfred Village	81	41.5	42	14.2	874,800	218,400
Alfred Station	36	18.5	36	12.2	388,800	187,200
Almond	15	7.7	27	9.2	162,000	140,400
Andover	5	2.6	53	18.0	54,000	275,600
Belmont	4	2.1	12	4.1	43,200	62,400
Hornell	21	10.8	59	20.0	226,800	306,800
Scio	3	1.5	9	3.1	32,400	46,800
Wellsville	18	9.2	28	9.5	194,400	145,600
Whitesville	0	0.0	11	3.7	--	57,200
9 other locations	12	6.2	--	--	129,600	--
14 other locations	--	--	18	6.1	--	93,600
Total	195	100.0	295	100.0	2,106,000	1,534,000
Alfred-Alfred Station	117	60.0	78	26.4	1,263,600	405,600

Note: Average staff salary for professional staff in 1967 was assumed at $10,800, and for auxiliary staff at $5,200 per year. Details may not add up to totals because of rounding.

Comparison with data from 1960 shows a tendency, especially for new professional staff, to reside in Alfred Station, on Jericho Hill, in Almond, Hornell, Wellsville, and other locations outside Alfred Village.[5] This results from the hiring of personnel from among county and area residents as well as from newcomers settling outside the village.

Officials and planners in Alfred Village are highly concerned about the fact that where new professional and auxiliary staff come from outside the general area and seek residences in the college town, they cannot be accommodated within village limits, where the scarcity of lots and the high cost of housing compel withdrawal to other nearby localities.[6] The village lies in a vise imposed by boundary limitations and terrain; its economic growth is hampered in construction, property development, retail trade, and other categories. Its tight little business district has expanded slightly by takeover of residential property--a difficult process, at best, in this village--and a new commercial strip has developed in the Tinkertown area, on the road to Alfred Station. This development has been attracting staff and students and competing with elements in the older center of town. In addition, Alfred's expanded nontaxable properties occupy a large proportion of the usable and centrally located land areas.

Some idea of Alfred's losses and gains can be obtained by examining the data in Table 2.2. Retail sales in its two-block commercial area have been extremely low and in 1963 were at $315 per capita.[7] In the same year, Alfred Village possessed 16 retail-trade establishments, 10 with payroll, and included 29 employees.[8] There were no stores for general merchandise, furniture, and lumber, and both retail trade and selected services indicated small operations.

On the plus side, persons in educational service made up slightly over 40 percent of Alfred's employed industrial labor force of 759 individuals. Those in professional and technical occupations contributed 33 percent to the total. Both groups were primarily

TABLE 2.2

Social and Economic Characteristics of Selected Locations in the Elmira-Syracuse Area, New York State

Location	Retail Sales per Capita, 1963 ($)	Persons in Educational Services, Percent of Employed Labor Force	Housing Median Value ($)	Median Family Income ($)	Full-Time Faculty Average Salary ($)	Full-Time Faculty Number on Staff
New York State	1,449	4.8	15,300	6,371		
Upstate New York	1,394	6.1	12,600	6,072		
Allegany County	1,039	12.2	7,600	4,828		
Alfred (T)	N.A.	41.2	12,000	5,649		
Alfred (V)	315	40.4	N.A.	5,800	6,994	82
Almond (T)	N.A.	21.7	N.A.	4,817		
Wellsville (T)	N.A.	7.7	11,300	5,715		
Wellsville (V)	3,281	8.8	11,800	5,828		
Steuben County Hornell (C)	1,278	5.6	9,400	5,607		
Hornells-ville (T)	N.A.	8.1	10,900	5,493		
Cortland County	1,502	8.0	10,600	5,505		
Cortland (C)	2,038	9.3	11,700	5,715	7,531	161
Cortland-ville (T)	N.A.	5.7	11,280	5,566		
Homer (T)	N.A.	6.3	11,460	5,771		
Homer (V)	2,581	8.9	11,500	6,018		
Cayuga County	1,191	6.2	10,300	5,384		
Auburn (C)	1,681	3.8	11,000	5,518	N.A.	N.A.
Madison County	1,346	9.6	9,800	5,451		
Cazenovia (T)	N.A.	14.9	14,500	6,604		
Cazenovia (V)	2,571	N.A.	14,500	6,808	N.A.	N.A.

C = City
T = Town
V = Village

Note: Data on Alfred faculty is for the Agricultural and Technical College only; data for the university was not published in the source given below.

Source: New York State Department of Commerce, Business Fact Book, Part I, Business and Manufacturing; Part II, Population and Housing (Albany, 1968 and 1963, respectively); American Association of University Professors, "The Economic Status of the Profession," AAUP Bulletin, XLVII, 2 (Washington, D.C., 1961).

associated with the colleges and were instrumental
in raising median family income levels in the village
and town above that for the county. Median housing
values in the Town of Alfred were at the peak level
for the county and considerably above those for
Steuben County. But it is evident that the village
and town are incurring a type of opportunity loss
relative to professional- and auxiliary-staff location, retail trade, and probably the tourist trade.[9]

     It is possible to estimate the outflow of the
Alfred Agricultural and Technical College payroll
from Alfred Village, as shown in Table 2.1. If we
assume an average annual salary for professional
staff of $10,800 in 1967 and note that 81, or 41.5
percent, of the professional staff reside in the village, the professional payroll distribution to village
residents is estimated at $874,800 per year before
taxes; for professional staff residents in Alfred
Station, this amounts to $388,800 annually. In total,
benefit in terms of professional-staff payroll to
residents in communities outside Alfred Village is
estimated at $1.2 million per year. Auxiliary-staff
payroll for residents outside the village is estimated at $1.3 million annually, when the average aux-
iliary-staff member's salary is $5,200 per year. It
should be emphasized here that some of this payroll
may still be brought back into the village through
purchases, transfers, and other means. Also, payroll
monies remaining outside the village serve to develop
other towns in the region.

     When residential settlement is considered from
the point of view of the county rather than the village, residence ratings are high, as shown in Table
2.3. About 85 percent of the professional staff
reside in Allegany County, and 12.8 percent in Steuben; for auxiliary staff, these figures are 76.5 and
22.7, respectively. Allegany County itself shows
strong benefit in payroll, housing, and related categories, but it exhibits opportunity losses in the
areas of retail trade and selected services. Steuben
County, through Hornell, is the beneficiary in the
latter categories.

TABLE 2.3

Counties of Residence of Staff at the State University of New York,
Alfred Agricultural and Technical College, 1967-68

| County | Number of Locations in Each County | Number of Staff in County | | | | | |
| | | Professional | | Auxiliary | | Total | |
		Number	Percent	Number	Percent	Number	Percent
Allegany	17	166	85.1	226	76.5	392	80.0
Chemung	2	1	0.5	1	0.3	2	0.4
Livingston	1	1	0.5	0	0.0	1	0.2
Steuben	7	25	12.8	67	22.7	92	18.8
Wayne	1	1	0.5	1	0.3	2	0.4
Tioga, Pa.	1	1	0.5	0	0.0	1	0.2
Total	29	195	100.0	295	100.0	490	100.0

Note: Details may not add up to totals because of rounding.

45

THE CITY OF CORTLAND
AND ITS COLLEGE

The situation at Cortland is quite different from that in Alfred. The City of Cortland had a population of 19,181 in 1960; 9.3 percent of its employed labor force of 7,617 was engaged in educational services and 11.6 percent was employed in professional and technical categories. Manufacturing plants in the area include Smith-Corona Marchant Corporation, which employed over 4,000 workers. The chief export industries for Cortland County are agriculture, manufacturing, and public education; the latter is represented by Cortland College.

The City of Cortland is amply planned compared to Alfred. The college is located on a hilltop a few blocks from the main commercial center of the city. Its campus of 140 acres is readily accessible to more distant areas by the north-south Interstate Highway 81, and, more locally, by Routes 13, 11, and 41. Ithaca, Syracuse, and Binghamton are, respectively, about 20, 25, and 35 miles distant. The college also operates the Hoxie Gorge Campus, a 140-acre natural preserve about 7 miles from the main campus and a 400-acre facility at Raquette Lake in the Adirondacks.

Cortland College had enrollments of 2,399, 3,195, and 3,611 in 1960, 1965, and 1967, respectively, and planned for a projected maximum enrollment of 4,000 undergraduates and 500 graduate students by 1971. The college's major academic divisions include the following: (a) Arts and Sciences, (b) Education, (c) Health, Physical Education, and Recreation, and (d) Graduate Studies and Research. The institution is primarily residential in character, and 91 percent of the college's students live on or in the immediate vicinity of the campus.[10] Accommodations in state dormitories were available for 2,164 students by 1967. Seven sororities and three fraternities offered room and board for their members, and some students lived in private homes and other buildings in the community.

Cortland College is surrounded by a residential district in the north and east, a cemetery and residences on the south, and a public water reserve on the west. At its current state of development, the campus and its $30.5-million complex of 22 buildings is fairly adequate, but an increased enrollment is expected to bring with it problems in expansion, especially in the categories of student housing, academic space, and parking.

The college staff is primarily housed in the Cortland-Homer area; the agglomeration is continuous with no sharp breaks in settlement at boundary lines. Ample room for additional residential settlement in the vicinity of the city is evident. However, commercial and residential construction in the city has not been very high, as indicated in Appendix Table G.3.

In 1967, 323 members (82 percent) of the professional staff and 261 auxiliary-staff members (80.6 percent) lived in the Cortland-Homer agglomeration, as shown in Appendix Table B.1. If we use these values and the data on average annual salary for staff at the College at Cortland, as indicated in Appendix Table G.4, the professional-staff payroll distribution to Cortland-Homer area residents is estimated at $3,779,100 before taxes. Residents in communities outside this area receive an estimated $830,700 in professional-staff payroll. If the average salary for auxiliary-staff members is assumed to be $5,400 per year, those living in the Cortland-Homer area draw $1,409,400, and $340,200 goes to auxiliary-staff residents living outside this area. It is likely that Cortland and Homer firms recapture some of the external $1,170,900 through local trade.

At the county level, as shown in Table 2.4, only a slight increase occurs in the residence rating for professional staff; 333, or 84.5 percent, live in Cortland County. The auxiliary-staff residence rating comes close to 90 percent, and 292 members live in Cortland County.

TABLE 2.4

Counties of Residence of Staff at the State University of New York at Cortland, 1967-68

County	Number of Locations in Each County	Staff in County					
		Professional		Auxiliary		Total	
		Number	Percent	Number	Percent	Number	Percent
Cortland	9	333	84.5	292	90.1	625	87.1
Broome	1	1	0.3	0	0.0	1	0.1
Cayuga	3	1	0.3	3	0.9	4	0.6
Chenango	2	1	0.3	3	0.9	4	0.6
Hamilton	1	1	0.3	2	0.6	3	0.4
Herkimer	1	1	0.3	0	0.0	1	0.1
Madison	1	0	0.0	2	0.6	2	0.3
Onondaga	10	27	6.9	1	0.3	28	4.0
Oneida	1	0	0.0	1	0.3	1	0.1
Seneca	1	1	0.3	0	0.0	1	0.1
Schuyler	1	0	0.0	1	0.3	1	0.1
Steuben	1	2	0.5	0	0.0	2	0.3
Tompkins	7	26	6.6	19	5.9	45	6.3
Total	--	394	100.0	324	100.0	718	100.0

In all, the Cortland-Homer area, the City of Cortland, and the county derive strong benefit from the location of the college in the city. Staff-residence characteristics indicate a strong effect on local housing and property-tax levels. As shown in Table 2.2, salaries for full-time faculty have a substantial effect in raising median family income levels for the City of Cortland and the general area.

It is difficult to separate out the effect of the college staff on retail trade in the City of Cortland. (See Chapter 4.) Table 2.2 shows Cortland with $2,038 per capita retail sales in 1963, somewhat below the Homer level but well above county, state, and Upstate New York levels. Per capita sales levels are lessened a bit for this city by the inclusion of dormitory students in the population base; if this is adjusted, the per capita sales level for the City of Cortland comes much closer to that of Homer.[11]

In conservative estimate, the average full-time student benefits retail trade in an area by spending $300 per year for occasional meals, clothing, entertainment, and personal services.[12] This amount varies for students living at home, in dormitories, and those living offcampus in private facilities; it is considerably higher for the latter group. For an enrollment of 3,700 students, if we use the $300 average, an expenditure of about $1.1 million per year spent in the Cortland area results. For Alfred, the sales potential for an enrollment of 2,000 students comes to $600,000. In addition to these expenditures, purchases by the colleges and auxiliary enterprises add to the income for the area. (These are discussed in Chapter 7).

SUMMARY

Alfred Village is an example of a college town with relatively high economic spillout. The village is small in population and has limited shopping facilities (sixteen retail establishments in 1963). It houses a private and a public college, in addition

to the Ceramics College, and it largely depends on
these institutions for growth and development. However, less than 50 percent of the colleges' professional staffs and below 20 percent of their auxiliary
staffs reside in the village. The spillout in payroll, residential construction, and related economic
benefits is accordingly substantial. The village is
limited in expansion by a topography and settlement
pattern that restrict expansion of its shopping district, housing, and institutions. This situation can
be ameliorated; however, the cost would be high, and
governmental assistance would probably be needed.[13]

On the other hand, the City of Cortland has retained a high proportion of the benefits generated
by its college. Residential ratings for both professional and auxiliary college staff are relatively
high, and there is a high college payroll input to
this city. The college is a factor in drawing new
industry to the Cortland area, and the city is additionally provided with a substantial export industry
in education, owing to the large number of nonlocal
students in attendance at the college.

NOTES

1. The full names of the colleges will be abbreviated or otherwise shortened to suit the exposition.
The Alfred Agricultural and Technical College is also
known as Ag. Tech., Alfred Tech., or SUNY Alfred.
The State University of New York College at Cortland
may be abbreviated to SUNY Cortland or simply Cortland. The Ceramics College at Alfred is a Contract
College of the State University of New York adminis-
tered by Alfred University.

2. In March, 1968, despite the high number of
students living in dormitories, the Alfred Technical
College office indicated that 806 students had registered cars on the campus. Faculty and staff added
737 vehicles to this, to make a total of 1,543 cars
registered on campus.

3. The source of this information is the State
University of New York Office of Institutional
Research.

4. _Ibid_.

5. New York State Division of the Budget, "The
Executive Budget, Fiscal Year April 1, 1968 to March
31, 1969," submitted by Nelson A. Rockefeller, Governor (Albany: New York State Division of the Budget,
1968), p. 572. Due to the restricted possibilities
for residential expansion, the proportion of professionals residing in the village drops at a rapid rate
with every increase in staff; for 1968-69, a 12-per-
cent increase in staff positions was recommended for
the college in the State of New York. Many of these
individuals would live outside the village. The number of professionals in the village stays almost constant over the years; those outside increase in
proportion rapidly.

6. This problem was discussed several times
with college, business, and town leaders and in a
group meeting at the Alfred Technical College on
April 26, 1968. At a meeting with President Leland
Miles of Alfred University, on December 18, 1968,
this issue was again mentioned.

7. Even when this figure is adjusted to include
only permanent residents in the college town, annual
retail sales are somewhere between $500-600 per capita.

8. New York State Department of Commerce, _Busi-
ness Fact Book, 1967-68_ Part 1, _Business and Manufac-
turing_ (Albany, 1968).

9. Phaichitr Uathavikul, "Decision Theory and
Regional Economic Growth: A Model of Resource Utilization in the Context of Regional Opportunity Loss"
(unpublished Ph.D. dissertation, Cornell University,
Department of City and Regional Planning, 1966),
treats the concept of opportunity loss at the regional
level at great length. See also William Woodbridge
Goldsmith, "The Impact of the Tourism and Travel Industry on a Developing Regional Economy: The Puerto

Rican Case" (unpublished Ph.D. dissertation; Cornell University, Department of City and Regional Planning, 1966), pp. 4-6; and Barclay G. Jones, Richard L. Ragatz, and Phaichitr Uathavikul, Regional Analysis for Economic Development: A Demonstration Study of Schoharie County (Ithaca, N.Y.: Cornell University Center for Housing and Environmental Studies, Division of Urban Studies, 1964), pp. 3-5.

10.   State University of New York, College at Cortland, General Catalog, 1968-69 (Cortland: State University of New York, 1968), p. 10.

11.   As shown in the Business Fact Book, op. cit., the City of Cortland had 264 retail-trade establishments in 1963.   Retail sales were $38.9 million, and had increased since 1958 at a faster rate than that of either New York State as a whole or Upstate New York taken as a region.   Cortland had 1,425 employees engaged in retail trade with a payroll of over $4.3 million, with 9 general-merchandise stores, 21 apparel stores, 22 furniture stores, 15 automotive dealers, 34 gasoline service stations, 36 food stores, 48 eating and drinking places, and other outlets.   In addition, in the category of selected services, 155 establishments were listed.   The Village of Homer supported 75 establishments engaged in retail trade and 32 in selected services.

12.   Frances S. Doody, The Immediate Economic Impact of Higher Education in New England (Boston: Boston University Bureau of Business Research, 1961), pp. 33-35, found in 1958 that the average undergraduate expenditure for New England students living in a college facility was $461.70 (26,886 students were sampled in 55 institutions), and state averages ranged from $302 to $549; in a private facility, away-from-home average expenditure was $826.10 (3,460 students sampled at 42 institutions); and for those living at home, the expenditure was $549.49 (17,619 students sampled at 56 institutions).   These expenditures are exclusive of tuition, board and room, and other fees paid directly to the institution.

13.   Pertinent discussions of governmental assistance are discussed in Edgar M. Hoover, <u>The Location
of Economic Activity</u> (New York: McGraw Hill, 1963),
pp. 272-78; Robert H. Haveman, <u>Water Resource Investment and the Public Interest</u> (Nashville, Tenn.:
Vanderbilt University Press, 1965), pp. 133-47; and
Spencer M. Hurtt, "The Impact of Institutional Growth
on Urban Land Use," <u>Urban Land</u> (January, 1968), pp.
3-100.

3

RESIDENCE
LOCATION
OF THE COLLEGE STAFF:
A MULTICOLLEGE
STUDY

Because staff-residence location is a key variable in determining social and economic impact of the
college on the community, the variation of this factor was studied for thirty-nine colleges in New York
State. This multicollege study was made to determine
the degree of correlation between the percent of
staff members living in the community, the population (size) of the community, and related factors.[1]

For purposes of this study, the college community is considered to include an area housing the
major proportion of the college family (staff and
students) and local businessmen, workers, and residents in frequent contact with the college family.
A college's impact may be felt in various areas of
the state and beyond, but, generally, distinctive
characteristics of the college community are strongly
evident within only 1-3 miles of the college campus.
Beyond this range, the college lineament is either
sharply diminished, sporadic, or not readily distin-
guishable from the operation of external factors.

The college community is frequently absorbed in
a single town or city. However, in some cases it is

more accurately defined and represented by <u>an agglom-eration</u> that includes the population of two adjacent villages or a city and a nearby village. These cases are clearly indicated in the tables and discussion that follow. (See Tables 3.1A and 3.1B.) For exam-ple, in the case of the State University at Cortland, the City of Cortland houses 296 professional- and 225 auxiliary-staff members. This represents 75.1 and 69.5 percent of the staff, respectively. The Village of Homer is within 2 miles of the city line and forms part of the total population agglomeration in the area. This village houses 27 professional- and 36 auxiliary-staff members or 6.9 and 11.1 per-cent of the staff, respectively. (Data for the two locations are listed individually in Appendix Table B.1 and summed to make up the Cortland-Homer agglom-eration.)

Other agglomerations listed in these tables are Fredonia-Dunkirk, Alfred-Alfred Station, St. Bonaven-ture-Allegany-Olean, Glens Falls-South Glens Falls-Hudson Falls-Fort Edward, Corning-Painted Post, Poughkeepsie-Hyde Park,[2] Johnstown-Globersville, and Jamestown-Falconer. Summary data on professional and auxiliary staff are listed in Table 3.1A along with other pertinent information on college charac-teristics. Data are aggregated for agglomerations as shown by asterisks. Table 3.1B lists data rela-tive to the locality; its population data conform to the individual and agglomerated college-community listings as discussed above.

The range of town-residence ratings for college staff is shown in Table 3.2. The highest profes-sional-staff rating (94.6 percent) was registered by Colgate University, a private four-year college; the lowest (51.7 percent) was obtained for Morrisville, a two-year college in the State University.

For colleges in agglomerated areas, the ranges listed in the table are based on combined data. This considerably increases town-residence ratings for staff. For example, if uncombined data are used for the two-year State University College at Alfred (and if only Alfred Village residency is considered), the professional-staff residence rating for the college town drops to a low of 41.5 percent, as indicated in Appendix Table B.3, in contrast to its rating of 60 percent based on the aggregate.

Highs in college-community residence for auxiliary staff are indicated for the St. Bonaventure-Allegany-Olean complex (88.6 percent) and the Fredonia-Dunkirk area (87.8 percent). Lows occur for the State University's four-year college at Geneseo (25.6 percent) and for the two-year college at Alfred (26.4 percent). If the latter is disaggregated, auxiliary-staff residence in Alfred Village alone stands at a low of 14.2 percent.[3]

REGRESSION ANALYSIS OF
PROFESSIONAL-STAFF LOCATION

In accordance with Hypothesis I, our basic task was to determine if the percent of college staff living in the college community varies with the size (population) of the college community. This must be done separately for professional- and auxiliary-staff members.

To determine the relationship between town-residence ratings for the college professional staff and community size (population), a scatter diagram using these two variables was made, as depicted in Figure 1. A clustering of values can be seen in the graph. In the larger rural cities, values for the percent of four-year professional staff living in the college town lie in the 80-90-percent range. Data from two-year colleges in the larger college communities form a group almost completely in the 60-70-percent range. The situation changes for the small community. For professional staff at four-year colleges, the values vary between the 70-95-percent levels; for two-year colleges, the variation is greatest of all in the small communities and lies between the 52-84-percent levels.[4]

From the distribution of values on the graph, it would appear that a critical range exists for the

TABLE 3.1A

Characteristics of Selected Public and Private Colleges in New York State, 1967

College	Degree Offered, Number of Years	Full-Time Undergraduate Enrollment		Professional Staff		Auxiliary Staff		Doctorates on Teaching Staff (%)	Number of Places Where Staff Reside	
		1959	1964	Number	Percent Live in College Community	Number	Percent Live in College Community		Prof.	Auxil.
Four-Year Colleges										
I. Public Colleges										
1. Brockport	27	1,366	2,130	451	70.3	291	45.2	34.0	22	18
2. Cortland*	28	2,246	3,045	394	82.0	324	80.6	42.8	29	24
3. Fredonia*	29	1,050	2,098	308	89.6	321	87.8	54.0	19	14
4. Geneseo	29	1,123	1,998	333	71.5	363	25.6	42.8	32	39
5. New Paltz	27	1,456	2,758	442	75.5	391	43.8	35.0	44	34
6. Oneonta	27	1,608	2,503	386	82.6	327	66.7	31.6	27	34
7. Oswego	27	2,256	3,573	498	87.4	N.A.	N.A.	36.0	20	N.A.
8. Plattsburgh	28	1,305	2,097	339	85.3	426	52.6	41.9	21	30
9. Potsdam	29	1,130	2,003	N.A.	N.A.	N.A.	N.A.	30.1	N.A.	N.A.
II. Private Colleges										
10. Alfred*	90	1,131	909	210	76.6	193	40.9	46.8	9	18
11. Clarkson	69	1,490	1,837	194	86.1	160	51.3	54.8	13	19
12. Colgate	147	1,342	1,492	244	94.6	147	63.3	58.0	9	21
13. Hartwick	37	577	1,256	114	88.6	112	72.3	44.6	12	13
14. Hobart	57	1,018	1,372	153	88.8	161	81.9	51.0	9	11
15. Houghton	44	719	1,024	96	92.7	98	83.1	35.2	4	9
16. Ithaca	73	1,319	2,330	252	87.3	177	69.5	30.0	17	17
17. St. Bonaventure*	95	--	1,619	231	89.2	229	88.6	33.0	15	13

18. St. Lawrence	104	1,355	1,537	199	93.9	304	55.3	46.8	9	30
19. Skidmore	45	1,250	1,334	195	79.9	126	77.0	46.5	24	14
20. Vassar*	102	1,410	1,598	293	91.7	534	79.0	74.8	17	28

Two-Year Colleges

I. Public Community Colleges

21. Adirondack*	8	--	525	66	72.8	36	80.5	8.2	15	9
22. Auburn	16	442	878	81	64.2	32	75.0	14.0	13	8
23. Corning*	3	130	1,040	127	66.1	101	77.1	8.9	12	13
24. Dutchess*	19	205	1,427	150	70.6	109	78.0	6.8	27	16
25. Fulton*	5	--	335	63	66.7	26	76.9	8.8	9	6
26. Genesee	--	--	--	63	42.9	20	75.0	N.A.	22	6
27. Jamestown*	35	154	546	68	67.6	27	66.6	6.7	13	8
28. Jefferson	7	--	359	56	76.8	31	77.4	2.9	11	7
29. Orange	19	405	1,147	132	60.6	81	70.4	9.5	24	16
30. Rockland	10	92	653	182	14.8	76	5.3	21.0	12	12
31. Sullivan	7	--	288	93	5.4	46	15.2	10.4	24	18
32. Ulster	7	--	369	81	11.1	46	21.8	35.0	20	8

II. Agricultural and Technical Colleges

33. Alfred*	21	1,308	1,598	195	60.0	295	26.4	5.8	17	23
34. Canton	32	530	828	149	79.2	198	56.1	3.3	7	13
35. Cobleskill	21	466	1,021	132	72.0	235	54.0	7.6	15	28
36. Delhi	21	420	999	122	83.5	240	60.0	3.4	13	15
37. Morrisville	21	673	1,046	91	51.7	154	32.5	6.8	22	28

III. Private Colleges

38. Cazenovia	35	280	410	84	75.0	72	54.2	18.4	9	16
39. Paul Smiths	23	--	821	56	50.0	68	41.1	13.0	7	3

Notes on methods and sources: See Table 3.1B.

TABLE 3.1B

Characteristics of Selected College Communities in New York State, 1960

College Location	Land Area, Square Miles	College Town Density, p/sq.mi.	Town and City Population	Village or City Population	Village or City Population, 1940	Monthly Rent
Four-Year Colleges						
I. Public Colleges						
1. Brockport	1.7	3,091	7,224	5,256	3,590	39.96
2. Cortland*	5.4	4,918	30,592	22,803	18,809	34.23
3. Fredonia*	10.2	1,513	31,205	26,682	23,451	31.62
4. Geneseo	2.7	1,216	4,337	3,284	2,144	46.79
5. New Paltz	1.0	3,041	5,841	3,041	1,492	39.98
6. Oneonta	4.1	3,271	17,480	13,412	11,731	31.77
7. Oswego	7.8	2,840	24,951	22,155	22,062	34.74
8. Plattsburgh	5.0	4,034	24,172	20,172	16,351	38.14
9. Potsdam	3.9	1,991	14,045	7,765	4,821	28.77
II. Private Colleges						
10. Alfred*	1.1	2,552	3,730	3,730	1,410	35.10
11. Potsdam	3.9	1,991	14,045	7,765	4,821	29.77
12. Hamilton	1.6	2,093	5,438	3,348	1,780	34.92
13. Oneonta	4.1	3,271	17,480	13,412	11,731	31.77
14. Geneva	4.1	4,216	19,889	16,286	15,555	41.21
15. Houghton	—	—	—	—	—	—
16. Ithaca	5.8	4,965	37,871	28,799	19,730	51.54
17. St. Bonaventure*	9.5	3,527	30,619	23,932	22,945	36.79
18. Canton	1.4	3,604	8,935	5,046	3,018	33.98
19. Saratoga Springs	26.8	621	20,145	16,630	13,705	37.94
20. Poughkeepsie*	5.3	9,126	83,175	40,309	40,478	32.48
Two-Year Colleges						
I. Public Community Colleges						
21. Hudson Falls	10.6	4,532	54,525	36,923	32,191	35.54
22. Auburn	8.5	4,147	35,249	35,249	35,753	31.15
23. Corning*	4.6	5,511	29,646	19,655	18,549	34.57

24. Poughkeepsie*	5.3	9,126	83,175	40,309	40,478	32.48
25. Johnstown*	8.4	2,474	37,251	32,131	33,995	31.75
26. Batavia	5.2	3,502	22,535	18,210	17,267	38.40
27. Jamestown*	10.9	4,224	52,269	45,161	45,860	28.01
28. Watertown	9.2	3,620	35,798	33,306	33,385	33.98
29. Middletown	4.1	5,725	31,651	23,475	21,908	34.30
30. Suffern	1.5	3,396	35,064	5,094	3,768	42.63
31. South Fallsburg	3.0	430	6,748	1,290	--	51.80
32. Stone Ridge	--	--	--	--	--	--
II. Agricultural and Technical Colleges						
33. Alfred*	1.1	2,552	3,730	3,730	1,410	35.10
34. Canton	1.4	3,604	8,935	5,046	3,018	33.98
35. Cobleskill	3.0	1,157	4,964	3,471	2,617	36.91
36. Delhi	1.5	1,538	3,398	2,307	1,841	29.81
37. Morrisville	1.0	1,304	3,196	1,304	666	30.53
III. Private Colleges						
38. Cazenovia	1.2	2,153	4,968	2,584	1,689	38.48
39. Paul Smiths	--	--	--	--	--	--

Notes on methods and sources: College communities represented by agglomerations are asterisked. Data on individual localities as well as on agglomerations are listed in Appendix Tables A.1 to A.3. As discussed in Chapter 2, where settlement around the college is more accurately represented by combination of the populations of several localities in close proximity (within 2 miles apart), the sums of the populations were used in the regression analysis for college staff-residence location. These agglomerations occur in the following areas: Cortland-Homer, Fredonia-Dunkirk, Alfred-Alfred Station, St. Bonaventure-Olean-Allegany, Poughkeepsie-Hyde Park, and Corning-Painted Post. Agglomerations not included in the regression analysis are at Hudson Falls-Fort Edward-South Glens Falls-West Glens Falls-Glens Falls, Johnstown-Gloversville, and Jamestown-Falconer. The values for density are not agglomerated in Table 3.1B and are for the college community only.

Sources: U.S. Office of Education, Total Enrollment in Institutions, 1959-60 (Washington, D.C.: U.S. Government Printing Office, 1960); State Education Department, Division of Higher Education, Going to College in New York State (Albany: University of the State of New York, 1965), pp. 112-45; U.S. Bureau of the Census, U.S. Census of Population: 1960, Volume I, Characteristics of the Population, Part 34, New York (Washington, D.C.: U.S. Government Printing Office, 1963); Otis A. Singletary, ed., American Universities and Colleges (Tenth edition; Washington, D.C.: American Council on Education, 1968), pp. 939-1082.

TABLE 3.2

Percent of Professional and Auxiliary Staff
Residing in the College Community of Employment,
Selected Colleges in New York State, 1967-68

	College Location	
	In a City of 10-40,000 Population	In a Village of 1-8,000 Population
1. Professional Staff		
Four-year colleges		
Public	82.0-89.6	70.3-75.5
Private	79.9-91.7	76.6-94.6
Two-year colleges		
Public and private	60.6-70.6	51.7-83.5
2. Auxiliary Staff		
Four-year colleges		
Public	52.6-87.8	25.6-45.2
Private	69.5-88.6	40.6-63.3
Two-year colleges		
Public and private	70.4-78.0	26.4-60.0

Note: Only those colleges that were included
in the regression analysis are used as a basis for
this table. Also, the ranges indicated include only
combined village data for certain colleges as discussed in the text. If, for example, the data were
uncombined for the two-year college at Alfred, the
percent staff college town-residence rating for professional and auxiliary staff would be at lows of
41.5 and 14.2 percent, respectively. Extremely low
staff inputs were indicated by Sullivan County and
Rockland County community colleges. The percents
for professional staff for these colleges were 51.4
and 14.8, respectively; for auxiliary staff, the inputs were 15.2 and 5.3 percent, respectively. However, these colleges were excluded from the regression
analysis for reasons mentioned in Chapter 2.

FIGURE 1

Scatter Diagram of Village (City) Population vs. Percent of
Professional Staff Living in the Community, 1960

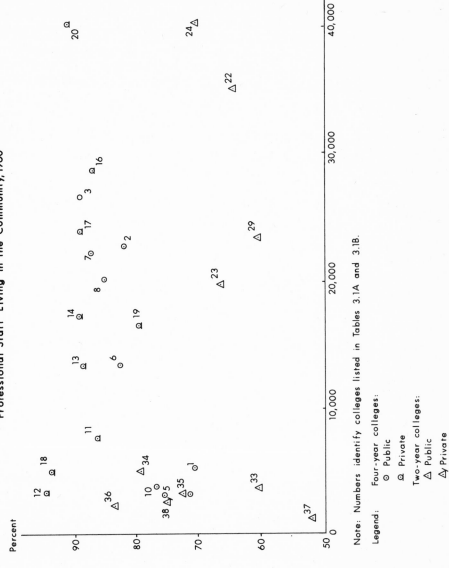

Note: Numbers identify colleges listed in Tables 3.1A and 3.1B.

Legend: Four-year colleges:
          ⊙ Public
          ⊿ Private

          Two-year colleges:
          △ Public
          △ Private

small college community, in which the professional
staff's college-community residence can go to either
an extremely low or a rather high level. This appears to depend on certain characteristics of the
college and the college community, and is discussed
later in this chapter. The lower level is predominantly represented by the two-year college and the
higher level by the four-year college, with a mix
occurring at intermediate levels. This juxtapositioning of values for two- and four-year colleges
holds throughout the scatter diagram.

Some relationship between the percent of professional staff living in the college community and the
population of the college community can be detected
by examination of the graph and the tabular data.
This is especially noted for four-year colleges in
the State University system. To examine the situation in more detail, regression analyses were made.
Their purpose was to statistically determine relationships and also to seek predictive factors relative
to professional-staff, town-residence ratings.

The distinct lineal pattern for the four-year
public colleges in Figure 1 suggested a regression
analysis for this group. Furthermore, the location
of data points on the scatter diagram suggested a
separate regression analysis for small and large college communities and a combined analysis for all communities. The clustering of values in separate and
distinct two- and four-year college groups indicated
that some variable should be found and applied to
reflect the difference between the junior college
and the baccalaureate institution. The variable decided on was the percentage of Ph.D.s on the full-
time teaching staff of each college; this variable
would not only help differentiate the above categories but it would also show differences within the
four-year college group.

Other independent variables selected for the
regression analyses relate to college and community
characteristics and are listed in Table 3.3 along
with their code names. These variables include density, square miles of land area of the college

TABLE 3.3

Variables Tested in Staff-Regression Analysis

Subscript Number	Variables	Code Names
	Dependent Variables	
4	Percent of college professional staff living in the college community	%-PROF-IN
6	Percent of college auxiliary staff living in the college community	%-AUXIL-IN
	Independent Variables	
1	Square miles of land area of the college community, 1960	SQM
2	Density, population per square mile, 1960	DEN
3	Number of individuals on the professional staff at the college, 1967	PROSTAF
5	Number of individuals on the auxiliary staff at the college, 1967	AUXSTAF
7	Percent of Ph.D.s on the teaching staff, 1967	T-PHD
8	Town (minor civil division) and city population, 1960	TOWN-CTY-POP
9	College community population, 1960	POPUL-60
10	Median contract monthly rent, 1960	RENT
11	Number of years degree offered by the college, as of 1969	DEGREE-YRS
12	Number of villages professional staff live in, 1967	PROF-VILL
13	Number of villages auxiliary staff live in, 1967	AUXIL-VILL
14	Population of nearby city, P_n	NER-CITY
15	Radial distance between the college town and nearby city, miles, d_{1-2}	DIST.
16	P_n/d_{1-2}^2	P/D^2
17	P_n/d_{1-2}	P/D
18	College community population, 1940	POPUL-40
19	Number of college-owned dwelling units for faculty and staff in the college community	HOUSG
20	Percent of Ph.D.s on the teaching staff of a four-year college in the State University system	%-PHD-4
21	College community population, 1960, for a community with a four-year college in the State University system	POPUL-60-4

Note: The above independent variables are important in explaining the value of the dependent variables for the college communities studied. All were used in the initial regression analysis. However, only the best explaining variables for college communities taken as a group were retained for the final regression analysis. These are listed in later tables. The deviation of a specific college community's dependent variable from the line of regression can be explained in part by use of one or more of the above-listed independent variables.

community, as well as college town (village or city)
population in 1940 and 1960, and township and city
population in 1960. Data for these variables are
listed in Table 3.1B.

First, a regression analysis for all colleges
in both large and small communities was made. Its
primary purpose was to note variation in staff-
residence input with factors related to town size.
The correlation matrix for this regression analysis
may be used to determine simple correlation of variables. An excerpt of correlation data pertaining to
Hypothesis I is presented in Appendix Table B.4;
this includes information relative to both professional and auxiliary staffs at the colleges and gives
information on small and large communities separately
and as a group.

The matrix for large and small communities as a
group shows very low correlation (0.06 to 0.11) between the percent of college professionals living in
the college community and community size (based on
population data). Also, population density and
square miles of land area of the college community
are in low association (0.02 and 0.13, respectively)
with the town-residence rating for professional
staff. (This was expected from the scatter diagram
discussed above.) The situation changes little for
small and large communities taken separately. However, the small communities do show a slightly greater
association (0.4) between professional-staff, town-
residence ratings and population. For large communities, there is a slightly negative association
(−0.17) between these two variables; as large-town
density increases, correlation (−0.25) with the professional-staff residence rating suggests a slight
tendency toward exurbia.

As mentioned previously, regression analysis
was used to test for Hypothesis I and also to determine more pertinent factors for explanation of the
variation in the town-residence ratings for staff.
Table 3.4 lists information relative to this regression analysis. The town-residence rating for professional staff is the dependent variable. When

TABLE 3.4

Data for Regression Equations for College Staff,
Multicollege Analysis

---

1. Percent of college professionals living in the community
   (town-residence rating), for large and small college communities.

   Dependent Variable: %-PROF-IN

   R squared   00.62   Significance level   0.001
   Constant   64.21   Standard error of estimate 7.49

Independent Variables	Beta	R Squared Without This Variable
%-PHD-4	0.02700	0.49
DEGREE-YRS	0.12700	0.54
POPUL-40	0.00002	0.62

2. Percent of college professionals living in the larger college
   (town-residence rating).

   Dependent Variable: %-PROF-IN

   R squared   00.82   Significance level   0.005
   Constant   63.75   Standard error of estimate 54.400

Independent Variables	Beta	R Squared Without This Variable
%-PHD-4	0.0280	0.69
DEGREE-YRS	0.1350	0.74
PROSTAF	0.0200	0.79
TOWN-CTY-POP	−0.0001	0.79

3. Percent of college auxiliary staff living in the community
   (town-residence rating), for large and small college communities.

   Dependent Variable: %-AUXIL-IN

   R squared   00.65   Significance level   00.005
   Constant   46.91   Standard error of estimate 11.650

Independent Variables	Beta	R Squared Without This Variable
POPUL-60-4	0.001	0.30
SQM	0.073	0.61
AUXSTAF	−0.028	0.61
DEGREE-YRS	0.084	0.62

Note: See Table 3.3 for definitions of code names.

both large and small college communities are examined
as a group, against selected community and college
characteristics, the value of the multiple correlation coefficient R is 0.78 (and R squared is 0.62).
Therefore, the variables indicated in the regression
equation account for 62 percent of the possible variance in the dependent variable.[5] The R-squared value
decreases if an important independent variable is
omitted from the regression equation. The values of
R squared without each of the several independent
variables is listed in the table, and these values
indicate the relative importance of the independent
variable under consideration.

As Table 3.4 demonstrates, the principal factors
in the equation are the percent of Ph.D.s on the
teaching staff (%-PHD) and the number of years a degree has been offered by the college (DEGREE-YRS).
Population of the community has virtually no effect
on the dependent variable.[6] The R-squared value remains at 0.62 when the variable for population is
omitted, but it changes appreciably without the
%-PHD or DEGREE-YRS variable.

The beta values and the constant term can be
used to form the multiple-regression equation:

$$Y_{41} = 64.21 + 0.027X_7 + 0.13X_{11} + 0.00002X_{18}$$

where Y_{41} is the percent of college professional
staff living in the college community (computed for
large and small rural college communities as a group)
and the variables are as defined in Table 3.3

A positive relationship exists for the variables
represented. Thus, the percent of professional staff
living in the college community will increase with an
increase in the percent of Ph.D.s on the teaching
staff and years as a degree-granting institution.
Because the four-year college is closest to this description, it generally will exhibit higher town-
residence ratings for the professional staff than
the two-year college. This was also expected from
the display in Figure 1.

The regression analysis for college professionals living in the larger college communities (or cities) resulted in higher predictive values. In this case, the multiple-correlation coefficient R is slightly over 0.9. The variables applied account for 82 percent of the possible variance in the dependent variable. However, as shown in Table 3.4, the population factor is still relatively low in importance. The principal explaining variables are again %-PHD and DEGREE-YRS. The beta values and the constant term can be used to form the following multiple-regression equation:

$$Y_{42} + 63.75 + 0.028X_7 + 0.135X_{11} + 0.02X_3 - 0.0001X_8$$

where Y_{42} is the percent of college professional staff living in the college community (computed for larger communities separately), and the variables are as indicated in Table 3.3.

Except for the population variable, all terms show a positive relationship; and as these variables increase, the town-residence rating increases. Again, this analysis indicates that town-residence ratings for the professional staff at the four-year college will be higher than at the two-year college.

A regression analysis was also made for college professionals living in the small college communities (villages). The R-squared value for this analysis was 0.69, but its level of significance was slightly above the 0.05 limit and is therefore not detailed.[7] Correlation matrixes for the independent variables used in the professional-staff regression analyses are exhibited in Appendix Table B.5. These show moderate relationships between institutional age, the percent of Ph.D.s on the staff, and the staff size.

As indicated at the beginning of this section, the scatter diagram (Figure 1) displayed a distinct pattern in residence ratings vs. community size (population) for professional staff at four-year

colleges in the State University system. Therefore,
a regression analysis was made to test this small
group of colleges. The results obtained are indicated in Table 3.5. The town-residence rating for
professional staff at these public colleges is the
dependent variable, and college-community size (population) is the independent variable. Both large and
small college communities were examined as a group
and the value of R is 0.91. Community size accounts
for 84 percent of the possible variance in the dependent variable. This indicates a strong variation
in professional-staff input to the college community
with community size.

The beta value and the constant term can be used
to form the following regression equation:

$$Y_{20} = 70.45 + 0.0067X_{21}$$

where Y_{20} is the percent of college-professional
staff at a four-year college in the State University
system who live in the college community (computed

TABLE 3.5

Data for Regression Equation for State University
Staff, Multicollege Analysis

Percent of college professionals at baccalaureate
institutions of the State University living in the
respective college communities (town-residence
rating vs. community size)

Dependent Variable: %-PROF-IN

R squared	00.8400	Significance level	0.005
Constant	70.4500	Standard error of estimate	3.200

Independent Variable: POPUL-60-4

Beta   00.0067

Note: See Table 3.3 for description of variables.

for large and small college communities as a group)
and X_{21} is college-community size as qualified in
Table 3.3. It can be readily seen in the equation
that as the college-community population increases
the percent of college professionals living in the
community increases, and the reverse is also true.
Cortland and Fredonia (agglomerated) are at the high
end of the pattern, and New Paltz and Geneseo are at
the low point. The important fact is that many of
the State University professional staff employed in
the smaller college communities live outside of
these towns. This contrasts with professional-staff
input to the small college community for private colleges; in the latter case, residence ratings do not
decrease with decrease in community size. This is
indicated particularly for Colgate University (in
Hamilton), St. Lawrence University (in Canton), and,
to a lesser extent, for Clarkson College (in Potsdam) and Hartwick College (in Oneonta).

There is a consistently high input (86-95 percent) to private college communities, except for
Skidmore College (somewhat lower, at 80 percent) and
Alfred University (at 77 percent). Thus, the small
college community, above a critical minimum, is generally as capable as the large community in attracting and containing a large proportion of the professional staff for the private colleges examined.

The situation is different for the four-year
State University colleges. As indicated in the analysis, professional-staff residence ratings vary with
community size for the four-year public colleges.
Those colleges in small communities draw a substantial number of professionals from the surrounding
villages and cities; Brockport (near Rochester),
Geneseo (near Rochester and Mt. Morris), and New
Paltz (near Poughkeepsie and Highland) are prominent
in this regard. These State University colleges
have larger enrollments and larger professional
staffs than the private colleges (see Table 3.1A),
and this may influence the situation. New staff
coming from distant points may be settling outside
the small college community, or new staff may be
commuting from residences previously established in
nearby towns or cities.

In sum, except for Alfred, most of the small
college communities with four-year private colleges
have high residential input for professional staff.
The relatively large State University colleges in
the small communities studied draw a substantial
proportion of their staff from towns and cities outside the college community; also, professional-staff
residence (input) ratings for these four-year public
colleges increase with town size.

REGRESSION ANALYSIS OF
AUXILIARY-STAFF LOCATION

To evaluate Hypothesis II, it is necessary to
determine if the percent of auxiliary-staff members
living in the college community varies with the size
of the college community. As was done previously
for the professional-staff analysis, the scatter
diagram depicted in Figure 2 was made using auxiliary
staff town-residence ratings and village or city
population data for 1960. The latter variable was
employed because it indicated fairly high correlation in initial analysis.

In examination of the graph, a relationship appears to exist between college-community size and
the percent of auxiliary staff living in the college
community when all the college communities are considered. However, this association is dubious for
small communities or large communities grouped separately. Generally, large communities can, and do,
supply a greater portion of the college auxiliary
labor force; but when the community labor force is
small, sources outside the community and county are
drawn upon. Commutation is a high factor for college-
auxiliary staff in the small college community, but
it is a much lower factor when professional staff
are considered. About half of the colleges in communities below the 8,000-population level indicated
that less than 50 percent of their auxiliary staff
lived in the college community. This is the case
for both two- and four-year colleges. Thus, much
of the college payroll for auxiliary-staff personnel
employed in the small college community is distributed
outside the immediate college area.

FIGURE 2

Scatter Diagram of Village (City) Population vs. Percent of Auxiliary Staff Living in the College Community, 1960

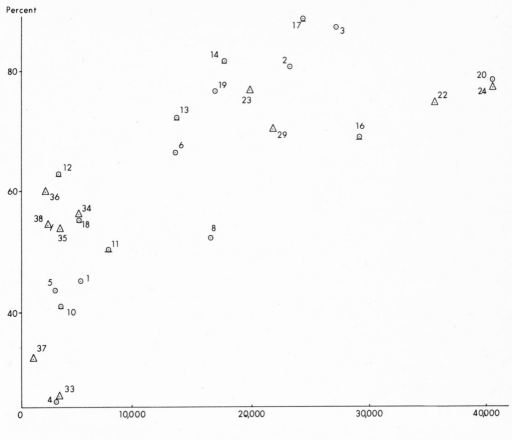

Legend: Four-year colleges:
      ⊙   Public
      Ω   Private
    Two-year colleges:
      △   Public
      △/   Private

Regression analysis was made for large and small communities individually and for all college communities as a set. Only the latter analysis was productive in yielding a substantial explanation of the dependent variable with a statistically significant result.[8]

Appendix Table B.4 can be used in noting the extent of simple correlation between community size and town-residence ratings for auxiliary staff. For the large and small community grouping, the correlations are rather high between variable 6 and the variables for size; correlation with 1960 and 1940 college-community population is at 0.74 and 0.73, respectively, and correlation with square miles of land area is 0.51. For small communities considered individually, only the correlation with towns (minor civil divisions) plus city population appears to yield a substantial result (0.59); low correlation (0.19) is indicated for the large-community (city) analysis.

Multiple-regression analysis confirmed the fact that community size (college-community population, variable 9) is a key factor in explaining auxiliary-staff, town-residence ratings. Other variables contributing slightly to the multiple-correlation coefficient are the square miles of land area of the college community, the number of individuals on the auxiliary staff, and the number of years a degree has been offered by the college.

The value of the multiple-correlation coefficient R is 0.81. The independent variables listed in Table 3.4 for the auxiliary-staff regression analysis explain 65 percent of the possible variance in the auxiliary-staff, town-residence rating. The R-squared value would show drastic change (to 0.30) if the factor for population (variable 9) were omitted.

The multiple-regression equation takes the following form:

$$Y_{63} + 46.91 + 0.001X_9 + 0.073X_1 - 0.028X_5 + 0.084X_{11}$$

where Y_{63} is the percent of college auxiliary staff living in the college community (computed for large and small college communities as a group), and the variables are as indicated in Table 3.3. Except for the variable for auxiliary-staff size, all terms in the equation are positive. In accordance with this, it is reasonable to suggest that as auxiliary staff at the college increases in size, more personnel will be drawn from outside the college community. This applies to both large and small communities.

ADDITIONAL EXPLANATIONS

Multiple-regression analysis is a partial explanation of the variation of community size and other factors with town-residence ratings. Many of the variables listed in Table 3.3 apply to some of the college communities but not to all of them and, therefore, do not enter the final regression equations. In offering an additional explanation for the above relationships, it is necessary to consider some of the unique situations that apply in several of the college communities.

As an over-all effect, general employment levels for professional and auxiliary personnel in the area will affect commutation or migration of individuals. For example, if a particular community loses a manufacturer, it is likely that the auxiliary staff of a newly established or expanding college will obtain a good part of its new employees from the local unemployed. Also, education and skills of the local labor force relate directly to possible employment at the college. The scope of this study does not allow for more than brief mention of these variables. The fact that the communities under consideration are in a limited region helps somewhat to equalize the situation in the above regard, but differences do exist; however, we are concerned with a search for commonalities.

At a more specific level, interesting comparisons can be made between colleges in small and large communities, between two colleges in the same community, and for other situations. (See Appendix

Tables B1, B2, and B3 for data on this part of the
discussion.) We are first concerned with factors
that corroborate the above regression analyses and
then with additional factors that have an effect on
certain college communities.

Three cases investigated involve college towns
that house both a four- and a two-year college.
These are Vassar and Dutchess County Community College, St. Lawrence and SUNY Canton, and Alfred University and SUNY Alfred. In each of these college
communities, the professional-staff residence ratings
for the four-year institutions (91.7, 93.9, and 76.6
percent, respectively) are considerably greater than
those for the two-year colleges (70.6, 79.2, and 60
percent). This is in part explained by four-year
colleges sponsoring some faculty housing, as well as
by the percent of Ph.D.s on staff and the age of the
institution, as shown in the regression analysis.

In all of the above locations, except for the
Town of Alfred, auxiliary-staff ratings for four-
and two-year colleges are extremely close (Vassar
and Dutchess, 79 and 78 percent; St. Lawrence and
SUNY Canton, 55.3 and 56.1 percent; and Alfred University and SUNY Alfred, 40.9 and 26.4 percent).
These are presented as additionally interesting parallels in the larger communities, and strengthen
the statistical evidence on variation of auxiliary-
staff residence location with community size.

In the case of Alfred, the auxiliary staff at
both colleges indicate low town-residence ratings,
and the two-year college draws a substantially higher
percentage of its auxiliary staff from outside the
village. This may, in part, be owing to recent expansion and a good wage level at SUNY Alfred for
auxiliary staff compared to that in surrounding
towns. Both colleges draw considerable personnel
from Alfred Station, Almond, Andover, Hornell, and
Wellsville. In this sense, Alfred Village is part
of a growing complex of towns. From another view,
it is a village that finds residential and other expansion difficult. (This was discussed in detail
in Chapter 2.) When we observe the pattern in

Figures 1 and 2 and review Appendix Table B.3, we
note that Morrisville and Alfred villages experience
an extremely low town-residence input for both professional and auxiliary personnel, and the villages
surrounding these communities gain a proportionate
share of benefits because of the presence of the colleges. In regard to professional-staff residence,
these college communities appear to be below what
could be a minimum level and substantially reduce
the moderate rating characteristic of the two-year
college in the small community.

Other cases studied involved two baccalaureate
insitutions in the same community. Evidence of a
narrow range for residential input is shown by the
fact that ratings closely resemble each other; thus,
SUNY Oneonta, and Hartwick, at the same location,
show only a 6-percent difference in their town-residence ratings for professional and auxiliary staff.
Full data are not available for a Clarkson-SUNY
Potsdam comparison, but their ratings for the total
staff are about 4 percent apart.

As previous discussion has shown, small college
communities vary considerably in their staff town-
residence ratings. Further discussion is warranted
for some with relatively high ratings. These include Hamilton (3,348 population) and Delhi (population, 2,307), homes of Colgate University and SUNY
Delhi, respectively.

As Appendix Table B.2 and other data indicate,
Hamilton Village serves the great majority of its
professional- and auxiliary-college staff and exhibits considerable centrality. Except for Oneida
and Norwich, each about 20 miles distant, it is the
largest central place in its area. Utica and Syracuse, close to 30 and 40 miles away, respectively,
house a little over 1 percent of the college's professional staff and none of its auxiliary staff.
Hamilton is an attractive village with a strong college tradition. With per capita retail sales in
1963 at $1,723, compared to that for New York State
at $1,449, and for Madison County at $1,346, it is
not a shopping mecca, but it is an attractive,
dominant marketing point in its locality.

Delhi lies somewhat isolated in a steep and pic-
turesque valley near the western gateway to the
Catskill Mountains. About 20 miles from Oneonta
(population 13,412), it draws less than 5 percent of
its professional staff and less than 3 percent of
its auxiliary staff from this city. It ranks high
in per capita income for its region, and it has adequate residential and commercial facilities with
room for some expansion.[9]

A perusal of the data on some of the newer two-
year colleges not included in the regression analysis may be helpful in further judgment of the factors
previously discussed. Appendix Table B.3 is useful
in this regard.

Although some colleges exhibit low town-residence ratings, most colleges compare well with other
institutions and industry, especially in drawing
professional personnel to an area.[10]

SUMMARY

It should be noted, relative to staff-population
input to the college community, that professional-
staff residence (input) ratings for public and private four-year colleges taken as a group show relatively small variation with community size (see
Table 3.2). However, when considered as a set, the
four-year public colleges studied show increasing
professional-staff input as town size increases;
these colleges are individually larger than the private institutions, and this may affect residence
ratings for small towns. Also of interest is the
fact that four-year colleges indicate higher professional-staff residence input than two-year colleges.

As for auxiliary staff, all the colleges studied
show an increase in residential (input) ratings as
town size increases; high occupational commutation
for the college in the small community generally occurs.

We can conclude that low spillout of professional-staff residence prevails in the large rural
town for all colleges and also for the private college in the viable small community. Through use of
regression equations, it is possible to predict professional-staff input for public four-year institutions and auxiliary-staff residence ratings for all
colleges. This can be used in long-range planning
for professional-staff housing, campus parking, college-staff expansion, and other related services.
For reasons of possible high spillout, caution should
be observed in selecting the small town for college
location; however, the active small community with
good potential for growth can do well relative to
professional-staff input and interaction.

For the college located in the large city and
metropolitan area, reversal of the above residence-
input characteristics can be anticipated; this may
vary in degree and should be verified by additional
investigation. For example, in large cities, unless
special provisions for housing are available, faculty
frequently reside in suburban locations. Also, professional staff may be drawn from districts in the
metropolis that are a substantial distance from the
college. With this case, a considerable spillout of
benefits from the college vicinity could occur. It
can be expected that auxiliary staff, especially office help, will be drawn primarily from the college
environs. However, depending on employment and manpower conditions, specialists, maintenance personnel,
and others could come from distant points in the
city.

NOTES

1. Where useful, the term "town-residence
rating" will be used to denote the percent of staff
members living in the college community.

2. The Dutchess Community College is located
near the northern boundary of the City of Poughkeepsie and within 2 miles of the Township of Hyde Park.

3.   See New York State Division of the Budget,
"The Executive Budget, Fiscal Year April 1, 1968 to
March 31, 1969," submitted by Nelson A. Rockefeller,
Governor (Albany: New York State Division of the
Budget, 1968), pp. 980-82. Some of the colleges not
included in the regression analysis, for reasons
previously given, show extremely low college town-
residence ratings for staff. For example, at Sullivan and Rockland County community colleges, professional staff native to the college community were at
5.4 and 14.8 percent, respectively; for auxiliary
staff, these figures were at 15.2 and 5.3 percent.
Among other economic and social considerations, this
indeed presupposes a low payroll input to the college
towns at this stage of the college's development.
It is interesting to note that these colleges grew
at a rapid rate. Rockland Community College listed
a full-time undergraduate enrollment of 92 in 1959,
and 653 in 1954, with its estimated Fall, 1967, enrollment at 1,824 full-time, and 1,658 part-time,
students. Sullivan Community College, established
after 1960, indicated a 1964 enrollment of 288 and
estimated full- and part-time enrollments at 905 and
151, respectively. Professional and auxiliary staff
at these colleges grew at a correspondingly rapid
rate, but many appear either to have been drawn from
outside the college community or to have obtained
residence in other localities. In Appendix Table
A.3, note the influence of New York City on Rockland
Community College staff residence.

4.   Figure 1 does not include data on colleges
excluded from the regression analysis. Some of
these, as shown in Appendix Table B.3, exhibit extremely low professional staff-residence ratings.

5.   The Mureg Ben David program was used for
multiple-regression analysis. This program was obtained through the School of Agriculture Department
of Agricultural Economics and was run on the IBM
360/65 computer. When the multiple regression was
begun, all of the variables in Table 3.3 were used.
The R-squared values obtained were in the 0.80-0.90
range; there were many small contributions by a large
number of variables, but they had low statistical

significance. Also, the variable for number of villages professional staff live in (LOC) contributed substantially to the explanation of the dependent variable; because this variable would be difficult to apply in planning, it was dropped from consideration along with others. The remaining variables shown in Table 3.4 result in a lesser R squared but yield a stronger statistical statement. The ECON Regression Program was used for the regression analysis for four-year colleges in the State University system.

6. The population variable is included in the regression equation only because of our special interest in this relationship.

7. For this regression analysis, the independent variables of importance were DEGREE-YRS and POPUL-40.

8. The variables listed in Table 3.3 were used in the initial multiple-regression analysis for this phase of the study. Only those indicating a significant and substantial effect on the multiple-correlation coefficient were retained for the final analysis. Only linear regression was used in this case. However, Figure 2 suggests that curvilinear regression would probably yield a higher R-squared value.

9. Barclay G. Jones and Jon T. Lang, Studies in Regional Development: Population, Activities, and Incomes in Chenango, Delaware, and Otsego Counties (Ithaca: Cornell University, New York State College of Agriculture, 1965), pp. 113-15.

10. Three major manufacturing plants surveyed in the Ithaca-Cortland area indicated town-residence ratings for the total staff between 35.1 and 42.1 percent. About 61 percent of the supervisory staff at the National Cash Register Company plant lived in Ithaca at the time of the survey.

4

COLLEGE-STAFF
INTERACTION
IN THE COMMUNITY:
ECONOMIC IMPACT
AND SOCIAL FACTORS

Although college staff and students reside in
the college community, many of their purchases are
made in neighboring villages or cities. Consequently,
their economic impact on the town is reduced substantially. As discussed previously and as will be further demonstrated in this chapter, economic spillout
depends on the size of the college community, the
extent of its commercial activity, its distance from
competing and attractive commerce centers, and other
factors.

In like manner, social interaction between the
college population and the townspeople may show a
high or a low level of exchange. Social attributes
of the college family can cause substantial change
in the community or may have only a moderate effect.

In this chapter, we will examine the social and
economic characteristics of the college population
and its interaction with community components. We
are concerned not only with the input of economic,
social, and human capital into a community but also
with the extent of the interaction of these inputs
with the community structure and population, at least
in the first round of transactions.

Many social and economic factors in the community
change when a college is established or expands. Only

a limited number of these factors can be examined in
this study. Our primary concern is to identify selected factors that act to build the community and
affect its institutions. In the economic sphere,
measures of these effects include per capita personal
income, retail sales, and property values.[1] When
these decrease, the community is less able to support
its services. Social factors of interest include
community-service activity by college-related persons
and interrelations of these individuals with other
residents in the community.[2] When these increase,
there is greater potential for community change and
development.

     This chapter further develops the earlier treat-
ment of information on SUNY Alfred Technical College
and SUNY Cortland. Data on Cazenovia College and the
Auburn Community College are presented to supplement
the argument. Cazenovia is a two-year private college
for girls in a small but viable town characterized
by a relatively high socioeconomic level. Auburn
Community College is a two-year college in a city of
close to 35,000 population.[3]

     Of special interest are the data on Alfred Uni-
versity vis-à-vis that for Alfred Technical College
because these two colleges are located in the same
town. Their comparison strengthens conclusions derived previously relative to community size and
spillout and affords an interesting contrast for the
two- and four-year college. Conclusions based on
these data apply only to the colleges examined, and
generalizations for other colleges should be made
with caution.

SELECTED ECONOMIC CHARACTERISTICS

Impact on Retail Trade

     Categories of retail trade that are especially
important to the college community include food
stores, eating and drinking places, and apparel
stores. These obtain a high proportion of the total
volume of retail sales and are key indicators of the

health of retail trade in a locality. College-staff
purchases in each of these categories can boost college community retail sales considerably unless spillout occurs.

Food Purchases

Per capita food sales are considerably higher
than sales in other categories, such as apparel,
furniture, drugs, gasoline, and restaurants. When
food sales are low in a college community, other con-
sumer goods on the shopping itinerary are generally
affected, and a major gap in the retail-trade sector
is thereby created.

Data obtained indicates that in 1968 the majority
of the professional and auxiliary staff at Alfred
Technical College made their food purchases outside
the college town. Auxiliary-staff purchases were
especially high in this regard. In this group, close
to 78 percent made no food purchases at all in Alfred
Village. Data in Table 4.1 indicate that less than
15 percent of the professionals and 5 percent of the
auxiliary staff bought 90 percent or more of these
staples locally; at a lesser purchasing level, only
35 percent of the professional staff and about 8 percent of the auxiliary staff purchases 50 percent or
more of their meats, groceries, and other foods in
the college town.

These data reflect the previous discussion on
staff location. Many staff members live outside
Alfred Village and therefore make their purchases
elsewhere. But in addition to this, the village is
not able to attract purchasing dollars from staff
who work in the college community and frequently pass
through its shopping district en route to work. In
fact, because the percentage of staff shopping for
food in the village is far less than the percentage
of staff living in the college town, a spillout of
purchasing dollars is indicated for these basic items.
Thus, not only do staff members at the college reside
outside the village in substantial numbers but also
many of those residing in the college town make their
food purchases elsewhere. Our data indicate that

TABLE 4.1

Staff Food Purchases in the College Town, in Percent

Percent Purchased in College Town	Alfred Tech.		Cortland		Alfred University		Cazenovia		Auburn		Total
	Prof.	Auxil.	Prof.	Auxil.	Prof.	Auxil.	Prof.	Auxil.	Prof.	Auxil.	
0-10	50.4	86.1	12.7	13.3	25.1	33.3	34.0	13.0	17.6	0.0	31.9
20-40	14.5	5.6	0.0	3.3	33.3	11.1	4.3	0.0	3.8	0.0	9.0
50-80	21.3	2.8	11.2	16.6	23.0	25.0	21.3	21.8	13.8	14.2	17.4
90-100	13.7	5.6	76.0	66.7	18.7	30.5	40.5	65.2	65.1	85.7	41.9
Total	100.0	100.0	100.0	100.0	100.0	100.0	100.0	100.0	100.0	100.0	100.0
N	117	36	71	30	48	36	48	25	80	14	502

Note: Details may not add up to totals because of rounding.

other places in Allegany County and the City of Hornell absorb the bulk of these purchases.

The situation at Cortland is quite different
from that at Alfred. In 1968, the majority of professional and auxiliary staff at Cortland College
made their food purchases in the City of Cortland.
Both staff groups exhibited similar behavior in this
regard, and 56 percent of each bought 100 percent of
their food staples in this city. Although some leakage in purchasing is apparent, a very high proportion
(79 percent) of the professional and auxiliary staff
bought 80 percent or more of these items locally.
When we review our data on staff residence at Cortland, a fair balance is noted between the proportion
of staff who live in Cortland and those who buy their
foods in this city.

Information from the university largely corrob-
orates the data from the Alfred Technical College.
The professional staff at Alfred University indicated
a slightly higher percentage of food purchases in the
village than those at Alfred Technical College. However, they are still considerably below levels at
Cazenovia, Auburn, and Cortland in this regard.[4] The
auxiliary staff at the university also made many more
of their food purchases in Alfred Village than did
those at the technical college, but they, too, fell
substantially below auxiliary staff at Cazenovia,
Auburn, and Cortland in this category. Details are
indicated in Table 4.1; 42 percent of the professional
staff at Alfred University made 50 percent or more
of their food purchases in the college town compared
to 35 percent at Alfred Technical College, 62 percent
at Cazenovia College, 79 percent at Auburn Community
College, and 87 percent at Cortland College.

Well over half (56 percent) of the auxiliary
staff at Alfred University made 50 percent or more
of their food purchases in the college town compared
to 8 percent at Alfred Technical College, 87 percent
at Cazenovia, 100 percent at Auburn, and 83 percent
at Cortland. The above difference between the two
institutions in Alfred is expected, as previous data
(Table 3.1A) indicate that more individuals on the

professional (77 percent) and auxiliary staff (41 percent) at Alfred University live in Alfred Town than those on staff at the technical college (60 and 26 percent, respectively). However, the fact remains that Alfred is incurring a high opportunity loss in its retail-food sales.

Cazenovia shows a far better situation. There, three fourths of the professional staff and more than half (54 percent) of the auxiliary staff live in the village, and, although Cazenovia shows some losses in food sales relative to professional staff, it appears to attract food purchasers among its auxiliary staff who live outside the village.

Clothing Purchases

In the category of clothing, the situation for Alfred in retail trade is even worse than for food. In 1968, about 90 percent of the staff at Alfred made 10 percent or less of their work-, dress-, and play-clothing purchases in the village (Table 4.2). Although a small clothing shop exists in the village, it caters mostly to college students and draws very few of the college staff. About 50 percent of the professional and auxiliary staff make half of their clothing purchases in nearby Hornell. Others are attracted to other incounty locations, and over 30 percent of the professional staff make 50 percent or more of their clothing purchases outside the county. The majority (over 80 percent) of professional and auxiliary staff living either in or outside of Alfred make the bulk of their clothing purchases outside the village.

Although the percentage of clothing purchases by college staff is far higher in Cortland, this city, with 21 apparel and 9 general-merchandise stores in 1963, lagged in attracting clothing purchases by staff. This is especially noticeable when these expenditures are compared with food purchases, discussed above. Only about 27 percent of the professional staff and 37 percent of the auxiliary staff buy 90 percent or more of their clothing in the City of Cortland. From the data in Table 4.2, it would appear that many faculty make their major clothing purchases outside this city. Syracuse, within a half hour's drive, draws slightly over 30 percent of the professional staff on 20 or more days during the year; during these visitations, clothing purchases are likely. Also, the fact that 50 percent of the auxiliary staff visit Syracuse during 10 or more days during the year and 36 percent make 50 percent or more of their clothing purchases outside of Cortland County indicates that Syracuse may also draw auxiliary-staff purchases for clothing.

In clothing sales, the larger cities surveyed demonstrate their centrality and attraction compared to the villages. As depicted in Table 4.2, well over half of the college professional staffs at Cortland and Auburn made 50 percent or more of their clothing purchases in their cities. Only a small percentage of the professional staff (1.8 percent at Alfred Technical College, 2.1 percent at Alfred University, and 11 percent at Cazenovia, did likewise in their college towns. Auxiliary staff at these colleges indicated somewhat higher clothing purchases in the college towns. Especially notable are the data on Cazenovia, Cortland, and Auburn, where 39, 70, and 93 percent of the auxiliary staff made 50 percent or more of their clothing purchases in the respective locations.

Demand for Restaurant Services

Restaurant services and eating and drinking places comprise substantial dollar volume in retail trade in New York State and are responsible for a considerable revenue to local and state government through the sales tax. In addition, good restaurants add to the social quality of a community and increase its attraction.

Relative to restaurant services, Alfred Village had only four establishments classified as eating and drinking places in 1963. These had luncheon facilities and attracted a good number of college students but few college staff. In 1968, 70 percent of the professional and auxiliary staffs at Alfred Technical

TABLE 4.2

Staff Clothing Purchases in the College Town, in Percent

Percent Purchased in College Town	Alfred Tech.		Cortland		Alfred University		Cazenovia		Auburn		Total
	Prof.	Auxil.	Prof.	Auxil.	Prof.	Auxil.	Prof.	Auxil.	Prof.	Auxil.	
0-10	89.8	91.9	32.4	20.0	83.4	77.8	66.7	43.5	15.0	0.0	31.9
20-40	8.6	5.4	7.0	10.0	14.7	19.4	22.2	17.4	17.6	7.1	12.6
50-80	0.9	2.7	33.8	33.3	2.1	2.8	8.8	34.8	37.6	28.6	16.8
90-100	0.9	0.0	26.8	36.7	0.0	0.0	2.2	4.4	30.0	64.3	13.2
Total	100.0	100.0	100.0	100.0	100.0	100.0	100.0	100.0	100.0	100.0	100.0
N	117	37	71	30	48	36	45	23	80	14	501

Note: Details may not add up to totals because of rounding.

College made almost no use of eating places in the village (Table 4.3). Forty-three percent of the professional and 80 percent of the auxiliary staff sought all of their restaurant services outside the village. In the latter case, many of the auxiliary staff living in Alfred left the village to obtain this service.

Cortland far surpassed Alfred Technical College in this regard; close to 50 percent of the college's professional staff and 53 percent of its auxiliary staff made 80 percent or more of their restaurant expenditures in this city. Cortland listed 48 eating and drinking establishments in 1963 with per capita sales ($142) well above those for Upstate New York ($110).[5] In spite of this, about 25 percent of the professional staff used restaurants outside the city most of the time.

The staff at Alfred University indicated somewhat higher local patronage for restaurants and eating and drinking places than did the staff at Alfred Technical College, but the predominant tendency here also was to obtain restaurant services outside the village. The situation in Cazenovia Village resembled that in Alfred Village. However, college staff in Auburn showed a pattern more related to that in Cortland. Thus, restaurants in the larger cities studied demonstrated greater attraction for college staff than those in the small towns.

Furniture Purchases

In this study, the data obtained relative to college-staff purchases of furniture also differentiates the small from the large community. The large community can generally support one or more furniture outlets that draw a substantial proportion of the college staff. Although furniture sales generally show a considerably lower dollar volume than do food sales, the former are a good source of local revenue through the sales tax. However, the small community usually lacks retail-furniture establishments.

TABLE 4.3

Staff Families' Restaurant Purchases in the College Town, in Percent

Percent Purchased in College Town	Alfred Tech.		Cortland		Alfred University		Cazenovia		Auburn		Total
	Prof.	Auxil.	Prof.	Auxil.	Prof.	Auxil.	Prof.	Auxil.	Prof.	Auxil.	
0-10	70.0	85.7	14.0	9.9	61.3	59.9	51.1	26.0	12.7	7.1	43.2
20-40	17.0	8.5	11.2	3.3	15.8	8.5	13.9	17.1	10.1	0.0	12.1
50-80	10.0	5.6	42.1	46.5	20.2	14.2	34.7	43.4	47.2	42.7	28.3
90-100	2.5	0.0	38.3	40.0	2.2	17.0	0.0	13.0	49.9	32.3	15.9
Total	100.0	100.0	100.0	100.0	100.0	100.0	100.0	100.0	100.0	100.0	100.0
N	117	35	71	30	44	35	43	23	78	14	490

Note: This table includes restaurant services, drinks, and ice cream purchases. Details may not add up to totals because of rounding.

Alfred Village has no real furniture outlets. Glidden Galleries may sell special pieces from time to time, and a few appliances are available through the local hardware store, but, generally, Hornell, Wellsville, or other cities are the primary sources in this category. This situation is reflected in Table 4.4. About 90 percent of the professional and almost 95 percent of the college's auxiliary staff buy their furniture and appliances outside the village.

At Cazenovia a like situation holds. About 8 percent of the professional and close to half the auxiliary staff make only a small fraction (10 percent or less) of their furniture purchases in the village. Over half of the professional and a fourth of the auxiliary staff choose Syracuse for almost all (90 percent or more) furniture purchases. Community size evidently is a big factor in furniture sales. Auburn indicates high performance in this category. Over 75 percent of the professional and 92 percent of the auxiliary staff make more than half their furniture purchases in this city of over 34,000 people.

The City of Cortland had 22 furniture and equipment stores in 1963. Sales in this category were at $111 per capita compared to county, upstate, and New York State values at $58, $54, and $71, respectively. About 60 percent of the college's professional and auxiliary staff made 80 percent or more of their furniture and appliance purchases in the city. Only 13 percent of the professional and 20 percent of the auxiliary staff made no purchases in Cortland. When this is compared to the percent of staff living outside the city, it is evident that, in the furniture category, Cortland attracts staff members living in other localities. This offers some evidence of Cortland's centrality in the area.

Additional data obtained indicate that primary reasons for shopping outside the college town are residence outside the community, unavailability of goods, and better variety elsewhere. Price of goods and comparative quality of goods in other localities

TABLE 4.4

Staff Families' Furniture Purchases in the College Town, in Percent

Percent Purchased in College Town	Alfred Tech.		Cortland		Alfred University		Cazenovia		Auburn		Total
	Prof.	Auxil.	Prof.	Auxil.	Prof.	Auxil.	Prof.	Auxil.	Prof.	Auxil.	
0-10	94.8	97.0	19.6	26.6	89.1	97.0	79.9	47.8	18.1	7.1	61.5
20-40	3.4	2.8	5.6	3.3	6.4	2.9	11.0	13.0	3.9	0.0	5.0
50-80	1.7	0.0	25.2	19.9	4.3	0.0	4.4	21.6	25.7	28.4	11.9
90-100	0.0	0.0	49.2	50.0	0.0	0.0	4.4	17.3	51.8	64.2	21.2
Total	100.0	100.0	100.0	100.0	100.0	100.0	100.0	100.0	100.0	100.0	100.0
N	117	35	71	30	46	34	45	23	77	14	492

Note: This table includes furniture, television, and appliance purchases. Details may not add up to totals because of rounding.

are minor factors in the college communities surveyed.
This would imply an opportunity loss for local entre-
preneurs, but its extent would depend on general demand by the entire community rather than only by the
college staff. The volume of local retail sales in
the small town may not warrant additional investment
by the entrepreneur in a greater variety of stock.
On the other hand, the larger city's centrality coun-
teracts staff-residential spillout, attracts people
from outlying areas, and may justify the added investment.

Additional Factors in Retail Trade

There are other retail and service categories
that could be additionally discussed. These indicate a condition similar to those analyzed above.

Comparison of data obtained in this study with
published data on retail trade shows some interesting
and useful parallels. As indicated in Table 4.5, retail trade at Alfred in all categories was extremely
low. Cazenovia, larger in permanent population than
Alfred but still a very small community, had a comparatively high retail-sales record, especially in
food, lumber and hardware, gasoline service stations,
and other retail stores; its eating and drinking
classification was at a lower level but was still
substantial. However, lower sales in furniture and
clothing appear evident in Cazenovia, and this con-
forms to our data--especially on professional staff
at the college, which indicate attraction to Syracuse
and other localities in these categories. Nearby
Hamilton, the home of Colgate University, does not
show as high a retail-sales record as Cazenovia. Its
over-all retail sales per capita was $1,723 compared
to $2,571 per capita at the latter location.

Cortland and Auburn, with retail sales per capita at $2,038 and $1,681, respectively, are well above
the upstate level ($1,394); however, neither city
displays an enviable record in this regard. Commercial areas in larger cities experience substantial
competition from shopping centers outside city limits
and from larger cities in the region. As indicated

TABLE 4.5

Retail Trade at Selected Locations in New York State, Number of Establishments and Per Capita Sales, 1963

	Population 1960[a]	College Enrollment 1964[b]	Sales Per Cap. 1963 ($)	General Merchandise Stores		Apparel Stores		Furniture Stores		Drug Stores	
				Est.	Per Cap. ($)	Est.	Per Cap. ($)	Est.	Per Cap. ($)	Est.	Per Cap. ($)
1. New York State	16,544,897	--	1,449	4,502	186	16,271	123	9,297	71	5,525	42
2. Upstate New York	5,977,137	--	1,394	1,759	163	4,128	77	2,990	54	1,740	43
Cities:											
3. Syracuse area	673,056	26,068	1,388	180	169	417	81	303	56	171	44
4. Auburn	33,607	878	1,681	16	275	41	119	22	--	8	42
5. Cortland	19,102	3,045	2,038	9	248	21	126	22	111	6	58
6. Oneida	11,648	--	2,208	9	213	12	84	10	112	5	124
7. Ithaca	28,727	16,053	2,204	15	238	33	148	20	113	12	63
8. Hornell	13,855	--	1,790	6	217	13	172	13	75	5	70
Villages:											
9. Alfred	2,807	2,507	315	0	0	0	0	0	0	1	--
10. Wellsville	5,945	--	3,281	3	254	13	157	7	74	4	72
11. Cazenovia	2,584	410	2,571	4	--	3	--	4	35	2	--
12. Hamilton	3,331	1,492	1,723	2	--	7	90	0	0	1	--
13. Potsdam	7,724	3,840	2,526	7	420	13	85	5	67	3	--
14. Canton	4,995	2,365	2,497	1	--	6	135	5	32	2	--
15. Cobleskill	3,455	1,021	3,693	2	--	12	202	4	67	2	--
16. New Paltz	3,041	2,758	2,278	3	--	8	114	1	--	3	--
17. Brockport	5,231	2,130	2,168	3	--	7	126	5	197	4	125

	Gasoline Stations Est.	Gasoline Stations Per Cap.($)	Lumber Hardware Dealers Est.	Lumber Hardware Dealers Per Cap.($)	Food Stores Est.	Food Stores Per Cap.($)	Eating Places Est.	Eating Places Per Cap.($)	Other Retail Stores Est.	Other Retail Stores Per Cap.($)
1. New York State	12,010	69	6,630	54	35,817	368	35,026	154	26,292	152
2. Upstate New York	6,669	84	3,397	77	11,386	384	14,356	110	9,459	135
Cities:										
3. Syracuse area	697	83	359	70	1,103	358	1,449	115	1,013	118
4. Auburn	42	86	25	116	82	434	79	102	83	152
5. Cortland	34	133	17	108	36	613	48	142	43	166
6. Oneida	20	147	7	83	31	659	35	97	27	243
7. Ithaca	42	157	18	80	35	470	75	176	57	298
8. Hornell	24	113	9	131	26	390	35	115	28	115
Villages:										
9. Alfred	2	--	0	0	5	131	4	32	4	96
10. Wellsville	9	148	13	216	25	683	21	179	18	160
11. Cazenovia	7	181	3	270	5	700	7	178	8	322
12. Hamilton	3	56	3	148	7	437	13	138	9	328
13. Potsdam	19	214	5	73	16	717	29	183	25	311
14. Canton	6	98	11	327	15	590	15	123	23	493
15. Cobleskill	10	179	4	228	7	1,046	9	104	21	814
16. New Paltz	6	256	6	407	6	--	14	189	10	292
17. Brockport	10	131	3	110	11	682	15	140	15	115

aPopulation data exclude inmates of institutions.

bCollege enrollment indicated was undergraduate full-time enrollment, 1964, except for Ithaca and Syracuse, for which data were obtained from the Business Fact Book and include only students enrolled for degrees, as of Fall, 1965.

Note: Stores listed above are classified in the Business Fact Book as follows: general merchandise stores; apparel accessory stores; furniture, home furnishings, equipment stores; drug stores, proprietary stores; gasoline service stations; lumber, building materials, hardware, farm equipment dealers; food stores; eating, drinking places; and other retail stores. Automotive dealers and nonstore retailers have been omitted from the above list. Est. indicates number of establishments. Per Cap. indicates per capita sales.

Source: New York State Department of Commerce, Business Fact Book 1967-68 (Albany, Part 1, Business and Manufacturing, 1968).

in our data, Cortland and Auburn show high retention
of college staff retail purchases. Although spillout applies to the large city as well as the village,
the smaller locality with less slack in its operation
and infrastructure may experience proportionately
greater fiscal difficulties owing to the concomitant
spillout of tax revenues and the added demand for
services related to the college presence.

    As our data indicate, the small community need
not necessarily exhibit low patterns in retail sales
and high spillout. It can do relatively well in food,
restaurant services, clothing, and other retail trade
with the proper entrepreneurship, attractive facilities, some amount of centrality in its area, and
boundaries that permit expansion. Relative to the
college, the degree of spillout of staff payroll and
student expenditures will largely determine the economic benefit and burden of the institution.

    In general, we can conclude that the small col-
lege community with a weak and static commercial district within a short distance from other competing
centers (with relatively high centrality) will experience high spillout of the purchasing dollar.
With low retail sales, a rapid outflow of funds occurs; with a low economic multiplier, the small
community's benefits from the college presence are
considerably lessened. When, in addition to this,
new faculty buy property and build homes in other
localities, additional sources of financial strength
are removed. The college may expand at a rapid rate,
which requires additional services, but the community
sometimes is forced to develop much more slowly and
is weakened by spillout and a low financial base that
cannot provide for growth. This is not to say that
the small town must inevitably experience this condition; as previously discussed, data on Hamilton
(Colgate University) and other villages indicate the
contrary.

    We can conclude that important qualifications
for college location in the small community are twofold: first, readily available room for town growth
to balance the expansion of the college and, second,

an attractiveness that will assure community development and growth. A college community cannot serve
every need of the college, its staff, and students,
but it must experience a reasonable amount of growth
as the college increases in size in order to carry
successfully the cost of services related to the
college operation.

The situation in Alfred Village can be ameliorated basically by expansion of its commercial operation and housing capability and probably by expansion
of the village boundaries. These courses of action
present difficulties, and the village will probably
need outside help in their accomplishment.

Impact on Housing

In addition to a college's effect on retail
sales, important gains in community economic health
and financial capability occur through an upgrading
of housing as well as occupational and personal income levels in a locality. Some of this has already
been discussed in previous chapters; what follows
will supplement this material.

Professional staff at the colleges studied generally live in homes that are above the average in
market value. Consequently, property values and tax
revenues in the expanding college community are increased by influx of these individuals.

Data obtained at the Alfred Technical College
(Table 4.6) indicate that a significant difference
exists between professional- and auxiliary-staff
housing in the area. Close to 50 percent of the
college's professional staff owning homes indicated
that their residences were in the $20,000-$35,000
range, compared to 10 percent for auxiliary employees
in this category. The great majority of auxiliary-
staff members (close to 80 percent) live in housing
valued below the $15,000 level; professional-staff
members show a much smaller group (22 percent) below
this mark. If these ranges are compared to the median housing value for Alfred Village in 1963
($12,000) as indicated in Table 2.2 considerable

TABLE 4.6

Current Market Value of Homes Owned by College Staff, in Percent

Market Value in Dollars	Alfred Tech.		Cortland		Alfred University		Cazenovia		Auburn		Total
	Prof.	Auxil.	Prof.	Auxil.	Prof.	Auxil.	Prof.	Auxil.	Prof.	Auxil.	
Below $10,000	2.4	41.3	2.0	15.0	6.6	31.0	0.0	21.4	1.7	16.6	9.7
$10-14,900	20.4	37.9	8.1	20.0	10.0	17.2	3.3	35.7	13.7	33.3	17.2
$15-19,900	24.1	10.3	24.4	35.0	23.3	20.6	10.0	14.2	24.1	33.3	21.8
$20-24,900	15.6	3.4	30.6	15.0	33.3	13.7	30.0	7.1	36.2	16.6	22.4
$25-29,900	19.2	6.9	18.3	10.0	20.0	10.3	16.6	14.2	10.3	0.0	14.6
$30-34,900	13.2	0.0	10.2	0.0	6.6	0.0	23.3	0.0	10.3	0.0	8.9
$35-39,900	3.6	0.0	4.0	0.0	0.0	3.4	3.3	7.1	0.0	0.0	2.3
$40,000 and over	1.2	0.0	2.0	5.0	0.0	3.4	13.3	0.0	3.4	0.0	2.8
Total	100.0	100.0	100.0	100.0	100.0	100.0	100.0	100.0	100.0	100.0	100.0
N	83	29	49	20	30	29	30	14	58	6	348

Note: Details may not add up to totals because of rounding.

upgrading of housing and property values by the college professional staff is apparent, although former
(1963) housing values have increased considerably
with time. However, in the case of Alfred Technical
College, the extensive spillout of professional staff
to residences outside the village (as previously discussed) drastically reduces the potential benefit of
additional good housing for the community.

Cortland shows a similar upgrading of housing
levels owing to the influx of professional staff.
But there is not a significant difference between
professional- and auxiliary-staff residential levels;
more of the latter group enter into the higher ranges
than at Alfred. About 60 percent of the college's
professional staff live in homes in the $20,000-
$35,000 range, and 25 percent of the auxiliary staff
occupy this category. In the lower cost range, fewer
(10 percent) professional and (35 percent) auxiliary
staff live in housing below the $15,000 level. It
is possible to conclude that the impact on housing
values is considerably greater in Alfred than in
Cortland if the housing levels for auxiliary staff
are considered typical for each area. Also, using
housing as an indicator, Alfred Technical College
appears to employ many more auxiliary-staff members
who come from lower socioeconomic levels than at
Cortland.

At Alfred University, Cazenovia, and Auburn,
professional and auxiliary staff also differ in the
market values of their homes. About half of the
auxiliary staff at these colleges live in homes
valued below $15,000; however, only about 15 percent
of the professional staff are at this level. Close
to 60 percent of these professionals live in homes
valued above $20,000, but only about 30 percent of
the auxiliary staff are in this category.

Rental housing is the characteristic mode for
newer staff members coming from outside the area.
Monthly rental costs for housing show a somewhat
greater spread in the Cortland area than in the Alfred vicinity. In the Alfred area, a small number
of staff have rentals below the $75 level, and

monthly rentals between $125 and $175 are fairly common for staff members who rent. In Cortland, rentals between $75 and $175 are frequent, and many staff members rent around the $125 monthly level. This form of housing, especially for professional staff, has raised property values and monthly contract rent levels in the college communities studied.

Impact on Local Employment

The community labor force is substantially affected by the new or expanding college. As previously discussed, an input of better paying jobs enters the area through the institution. The bulk of the college's auxiliary-staff positions go to individuals already resident in the county. However, professional staff are generally attracted from outside the county.

The four-year college tends to have higher town-residence ratings for professional staff than the two-year college. However, the college in or near a large city generally draws a high proportion of auxiliary and professional staff from that locality. The college community's labor-force statistics vary for each situation accordingly.

Chi-square values for both Alfred Technical College and Cortland College show that a significant difference exists between professional- and auxiliary-staff members relative to the location of their previous employment.[6] This conclusion was readily anticipated, but the proportions obtained in the survey are of interest. Close to 70 percent of the professional staff at both colleges were previously employed at distant locations outside the county or adjacent counties (Table 4.7). And conversely, for the auxiliary staffs at both colleges, close to 70 percent (a bit higher for Cortland College and a bit lower for Alfred Technical College) were previously employed in the local area, including the college community, county, or adjacent counties. At Alfred, 26 percent of the professional and 6 percent of the auxiliary staff were employed outside New York State; at Cortland, this proportion was considerably higher,

TABLE 4.7

Location of Previous Employment by College Staff, in Percent

Location	Alfred Tech.		Cortland		Alfred University		Cazenovia		Auburn		Total
	Prof.	Auxil.	Prof.	Auxil.	Prof.	Auxil.	Prof.	Auxil.	Prof.	Auxil.	Total
College-town	4.2	16.1	8.4	32.1	14.8	32.3	8.3	33.3	15.1	66.6	15.5
This county	14.2	38.7	2.8	7.1	2.1	17.6	4.1	16.6	10.1	6.6	11.0
Adjacent county	11.7	12.9	19.7	35.7	6.3	17.6	39.5	33.3	18.9	6.6	18.9
New York State	43.7	25.8	30.9	14.2	29.7	20.5	29.1	8.3	32.9	13.3	30.4
Outside New York State	26.0	6.4	38.0	10.7	46.8	11.7	18.7	8.3	22.7	6.6	23.9
Total	100.0	100.0	100.0	100.0	100.0	100.0	100.0	100.0	100.0	100.0	100.0
N	119	31	71	28	47	34	48	24	79	15	496

Note: Details may not add up to totals because of rounding.

at 38 percent and 11 percent for these staff groups,
respectively.

Another important consideration is the fact that
Alfred Technical College has a far greater draw of
individuals previously employed in the county than
Cortland College has. At Alfred Technical College,
19 percent of its professional and 55 percent of its
auxiliary staff were so employed, compared to 11 percent and 39 percent, respectively, for Cortland College. Thus, at the county level, Alfred Technical
College has a greater effect as an employer of area
residents. Industry in Cortland probably offers more
competition for the area employee than is the case
in Allegany County. The situation evens out when the
area under consideration is extended to adjacent
counties. Relative to college town-residence ratings,
it is possible that individuals who worked in the
county prior to their employment at the college also
had lodging fairly near the college community; many
of these individuals probably maintained their former
lodging rather than move into the college community.
Alfred Technical College had 14 percent of the professional and 39 percent of the auxiliary staff previously employed in the county, and this would considerably lower its town-residence ratings.

Auxiliary staff at Alfred University, Auburn,
and Cazenovia also indicate that a considerable amount
of local recruitment occurs. The latter college draws
heavily on the Syracuse area for auxiliary personnel.
However, professional staffs at these colleges are
primarily nonlocal in origin. Over three fourths of
Alfred University's professionals were attracted from
outside the region of the college, and Auburn Community College and Cazenovia College required extra-
regional recruitment for about two thirds and one
half of their professional staffs, respectively.

Spouse Employment

When newcomers enter an area in considerable
numbers, as do professional staff at a college, there
is a good possibility that employment of their spouses
will bear upon economic and social factors in the

area. At the five colleges studied, between 40 and
70 percent of the professional staff indicated that
their spouses were employed. The higher percentages
occurred at the two-year colleges.

Faculty wives frequently engage in teaching or
in other professions, and communities in which these
skills are scarce generally benefit by this increased
supply of qualified personnel. In Table 4.8, the
high percentage of employed spouses engaged in teaching is indicated. Many of these individuals find employment in community schools, nurseries, and other
educational institutions.

For the professional staff, the percentages of
employed spouses engaged in teaching, professional,
and technical activities were high at all the colleges
studied, with Cazenovia at 82 percent, Cortland at
70 percent, Alfred Technical College at 67 percent,
Auburn at 60 percent, and Alfred University at 56
percent. In most cases, employment was in the county
or the college community, but many of the professional
and auxiliary staff at these colleges indicated that
their spouses worked in an adjacent county.

SELECTED SOCIAL CHARACTERISTICS

In addition to their economic input, incoming
professionals bring social qualities that have value
to the community or affect its change and growth.
A quantitative measure of a part of this input to a
locality can be obtained by utilization of common
statistical information on age, sex, educational
level, occupational level, intelligence quotient,
and other characteristics that can be summed, averaged, or otherwise manipulated.

Measurement of Input and Spillout
of Human and Social Capital
by Use of Indexes

Statistical measures for determining input of
human and social capital to a community can be obtained by the use of reliable indexes that are formed

TABLE 4.8

Major Occupation of Spouse, as Indicated by College Staff, in Percent

Occupation	Alfred Tech. Prof.	Auxil.	Cortland Prof.	Auxil.	Alfred University Prof.	Auxil.	Cazenovia Prof.	Auxil.	Auburn Prof.	Auxil.	Total
Teacher	45.9	4.7	53.3	14.2	35.7	13.6	45.8	0.0	39.5	12.5	33.0
Professional[a]	22.9	4.7	20.0	0.0	21.4	13.6	37.5	11.1	20.9	0.0	18.5
Craftsman[b]	3.2	19.0	3.3	14.2	0.0	9.0	0.0	22.2	6.9	62.5	8.5
Clerk[c]	21.3	23.8	10.0	7.1	10.7	9.0	4.1	0.0	2.3	0.0	10.7
Other	6.5	47.4	13.3	64.1	32.1	54.3	12.4	56.5	30.2	25.0	28.9
Total	100.0	100.0	100.0	100.0	100.0	100.0	100.0	100.0	100.0	100.0	100.0
N	61	21	30	14	28	22	14	24	43	8	269

[a]Includes other professional or technical personnel.
[b]Includes craftsmen, foremen, service workers, and equipment operators.
[c]Includes clerks, salesworkers, and secretaries.

Note: Details may not add up to totals because of rounding.

from a composite of basic characteristics. Examples of indexes used to describe social and economic characteristics of a community include indexes of socioeconomic status, community solidarity, neighborliness, and others; these have been demonstrated by a number of sociologists, planners, and human ecologists.[7]

It is possible to measure socioeconomic development in a community by use of the above quantitative values. It is also possible, in some degree, to plan an input of human and social qualities into a locality, just as an input of dollars is plannable as previously discussed relative to college establishment or expansion. However, to assess this input, spillout must be considered.

Application of the Community Service Activity Index can illustrate how an element of human and social input to the college community can be measured. The Community Service Activity Index was used to determine professional- and auxiliary-staff participattion in community activity.[8] This and related measures offer quantitative indications of the potential of the college, through its personnel, as an instrument for social development and change. Fifteen behavioral items related to community-service activity form the index. The individual scores 1 point for each activity he has engaged in. Scores have been standardized, and a score of 0-5 indicates a low participating member, 6-9 is average, and 10-15 is the range for an outstanding member of the community. The input of outstanding individuals to a town can be considered an asset in community development.

Survey results are indicated in Table 4.9. Chi-square values indicate a significant difference between professional- and auxiliary-staff personnel in community-service activity scores. As previously indicated, professionals are generally imported to the area while auxiliary staff are primarily local in origin.

At Alfred Technical College, 28 percent of the professional and 11 percent of the auxiliary staff

TABLE 4.9

Community Service Activity Scores of College Staff, in Percent

Score	Alfred Tech.		Cortland		Alfred University		Cazenovia		Auburn		Total
	Prof.	Auxil.	Prof.	Auxil.	Prof.	Auxil.	Prof.	Auxil.	Prof.	Auxil.	
0-5	20.6	54.3	25.4	48.2	31.3	44.5	25.1	52.0	22.0	42.8	30.7
6-9	51.3	34.2	38.0	41.3	47.9	55.6	45.8	32.0	45.2	42.9	44.9
10-15	28.2	11.5	36.6	10.5	20.9	0.0	29.2	16.0	33.0	14.3	24.4
Total	100.0	100.0	100.0	100.0	100.0	100.0	100.0	100.0	100.0	100.0	100.0
N	117	35	71	24	48	36	48	25	82	14	505

Note: Details may not add up to totals because of rounding.

108

scored as outstanding members in the community; 21 percent of the professional and 54 percent of the auxiliary staff scored as low participants in community activity. Mean score for the professionals was close to 8; for auxiliary-staff members, it was close to 5.5. The proportions of individuals in the outstanding-service category are most important, as it is this group that would be most active in creating change in the area.

At Alfred University, a lower percentage of staff members rated high scores; only 21 percent of the professional and none of the auxiliary staff scored as outstanding members of the community. At Cortland, close to 37 percent of the professionals scored in the outstanding community-activity range, and the percentages were somewhat lower at Auburn (33 percent) and Cazenovia (29 percent). However, at all the colleges studied, the proportion of professionals indicating outstanding service was at least double that of the auxiliary staff.

It is possible to calculate the input of community-service potential to each locality and to the general area around the college community owing to the influx of professional staff, in similar manner to the payroll input exhibited in Table 2.1. For example, for Alfred Technical College, with an assumed 70 percent of the 195-member professional staff newly entering the area and bringing a community-service potential score of 8, the community-service activity input amounts to 0.7 x 195 x 8 = 1,092 units. This represents an input of human and social capital to the area, which is of value in its growth. In per capita form, or when totaled as a neighborhood or community rating, it may represent a potential for development. The precise value of this potential for a community is difficult to assess fully at present. Delbert C. Miller suggests research to indicate the relationship between community-service activity and other community characteristics, such as solidarity and quality of community life.[9]

Political Input

Related to community-service activities are the political views of the college staff. These may effect change in an area if they differ substantially from those of other residents in the community (businessmen, farmers, etc.), and especially if the college professional staff is politically active and potent in the locality. The professional staff are largely newcomers. Except in the small villages, the size of this group makes it a minority. Generally, the rural areas of Upstate New York are strongly conservative and predominantly Republican. They resist change. Any differing political input via the college's professional staff may represent a threat to the conservative position.[10] As expected, the five colleges studied indicate that auxiliary staff generally have political views that closely resemble those of other townspeople. However, professional-staff members at the colleges are considerably less conservative.

At Alfred Technical College, close to half (46 percent) of the professional staff indicated that they held less conservative political views than other residents in the community. (See Table 4.10.) About 15 percent considered themselves far less conservative, and if political change were to come, it would probably be stimulated by individuals in this minority. The auxiliary staff, primarily native to the area, indicated political views largely similar (at 78 percent) to those of the townspeople in the general area, and the chi-square value indicated that a significant difference existed between professional- and auxiliary-staff groups.

At Cortland College, a still higher number (75 percent) of the professional staff showed less conservative political views than other local residents. A substantial number (38 percent) indicated that they were far less conservative. About 29 percent of the auxiliary-staff members also indicated less conservative views, and a sizable potential for community change was apparent at the college.

TABLE 4.10

Political Views of College Staff Compared to Other Residents in the Area, in Percent

Political Views	Alfred Tech.		Cortland		Alfred University		Cazenovia		Auburn		Total
	Prof.	Auxil.	Prof.	Auxil.	Prof.	Auxil.	Prof.	Auxil.	Prof.	Auxil.	
Far more conservative	0.8	2.7	2.9	3.5	2.0	3.0	0.0	0.0	0.0	7.1	1.6
Fairly more conservative	10.2	11.1	4.4	21.4	14.5	9.0	2.0	20.0	8.5	21.4	10.2
At same level of opinion	42.7	77.7	17.6	46.4	29.1	69.7	20.8	64.0	26.8	57.1	39.2
Fairly less conservative	30.7	8.3	36.7	21.4	35.4	12.1	39.5	12.0	34.1	14.2	28.6
Far less conservative	15.3	0.0	38.2	7.1	18.7	6.0	37.5	4.0	30.4	0.0	20.2
Total	100.0	100.0	100.0	100.0	100.0	100.0	100.0	100.0	100.0	100.0	100.0
N	117	36	68	28	48	33	48	25	82	14	499

Note: Other residents in the community were defined as businessmen, farmers, and workers in the area. Details may not add up to totals because of rounding.

111

112   THE COLLEGE AND COMMUNITY DEVELOPMENT

Several factors may influence the relative con-
servativeness of Alfred Technical College's professional staff, compared to that at Cortland. As
indicated in Table 4.7, a higher proportion of the
Alfred Technical College contingent previously worked
and lived in the county or came from adjacent counties that were predominantly rural and generally
conservative. Additional data from this survey indicate that close to 70 percent of the professional
staff at Cortland have lived in a large city or its
suburb for at least one year, compared to 50 percent
of those at Alfred Technical College. Conversely,
45 percent of the professionals at Alfred Technical
College never lived in a large city, compared to 23
percent at Cortland. Other factors influence political views (and certainly, individuals coming from
large cities need not be less conservative), but the
above-mentioned variables appear to suggest a relationship.

The professional and auxiliary staff at Alfred
University do not differ significantly from the respective staffs at Alfred Technical College in conservative tendencies. However, a considerable proportion (77 percent) of the professional staff at
Cazenovia indicated their political views were less
conservative than those of other residents in the
community. Many (88 percent) of the professional
staff at Cazenovia come from outside the county, and
a considerable number (68 percent) previously lived
in a large city or its suburb. This, again, may
substantially account for the less conservative view
of these professionals. Also, from the standpoint
of community residents themselves, historical data
on gubernatorial elections in New York State indicate
a predominantly conservative inclination for the town.

The data obtained from Auburn Community College
again indicate that a high proportion (65 percent) of
the professional staff are less conservative politically than other residents in this city. This information is also supported by additional survey data
that indicate that a large number of these professionals come from large cities outside the county.

Staff Influence on Local Policy

An important area of interaction between college staff and other residents in the community can occur, especially in the establishment of school-district policy. This area of decisionmaking is usually of special concern to the professionals. As educators, the faculty and administrators tend to favor greater expenditures for schools. The community residents are frequently divided on this issue. A proportionately large and active professional group may swing the vote and substantially influence school-district policy.

The opinions of college staff on the influence of the college in local government and school-district policy were solicited in this survey. The results are indicated in Tables 4.11 and 4.12. At Alfred Technical College, over 50 percent of the professional and auxiliary staff were of the opinion that college and staff influence is high or fairly high; both groups were quite agreed in this opinion, especially relative to local government policy as can be seen in the chi-square value. The staff at Alfred University corroborated this opinion.

At Cortland, the college was rated as a moderate or fairly low influence. However, some disagreement is evident in that the professional group assigned lower influence to the college than the auxiliary group; at Cortland, close to half (49 percent) of the professional staff felt that the college had fairly low or no influence in local government and school-district policy, but only about a quarter of the auxiliary staff gave this opinion. On the other hand, there is much agreement between the two groups in that only a small number of professional and auxiliary staff indicated fairly high or high influence on school-district and local-government policy.

It appears, for both Alfred and Cortland, that the size of the college professional staff relative to the size of the college community's total labor force has considerable bearing on the influence of the college. As indicated previously, in 1960 in

TABLE 4.11

Influence of the College and Staff on School-District Policy, in Percent

Influence Indicated By Staff	Alfred Tech.		Cortland		Alfred University		Cazenovia		Auburn		Total
	Prof.	Auxil.	Prof.	Auxil.	Prof.	Auxil.	Prof.	Auxil.	Prof.	Auxil.	
High	19.6	7.4	4.6	8.0	34.8	32.2	0.0	13.6	1.2	18.1	13.0
Fairly high	30.8	44.4	13.8	8.0	25.5	29.0	0.0	31.8	29.6	45.4	24.6
Moderate	31.7	40.7	32.3	60.0	30.2	29.0	37.2	36.3	38.2	26.3	35.6
Fairly low	14.0	7.4	36.9	16.0	9.3	9.6	48.8	13.6	27.1	0.0	21.5
None	3.7	0.0	12.3	8.0	0.0	0.0	13.9	4.5	3.7	0.0	5.2
Total	100.0	100.0	100.0	100.0	100.0	100.0	100.0	100.0	100.0	100.0	100.0
N	107	27	65	25	43	31	43	22	81	11	455

Note: Details may not add up to totals because of rounding.

TABLE 4.12

Influence of the College and Staff on Local-Government Policy, in Percent

Influence Indicated by Staff	Alfred Tech.		Cortland		Alfred University		Cazenovia		Auburn		Total
	Prof.	Auxil.	Prof.	Auxil.	Prof.	Auxil.	Prof.	Auxil.	Prof.	Auxil.	
High	15.3	12.1	1.5	11.5	23.2	29.4	0.0	12.5	0.0	7.6	10.3
Fairly high	37.8	42.4	19.7	11.5	34.8	20.5	7.1	33.3	18.2	53.8	26.7
Moderate	34.2	36.3	30.3	53.8	27.9	47.0	38.1	33.3	32.9	23.0	35.0
Fairly low	10.8	9.0	42.4	15.3	13.9	2.9	52.3	12.5	36.5	15.3	23.4
None	1.8	0.0	6.0	7.6	0.0	0.0	2.3	8.3	12.2	0.0	4.4
Total	100.0	100.0	100.0	100.0	100.0	100.0	100.0	100.0	100.0	100.0	100.0
N	111	33	66	26	43	34	42	24	82	13	474

Note: Details may not add up to totals because of rounding.

Alfred Village, the percentage of employed persons engaged in educational services was 41.2 percent of those employed in industry; on an occupational basis, 31.6 percent of those employed in Alfred Village were professional and technical workers. Since the Alfred school system includes Almond Village, where several of the college professional staff reside, Almond's labor-force proportions also bear influence. In 1960, in Almond, 21.7 percent of those employed in industry were engaged in educational services, and professional and technical workers made up 16 percent of the occupation groups.

The data for Alfred and Almond can be compared to that at Cortland where individuals engaged in educational services amounted to 9.3 percent of those in industry. On an occupational basis, 11.6 percent of those employed were professional and technical workers. Because there are many firms in Cortland that employ professional and technical help, the latter percentage should be reduced in assessing the number connected with the college. When this is approximated, the difference in the situation at Alfred and Cortland is considerable. At Alfred, the colleges (both Alfred Technical College and Alfred University) are the major employers; the professional group comprises a large proportion of the college staff, as indicated in Appendix Tables B.2 and B.3. In Cortland, the college staff is a small segment of the labor force. The influence of these colleges on local government and school policy appears to relate somewhat to their impact on the total labor force. However, other factors, such as the extent of faculty involvement in community affairs, are important.[11]

The situations at Cazenovia and Auburn strengthen these conclusions in that persons in educational services comprise only 15 and 4 percent of the employed labor force in each of these college communities, respectively. In these localities, close to 50 percent of the professional staff indicated low influence of the college and staff on local school-district and government policy. However, interviews at Auburn indicated that college-staff participation in community affairs helped in problem areas and somewhat increased college and staff influence in the formation of local policy.

Social Ties Between College Staff and Other Residents in the Community

The nonpolitical contact or interaction of the college family with other residents in the community (such as businessmen and farmers) is also important in social impact, development, and change. This can involve social relationships or frequent conversations with townspeople in which work, problems, recreation, family, social activities, or current events are discussed. A predisposition for accepting innovation and change may be established through repeated and routine social contact, especially when this interchange is constructive. What is important is the amount of interaction between the professional staff and local townspeople, as these two groups probably feature the greatest differences in ideas, customs, and actions.

Staff members at Alfred Technical College and Cortland College were asked to give their opinions on the strength of their social ties with other residents in the community (businessmen, farmers, etc.). A qualitative measure was provided the respondent in that ties were classified as very strong, fairly strong, moderate, fairly weak, or nonexistent (Table 4.13). A second question utilized a quantitative device to indicate contact between the college staff and other residents in the community. Staff were asked to indicate with how many townspeople they fairly frequently discussed town problems, work, recreation, family, or social activities. The answers varied between none and six or more.[12]

At both Alfred Technical College and Cortland College, there is no significant difference between the professional and the auxiliary staff relative to social ties with other local residents (Table 4.13). Both indicate primarily moderate or close-to-moderate ties. At Alfred Technical College, one

TABLE 4.13

Strength of Social Ties Between College Staff and Other Residents in the Area, in Percent

Social Ties	Alfred Tech.		Cortland		Alfred University		Cazenovia		Auburn		Total
	Prof.	Auxil.	Prof.	Auxil.	Prof.	Auxil.	Prof.	Auxil.	Prof.	Auxil.	
Very strong	5.9	2.7	9.8	7.1	8.5	16.6	4.3	16.0	17.0	14.2	9.7
Fairly Strong	27.1	16.2	16.9	14.2	25.5	27.7	19.5	32.0	18.2	28.5	22.2
Moderate	31.3	51.3	30.9	42.8	27.6	36.1	34.7	44.0	31.7	35.7	34.5
Fairly weak	27.1	16.2	28.1	14.2	27.6	13.8	30.4	8.0	28.0	14.2	24.0
None	8.4	13.5	14.0	21.4	10.6	5.5	10.8	0.0	4.8	7.1	9.5
Total	100.0	100.0	100.0	100.0	100.0	100.0	100.0	100.0	100.0	100.0	100.0
N	118	37	71	28	47	36	46	25	82	14	504

Note: Details may not add up to totals because of rounding.

third (33 percent) of the professional staff show
fairly strong or very strong social ties with townspeople, compared to about one fifth (19 percent) of
the auxiliary staff. On the other hand, 36 percent
of the former show fairly weak or nonexistent social
ties, compared to 30 percent of the latter. At
Cortland, a similar situation prevails with only 26
percent of the professional and 22 percent of the
auxiliary staff indicating strong ties with other
residents in the community.

At Alfred University and Auburn, the auxiliary
staffs show somewhat stronger social ties with townspeople than do professionals, but great differences
do not exist between these groups. However, at
Cazenovia a substantial difference in social ties
is shown between auxiliary- and professional-staff
members; close to half (48 percent) of the former
and only about a fourth (24 percent) of the latter
show strong social ties with other local residents.

In quantitative assessment of social contact
with townspeople, there is no significant difference
between professional and auxiliary staff at Alfred
Technical College, Cortland, and Auburn (Table 4.14).
However, at Cortland, professional and auxiliary
staff indicate a far greater contact with townspeople than at Alfred Technical College; in the former
location, slightly over 60 percent of the staff have
fairly frequent discussions with four or more other
residents in the community, while in the latter case,
only about 35 percent do so. A rather high percent
among the professional (34 percent) and auxiliary
staff (48 percent) at Alfred Technical College indicate contact with none or one of the townspeople.
This may relate to college-town size and town-residence ratings, but further study would be necessary
to validate that conclusion.

When the quantitative measure is applied to
Alfred University, considerably closer contact between staff and other local residents is evident
than for Alfred Technical College. About half of
the professional and auxiliary staff contact four
or more townspeople frequently. Cazenovia professionals are also near this level of contact, but

TABLE 4.14

Number of Other Local Residents Contacted Fairly Frequently by College Staff, in Percent

Number Contacted	Alfred Tech.		Cortland		Alfred University		Cazenovia		Auburn		Total
	Prof.	Auxil.	Prof.	Auxil.	Prof.	Auxil.	Prof.	Auxil.	Prof.	Auxil.	
None	26.3	34.4	13.6	26.9	15.9	22.5	19.5	0.0	7.5	16.6	18.2
1	8.1	13.7	3.0	0.0	4.5	6.4	4.8	0.0	0.0	0.0	4.5
2 to 3	30.0	17.2	22.7	11.5	25.0	19.3	24.3	15.7	25.0	33.3	24.0
4 to 5	12.7	6.9	6.0	19.2	11.3	12.9	7.3	26.3	15.0	0.0	11.7
6 or more	22.7	27.5	54.5	42.3	43.1	38.7	43.9	57.8	52.5	50.0	41.0
Total	100.0	100.0	100.0	100.0	100.0	100.0	100.0	100.0	100.0	100.0	100.0
N	110	29	66	26	44	31	41	19	80	12	458

Note: Details may not add up to totals because of rounding.

Auburn indicates the highest contact with other
residents in the community by 67 percent of their
professional staff.

College-Community Problems

The college community may experience problems
that may or may not be attributed to impact of the
college. Some insight into these problems was obtained through analysis of data in Appendix Table
E.1. There was high consensus by staff at both Alfred University and Alfred Technical College on the
need for housing. Well over half of the professional-
and auxiliary-staff members at these colleges ranked
housing as the primary problem of the college community. Housing needs at Auburn, Cortland, and Cazenovia were also considered a problem; however, less
than one fourth of the staff at these colleges saw
this as primary. The second major problem for the
college communities was high taxes. Auxiliary-staff
members at the colleges were especially concerned
with this situation. Lesser numbers of the staff
indicated the need for shopping facilities and industrial development, and others were concerned with
poor entertainment and recreational facilities.
Difficulties between students and townspeople were
seen as minimal. Other problems listed were indicated as minor in the college communities examined.
Generally, attitudes of the townspeople toward the
colleges were favorable (see Appendix Table E.3).

SUMMARY

In conclusion, the regression and questionnaire
analyses indicate broad likes and differences in impact for the college communities studied and suggest
additional research. Although not within the scope
of this study, a more detailed analysis of staff impact and spillout could be made by using current-
and previous-residence location as control variables.

This chapter reinforced the findings of Chapter
2 and Chapter 3. It further demonstrated how college
communities are affected in the interaction phase by

the college staff. Alfred Village obtains a relatively low staff-residential input (Phase I) and a
low rating on staff purchases in its commercial district (Phase II). On the other hand, Cortland indicates substantial benefits owing to the college
presence in both phases of institutional input. Auburn and Cazenovia also show relatively favorable
input in both stages.

     As demonstrated, the small college community
need not inevitably experience a low economic and
social input. The situations at Cazenovia and other
viable college towns indicate favorable college impact in both stages. To realize benefit from college
input, the small college community must be capable of
ready expansion to balance growth of the college,
and it should have a centrality and attractiveness
that provide for growth and development.

     The community planner and decisionmaker should
be apprised of the social and political input that
enters with the college population as well as the
resultant economic consequences. The former input
may be of greater importance, in the long run, in
determining social and political outcomes for the
college community. The institutional population
brings a potential for social change. The professional staff are generally above average in community-
service potential and are less conservative than other
community residents. College influence on school-
district policy and local government can be substantial, especially in the small college town, with a
relatively large and locally active college staff.

     Although the above data can provide insight on
impact of the college on a district in the large city
and metropolitan area, caution is advised in this
application. As indicated previously, unless special
provisions for local housing are made, a large proportion of the professional staff tend to reside at
a considerable distance from the college. Consequently, city and suburban districts outside the
college vicinity absorb many of the social and economic benefits derived from the professional-staff
input. It should be expected that influence of the

professional staff on local government would be diluted in the large city. However, with active programs in college extension work and community development, the college could have substantial impact on target areas of the metropolis.

NOTES

1.   See Lloyd L. Hogan, <u>Measurement of the Ability of Local Governments to Finance Local Public Services</u> (Albany: Bureau of Educational Finance Research, State Education Department, University of the State of New York, 1967).

2.   Answers received in a questionnaire survey of staff and students are used in this part of the study.   The responses to questions are displayed in tables indicating the percentage distribution for the variables considered.   Juxtapositioning data and using one table for the several colleges examined is not done with the intent of comparison, but rather to contrast college-community situations.   The small town with a two-year college should not exhibit the same characteristics as the city with a four-year institution.   This would not be possible.   Nor are two small towns or colleges necessarily alike.

Chi-square analysis was used where applicable to test for the existence of a possible association between the variables.   The 0.05 probability level was taken as the level determining acceptance or rejection of association.

The survey was made in Fall, 1968.   Unfortunately, resources and time did not permit distribution of a similar questionnaire to residents (not associated with the college) in the respective areas.   This would have been helpful.   Instead, interviews and meetings with townspeople were held to supplement data obtained through the questionnaires.

3.   In 1960, Auburn's industrial labor force included 38.6 percent in manufacturing, 15.7 percent in retail trade, and 12.8 percent in professional and related services.

4.   In 1940, Cazenovia Village had a population of 1,689 compared to 694 for Alfred Village; their town populations were 3,424 and 1,410, respectively. In 1960, the Alfred Town population was at 3,730 (including resident college students), and that for Cazenovia was at 4,968.   (Refer to Appendix Table B.3 for information on staff-residence location and to Table 4.5 for data on retail sales.)   The 1959, full-time undergraduate enrollments were 1,308 at Alfred Technical College, 1,131 at Alfred University, and 280 at Cazenovia.

5.   New York State Department of Commerce, Business Fact Book, 1967-68 (Albany, Part 1, Business and Manufacturing, 1968).

6.   This is also indicative of their residence location before joining the college staff.

7.   Delbert C. Miller, Handbook of Research Design and Social Measurement (New York: David McKay Company, Inc., 1964), pp. 91-327, compiled selected sociometric scales and indexes.   Eshref Shevsky and Wendell Bell, Social Area Analysis (Stanford, Calif.:   Stanford University Press, 1955), utilized indexes of social rank, urbanization, and segregation.   Douglass B. Lee, Jr., "Urban Models and Household Disaggregation, An Empirical Problem in Urban Research" (unpublished Ph.D. dissertation, Cornell University, Department of City and Regional Planning, 1968), pp. 308-15 and 334-44, developed similar indexes.   Raymond A. Bauer, ed., et al., Social Indicators (Cambridge: Massachusetts Institute of Technology Press, 1966), pp. 154-271, included a section on social-systems accounting. See also U.S. Department of Health, Education, and Welfare, Toward a Social Report (Washington, D.C.: U.S. Government Printing Office, 1969).   "A General Social Welfare Index," which includes factors such as purchasing power, home ownership, housing adequacy, health needs, educational provisions, political expression, and municipal wealth and service, is used in Irving A. Fowler, Local Industrial Structures, Economic Power, and Community Welfare, Thirty Small New York State Cities, 1930-1950 (Totowa, N.J.:

Bedminster Press, 1964), pp. 68-69. For selected
readings and current papers on social-reporting
techniques, see Political Intelligence for America's
Future, The Annals, CCCXXCVIII (Philadelphia: American Academy of Political and Social Science, March,
1970).

    8. Miller, op. cit., pp. 205-7.

    9. Ibid., pp. 192-207. Other socioeconomic
and political indexes may be used in the same manner.
Each index and its total value is an indication of
the extent of vested human and social capital that
determines the characteristics of the locality.

    10. See Delbert C. Miller, "Town and Gown: The
Power Structure of a University Town," American Journal of Sociology, LXIII, 4 (January, 1963), pp. 432-
43; Miller studied a university town and found that
business and governmental associations dominated the
educational institutions in resolving community
issues. For additional discussion of political power
in the small town, see A. J. Vidich and J. Bensman,
Small Town in Mass Society (Princeton, N.J.: Princeton University Press, 1958), pp. 79-105. For a more
general discussion, see Robert A. Dahl, Who Governs?
Democracy and Power in an American City (New Haven,
Conn.: Yale University Press, 1961), pp. 63-103 and
150-59.

    11. Miller, "Town and Gown," op. cit., indicated
that although the university was the largest employer
in the city (population 32,000, including 13,000
students), with 3,600 faculty and staff personnel,
its influence was subordinated to business and governmental associations in resolving community issues.
Miller indicated that the university housed over
1,000 faculty in the city; two large industrial
plants employed about 2,500 workers each, and an
extractive industry employed 2,000 more. In the
county, with a population of about 60,000, there
were about 15,000 nonagricultural jobs. The university community was "in the center." Miller pointed
out that the university was "well represented in
community affairs by university officials" but that

faculty were underrepresented, owing to the fact
that the latter were more involved with state, national, and international roles rather than in local
participation. At Alfred Technical College, a two-
year college without a research emphasis, the faculty
were considerably more local in outlook; a former
faculty member served as mayor of the village, and
others were on the school board. However, it did
take a considerable number of years and growth of
the college before the political transformation
occurred. With recent occurrences on campuses as
a gauge, it appears that greater involvement by
faculty in community affairs is the trend.

12. See Paul Wellin, "A Guttman Scale for
Measuring Women's Neighborliness," in Miller, Handbook of Research, op. cit., pp. 220-21, especially
questions 6 and 9. Greater neighborliness (GN) and
lesser neighborliness is scored based on qualitative
and quantitative query. The reliability is high.
Or see Paul Wellin, "A Guttman Scale for Measuring
Women's Neighborliness," The American Journal of
Sociology, LIX (1953), pp. 243-46.

5

LOCAL
STUDENT
ENROLLMENT
AND
COMMUTATION

Another major factor affecting impact of the college on the community is the characteristic of its local and nonlocal student enrollment. The locality with a college benefits by offering a readily accessible program in higher education to local students and by supplying educational services to nonlocal students. In the latter case, a substantial increase in the community's economic base can occur due to this export. In addition, educational and social benefits accrue to the college community because broader and more diversified educational programs can be planned, and a greater interchange of ideas and experiences takes place. Consequently, of primary interest to the educational and town planner is the size of the local and nonlocal enrollment and the size of the commuter, dormitory, and offcampus student components.

At colleges located outside of metropolitan areas in New York State, the great majority of the students come from homes beyond a 50-mile radius. In the Elmira economic area, for example, in 1963, with enrollments at local colleges totaling 13,338 students, only 2,429 (18.2 percent) were local residents. In the Binghamton area, only 1,742 (27 percent) were local students out of a total of 6,476 full-time undergraduates. On the other hand, only

48 percent of the Elmira-area college students, out
of a total of 5,026 undergraduates, chose to enroll
at local colleges; in the Binghamton area, this figure was 37.3 percent. Extensive intrastate student
migration between economic areas is evident in
Table 5.1.

When one examines the situation at individual
rural colleges, the above data are reflected in enrollment patterns of four-year institutions and also
at two-year agricultural and technical colleges.
However, two-year community colleges located in cities
throughout New York State draw much of their student
enrollment from the city itself and from the local
economic area. For example, Auburn Community College
records indicate that 35 percent of its full-time
student enrollment came from the Auburn School District in 1965.[1] In total, the Syracuse economic
area, of which Auburn is a part, provided 76.5 percent of Auburn Community College's student body, as
indicated in Table 5.2. Additional data indicate
that, in 1963, community colleges outside of New
York City drew 69.7 percent of their students from
the county in which the college was located.[2]

A primary factor in state-college location has
been the intent to serve students in the local area
who can commute from their homes and thus incur minimal expenditures for their college education.[3] The
community that provides higher education delays the
departure of both youth and dollars spent for education. However, at the same time, the rural college
provides educational skills with which the local
graduate can obtain employment outside the college
town or region. If we consider this college impact,
these rural institutions serve to pump local youth
into the larger cities where more opportunities are
available.

Our purpose in this phase of the study is to
find probable maximums for local-student enrollment
and commutation at rural colleges. This will also
yield insight into enrollment (and commutation) po-
tentials for colleges in the highly populated urban
areas.

TABLE 5.1

Intrastate Migration Matrix by Economic Area of Full-Time Undergraduate Students, Fall, 1963

Location of College Attended (Economic Area)	Bing-ham-ton	Buf-falo	Cap-ital Dis-trict	El-mira	Mid-Hud-son	Mo-hawk Val-ley	New York Metropolitan			North-ern	Roch-ester	Syra-cuse	Total
							New York City	Nassau-Suffolk	Rock-land-West-chester				
Binghamton	1,742	219	519	273	450	325	836	1,179	350	94	227	262	6,476
Buffalo	282	14,520	444	448	276	401	999	1,066	381	246	1,478	593	21,134
Capital District	426	410	5,663	225	1,002	823	822	1,092	643	327	457	382	12,272
Elmira	536	1,379	711	2,429	571	390	2,065	1,688	927	275	1,593	774	13,338
Mid-Hudson	65	74	205	25	3,415	73	1,239	906	612	25	68	58	6,765
Mohawk Valley	105	99	95	37	47	563	40	89	51	109	138	259	1,632
New York Metro-politan													
New York City	147	183	294	60	579	120	73,491	8,569	4,067	83	136	94	87,823
Nassau-Suffolk	15	27	50	13	92	29	2,318	9,088	199	19	25	15	11,890
Rockland-West-chester	40	71	129	30	115	49	2,409	459	3,161	31	60	73	6,627
Northern	249	424	788	178	334	530	322	950	392	2,181	586	565	7,499
Rochester	297	1,272	407	633	288	380	670	833	396	256	6,514	614	12,560
Syracuse	769	910	745	675	601	1,804	1,613	1,971	1,148	631	1,319	5,745	17,931
Total	4,573	19,588	10,050	5,026	7,770	5,487	86,824	27,890	12,327	4,277	12,601	9,434	205,947

Source: State University of New York, The Regents Tentative Statewide Plan for the Expansion and Development of Higher Education, 1964 (Albany: State Education Department, 1965), p. 130.

TABLE 5.2

Geographic Origin of Full-Time Students at Selected
Colleges in New York State, 1965-67

New York State Economic Area	Percentage Distribution			
	Alfred Ag. & Tech. 1966	Cort-land 1966	Auburn C.C. 1965	Caze-novia[a] 1967
Binghamton	4.3	10.1	1.5	7.1
Capital District	3.2	4.4	0.4	8.0
Elmira	14.9	7.2	2.2	6.8
Mid-Hudson	1.6	5.2	0.0	3.2
Mohawk Valley	5.2	4.0	1.9	6.2
New York Metropoli-tan	4.2	41.4	0.3	26.8
Niagara Frontier	16.0	3.3	0.5	6.8
Northern	1.6	2.5	0.5	3.2
Rochester	28.2	5.9	16.2	10.3
Southwest Gateway	17.4[b]	1.8	0.2	2.7
Syracuse	7.0	14.2[b]	76.5[b]	18.6[b]
New York State total	1,783	3,296	1,137	a
U.S. total, exclud-ing New York and territories	79	31	8	0
Foreign countries and U.S. terri-tories, total	6	8	4	3
Total	1,868	3,335	1,149	a

[a]The Cazenovia distribution is based only on 339
new students who enrolled in September, 1967.
[b]The college is located within this economic
area.

Source: Data supplied by the admissions offices of the above colleges.

130

When a two- or a four-year college is placed in a rural area, what is the probable full-time enrollment and commutation by the local students, and how does this vary with the size of the college town? The answer to this question is important because a substantial part of the educational, social, and economic impact of the college on the local community depends on the size of its local and nonlocal student enrollment.

ANALYSIS OF THE STATE UNIVERSITY OF NEW YORK AT CORTLAND

In this study, the term <u>local</u> is defined to include an area within about 50 radial miles of the college. However, the analysis utilizes separate data for the college town and for its outlying student commuter area.

In 1967, out of 950 local students enrolled at SUNY Cortland, 463 (48.8 percent) lived in dormitories, 239 (25.2 percent) commuted from their homes, and 248 (26.1 percent) lived in offcampus housing. All had permanent residences within a 54-mile radius around the college.

Among 157 students with permanent residences in Cortland, 12 (7.6 percent) chose dormitory residency (as shown in Table 5.3), but by far the greatest number (87.9 percent) commuted from their homes. A small number of the students living in Cortland (4.5 percent) chose to live away from their permanent residence at another location in the city. Up to about 4 miles outside the town, commutation is high (88.5 percent), but as the 8-mile mark is approached, the number of commuters decreases considerably (to 52.2 percent), and there are corresponding increases in the number of students who move into dormitories or offcampus housing. When the 20- and 30-mile marks are reached, commutation probabilities again take severe drops, and around the 35-40-mile point, the proportion of students commuting drops close to zero. As shown in Figure 3 and Table 5.3, dormitory

TABLE 5.3

College Residence Distribution of Local Students Attending Cortland College of the State University of New York, Fall, 1967

Permanent Residence Ring	Average Distance in Miles[a]	Number in Dorms				Number Commuting				Number Offcampus				Sum		Ring Totals	Ring Percent of Overall Total	Grades 7-12 ADA, 1964-65[b]	Ratio of College Enrollment to ADA, in Percent[b]
		M.	F.	Total	(%)	M.	F.	Total	(%)	M.	F.	Total	(%)	M.	F.				
C-T	1.1	3	9	12	7.6	47	91	138	87.9	4	3	7	4.5	54	103	157	16.5	1,464	10.724
1	3.8	0	2	2	7.7	10	13	23	88.5	1	0	1	3.8	11	15	26	2.7	1,330	1.954
2	8.1	2	7	9	39.1	4	8	12	52.2	2	0	2	8.7	8	15	23	2.4	1,397	1.646
3	13.5	1	7	8	30.8	7	7	14	53.8	2	2	4	15.4	10	16	26	2.7	2,523	1.030
4	18.9	5	21	26	40.6	1	19	20	31.3	7	11	18	28.1	13	51	64	6.7	5,945	1.076
5	24.4	3	14	17	68.0	1	5	6	24.0	1	1	2	8.0	5	20	25	2.6	3,976	0.628
6	29.6	40	57	97	56.7	3	12	15	8.8	27	32	59	34.5	70	101	171	18.0	29,732	0.575
7	35.1	43	112	155	60.5	4	6	10	3.9	54	37	91	35.5	101	155	256	26.9	20,905	1.224
8	40.5	16	43	59	73.7	0	0	0	0.0	13	8	21	26.3	29	51	80	3.4	15,252	0.524
9	45.9	13	33	46	61.3	0	0	0	0.0	18	11	29	38.7	31	44	75	7.9	9,467	0.792
10	51.2	10	22	32	68.1	0	1	1	2.1	7	7	14	29.8	17	30	47	4.9	12,087	0.388
Total	--	136	327	463	--	77	162	239	--	136	112	248	--	349	601	905	100.0	104,078	0.912

[a]Distances indicate radial miles from the college to the permanent residence ring.
[b]Average daily attendance.

Note: Data combined for rural, suburban, and urban students. Details may not add up to totals because of rounding.

and offcampus housing act as complements and increase
correspondingly as the number of students commuting
from home drops.

The location of the college in the City of Cortland and the presence or absence of nearby towns
within commuting limits bear on the resulting pattern
of student commutation but are of lesser consequence
once the 15-mile range is past. The absolute number
of commuters from outside of Cortland is indeed
small and is less than those coming from within the
city. At the 13.5-mile mark, the downward trend in
the proportion of commuters turns upward, with a
fairly high percentage of the students who commute
from Marathon and Moravia, but beyond this point, the
majority of the students seek dormitory or offcampus
accommodations. Ithaca commuters at about 19 radial
miles from the college are only 26.8 percent of the
total Ithaca contingent. Between the 25-35-mile
rings, although cities such as Auburn, Syracuse, and
Binghamton come into the commuter range, over 90 percent of the students from these cities prefer living
at the dormitory or in offcampus rentals.[4]

Figure 4 shows the commuter zone for Cortland
College and indicates the effect of Ithaca, Syracuse,
Binghamton, and other areas on commutation. As expected, in areas with sparse population, enrollment
and commutation drop precipitously. This is especially the case in the southeastern sectors where
small villages and minor roads predominate. Student
commutation and enrollment are indicated for each
sector in Appendix Table C.1. For example, out of
41 Ithacans enrolled at the college (from ring 4,
channel I) 11 commute. In the Binghamton vicinity,
9 commute out of the 157 enrolled (ring 7, channel
F). Channel totals and subtotals are also given.
These values do not include amounts for the City of
Cortland at the center of the circle because this
cannot be assigned to any particular channel.

The patterns of local college enrollment and
commutation are also indicated in Figure 4. The
rings drawn around the college town are used to establish the scale from 0 to 300, as indicated in

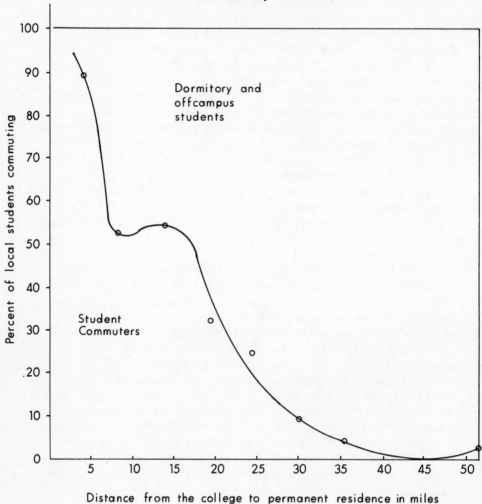

FIGURE 3

Decrease in Percent of Local Students Commuting to College With Distance to the Permanent Residence, State University of New York at Cortland, Fall Term, 1967

Dormitory and offcampus students

Student Commuters

Percent of local students commuting

Distance from the college to permanent residence in miles

FIGURE 4

Average Daily Attendance (ADA) for Grades 7-12 in the Cortland Area and Local Student Enrollment and Commutation, by Channels, for the State University of New York at Cortland, Fall Term, 1967

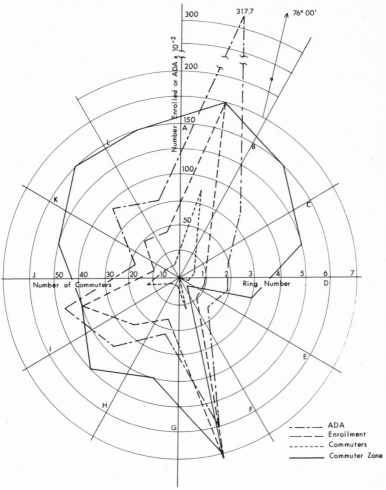

Notes: The graph is imposed on a map of the Cortland area, with the State University of New York at Cortland at the center. The 76° 00' longitude is indicated in channel A to orient the graph to the map of New York State.

Scale for the map is 1 inch = 10.8 miles. Channels A through L, and rings 1 through 7 are indicated.

Major cities are located in sectors as follows:

City	Sector
Binghamton	F-7
Ithaca	I-4
Auburn	L-6
Syracuse	A-6
Cortland	C-T (at center)

Interstate Highway 81 is in channels A and F.

See Appendix A and Figure 6 for additional details on channel, ring, and sectors construction.

channel A. It is thus possible to graph local student
enrollment and commutation for each channel radiating
outward from the college. For example, villages in
channel A are the locations of permanent residences
for 34 commuters out of 177 local students enrolled
at the college. Commutation is closely related to
increases and decreases in college enrollment in
many of the channels.

Beyond 5 miles from the college, we are working
with small numbers relative to local student commutation. The City of Cortland itself supplies more than
50 percent of the 239 students commuting from home.
But when one considers that the enrollment at Cortland is well over 3,000 and is growing, the locating
of baccalaureate institutions, even in sizable rural
cities, is not primarily a matter of local commutation. It is evident that city and regional development are important factors in college location. Also
important is the enrollment of a large number of
local students from outside the college town and
others from nonlocal areas who may wish to attend the
college for various reasons.

Because colleges are placed in rural cities and
villages, it is profitable in planning to seek deter-
minative factors in local student enrollment and commutation. The question raised by Hypotheses III and
IV is as follows: Does local student enrollment and
commutation at a college placed in a rural area vary
with the size of the college town? To investigate
these hypotheses, population-related factors were
utilized, and a study of the situations at Cortland
and Alfred Agricultural and Technical College was
made.

The average daily attendance (ADA, grades 7-12)
of students in sectors of a 54-mile circle around
Cortland College in 1964 was obtained. Regression
analysis was used to determine a predictive relationship between college enrollment and high school attendance four years previous. The ADA totals for
each channel around Cortland are graphed in Figure
4, based on sectoral ADAs in Appendix Table D.1.[5]
ADAs were matched against the local student enrollment

TABLE 5.4

Data for Regression Equations, Local Student Enrollment and Commutation,
State University of New York at Cortland

	Analysis by		
	Multi-	Sector	Channel
1. College Enrollment			
Dependent variable	CORT-NROLL-S	CORT-NROLL-S	CORT-NROLL-C
R squared	0.690	0.650	0.840
Constant	-0.210	0.240	-16.800
Significance level	0.001	0.001	0.005
Standard error of estimate	4.680	13.490	24.600
Independent variable	ADA-S/D	ADA-S	ADA-C-10
Beta	0.183	0.007	0.009
2. College Commutation			
Dependent variable	CORT-CMUTE-S		CORT-CMUTE-C
R squared	0.680		0.710
Constant	-0.310		5.640
Significance level	0.001		0.001
Standard error of estimate	2.020		5.640
Independent variable	ADA-S/D		ADA-C-7
Beta	0.046		0.156-02

Note: See Table 5.5 for description of code names.

and commutation data for Fall, 1967, at Cortland.
Note the similarity of the ADA and the channel enrollment and commutation patterns.[6]

Input data for the regression analysis included
local student enrollment and commutation data for the
State University College at Cortland and ADA information. Both multisector and channel analyses were
made.[7] For the former analysis, sectors within the
54-mile circle were used to obtain the variables.
In the latter case, channel totals for enrollment
and ADA in grades 7-12 provided the necessary data.
However, data for the City of Cortland at the center
of the circle are excluded, and the college-town information is retained for separate analysis.

When channel analysis is used with local student
enrollment as the dependent variable and high school
attendance as the independent variable, the value of
R is 0.92, and R squared is 0.84, as shown in Table
5.4. ADA in grades 7-12, therefore, accounts for 84
percent of the possible variance in local student
enrollment for the local areas outside the City of
Cortland.

The regression equation for the channel analysis
takes the following form:

$$Y_{21} = -16.80 + 0.009X_{27}$$

where Y_{21} is the local college student enrollment in
channels outside the City of Cortland, and X_{27} is
the independent variable (ADA) as defined in Table
5.5. Values for the independent variable, as depicted in Figure 4, are sufficiently high to contra-
vene the negative constant term. The equation gives
the expected local student enrollment within the 54-
mile circle outside of the City of Cortland.

The total number of local students enrolled at
the college is, of course, the sum of those coming
from the college town itself and those from its hinterland. In the City of Cortland, 10.7 percent of
its ADA enroll at the local college (Table 5.3).
This compares with about 15 percent of the ADA for

TABLE 5.5

Variables Used in Student Regression Analysis of Enrollment and Commutation

Sub-script Number	Variables	Code Names
	Dependent Variables	
20	Local student enrollment, by sector[a]	CORT-NROLL-S
21	Local student enrollment, by channel[a]	CORT-NROLL-C
22	Local student commutation, by sector[a]	CORT-CMUTE-S
23	Local student commutation, by channel[a]	CORT-CMUTE-C
24	Local student enrollment, by sector[b]	Alf-nroll-S
25	Percent of local students commuting to both colleges from a given distance	%-MUTA
	Independent Variables	
26	Average daily attendance, grades 7-12, by sector	ADA-S
27	Average daily attendance, grades 7-12, by channel to ring 10[c]	ADA-C-10
28	Average daily attendance, grades 7-12, by sector, divided by distance	ADA-S/D
29	Average distance to a sector	Dist-S
30	Average distance to a ring about a college	Dist-R

[a]At Cortland College.
[b]At Alfred Technical College.
[c]If 7 is used in code name, to ring 7.

the City of Auburn who attend the community college
and a somewhat higher percentage of the ADA enrolled
at Alfred Technical College.[8] With 1964 ADAs of
2,643, 1,464, and an estimated 218, for Auburn, Cortland, and Alfred, respectively, by far the greatest
number of local residents enrolled at the local college occurs in the case of Auburn.

There is strong evidence that population-related
factors operating both in the city and in its local
area have a decided effect on local student enrollment. Undoubtedly, in addition to population factors,
the characteristics of the college and its curriculum
and the college community affect the number of local
students attending.[9] Two-year community college enrollment will have a greater proportion of local
students than the four-year college.

A multisector regression analysis was made to
achieve sharper definition for the dependent variable.
This analysis, for local student enrollment, operated
on smaller land areas and, as expected, the R-squared
value (0.65) is lower, as shown in Table 5.4. Sixty-
five percent of the variation in the dependent variable is explained by ADA values. Thus, size of the
population generally plays a considerable part in
local student enrollment. However, other factors
are important, as indicated above.

An increase in the R-squared value to 0.69 was
obtained when the inverse distance (D) to each sector
was entered into the analysis as the independent
variable. Thus, a small part of the variation in
local student enrollment is explained by distance
(D) from the college of the sector under consideration. If we use the data in Table 5.4, the regression
equation takes the following form:

$$Y_{20} + -0.21 + 0.183X_{28}$$

where Y_{20} is the local student enrollment for a sector in the 54-mile ring, and X_{28} is equal to the ADA
(grades 7-12) for that sector, divided by its distance
from the college.

The data obtained from regression analysis of commutation by local students is indicated in Table 5.4. By using channel analysis, the R-squared value came to 0.71, with ADA as the independent variable. For multisector analysis, and the inverse distance considered as previously, the R-squared value (relatively high) was at 0.68. In both these cases, the ADA values only to ring 7 were considered, as this was the outer limit for student commutation.

ANALYSIS OF THE STATE UNIVERSITY OF NEW YORK AT THE ALFRED AGRICULTURAL AND TECHNICAL COLLEGE

Alfred Technical College, a two-year institution, is located in a small village with a 1940 population that numbered 694 individuals; in 1960, the Census inflated this number by including resident students from both the Alfred Technical College and Alfred University in the population count, along with other new residents. This made the total population 2,807.

In 1967, out of 856 local residents enrolled at the college, 516 (60.4 percent) lived in dormitories, 276 (32.3 percent) commuted from home, and 64 (7.5 percent) lived in offcampus housing. All had permanent residences within a 52.5-mile radius of the college.[10]

The two-year technical programs, including agriculture, business, and technology, at the college attracted a substantial commuter group of up to about a 15-mile radius from the campus. Of the students with permanent residences in Alfred and Alfred Station, 41 of the 45 commuted from home. Approximately 65 percent of the students coming from a distance of about 13 radial miles from campus commuted, as indicated in Table 5.6. This proportion was down to 20 percent at around the 24-mile radial distance, and it dropped to near 0 a bit beyond this point.

A graph of the proportion of local students commuting to Alfred Technical College from successive

TABLE 5.6

College Residence Distribution of Local Students Attending Alfred Agricultural and Technical College, 1967-68

Permanent Residence Ring	Average Distance in Miles[a]	Number in Dorms				Number Commuting				Number Offcampus				Sum		Ring Totals	Ring Percent of Overall Total	Grades 7-12 ADA 1964-65[b]	Ratio of College Attendance to ADA, in Percent
		M.	F.	Total	(%)	M.	F.	Total	(%)	M.	F.	Total	(%)	M.	F.				
C-T	1.1	0	1	1	3.9	13	10	23	88.4	1	1	2	7.7	14	12	26	3.0	} 218	} 20.20
1	2.6	0	0	0	0.0	12	6	18	100.0	0	0	0	0.0	12	6	18	2.1		
2	7.9	14	19	33	21.9	89	23	112	74.1	5	1	6	4.0	108	43	151	17.6	2,598	5.82
3	13.1	11	24	35	30.4	52	23	75	65.2	4	1	5	4.3	67	48	115	13.4	2,383	4.82
4	18.4	5	9	14	48.4	10	2	12	41.4	3	0	3	10.3	18	11	29	3.4	731	3.92
5	23.6	56	21	77	64.6	24	7	31	20.1	11	0	11	9.2	91	28	119	13.9	5,129	2.32
6	28.9	19	12	31	94.0	0	0	0	0.0	2	0	2	6.0	21	12	33	3.9	2,447	1.35
7	34.1	54	28	82	84.5	3	0	3	3.1	12	0	12	12.4	69	28	97	11.3	4,061	2.39
8	39.4	44	18	62	86.1	1	0	1	1.4	9	0	9	12.5	54	18	72	8.4	7,452	0.97
9	44.6	39	22	61	93.9	0	1	1	1.5	3	0	3	4.6	42	23	65	7.6	5,163	1.26
10	49.9	71	49	120	91.6	0	0	0	0.0	10	1	11	8.4	81	50	131	15.3	17,053	0.77
Total	--	--	--	516	60.4	--	--	276	32.3	--	--	64	7.5	--	--	856	100.0	--	--

[a]Distances indicate radial miles from the college to the permanent residence ring.
[b]Average daily attendance.

Note: The ADA in grades 7-12 is estimated for the college town (C-T), and Alfred Station in ring 1 because this is not directly obtainable from the Annual Educational Summary, 1964-65. Alfred and Almond town's ADA is combined (at 403 ADA) in the listing. The estimate is based on the 5-14 age groups listed in "The Census of Population for 1960 for Alfred and Almond Town," Table 26. Almond Town indicated 46 percent of the total age group, and its ADA was estimated at 185, with Alfred Town at 218 ADA. Rural, suburban, and urban students combined. Details may not add up because of rounding.

Sources: State Education Department, Bureau of Statistical Services, Annual Educational Summary, 1964-65 (Albany: University of the State of New York, 1965), pp. 84-95; U.S. Bureau of the Census, U.S. Census of Population: 1960, Volume I, Characteristics of the Population, Part 34, New York (Washington, D.C.: U.S. Government Printing Office, 1963); data on dormitories, commuting, and offcampus students obtained by computer analysis of college records.

distances showed a slope similar to that for Cortland College, depicted in Figure 3. Because of this similarity, a regression analysis was made combining data for SUNY Cortland and Alfred Technical College in an effort to find a statement on commutation that could be applied to both of these colleges, and perhaps to others in college towns of varying size. A rather high multiple correlation was obtained, which encourages broader application of the results to other public colleges in the region and makes a strong statement relative to Hypothesis IV.[11]

As the dependent variable, input data for the regression analysis included the percent of local students commuting from a permanent-residence ring. The independent variable was the average distance, in miles, of these rings from SUNY Cortland and the Alfred Technical College, as listed in Tables 5.3 and 5.6.

The results of the regression analysis are listed in Table 5.7, and 93 percent of the variance in the dependent variable (percent commuting) is accounted for by the independent variable (distance). The regression equation is formed as follows:

$$Y_{25} = 90.5 - 0.965X_{30}$$

where Y_{25} is the proportion of local students commuting to both colleges from a given distance, and X_{30} is as defined in Table 5.5.

The negative coefficient for the independent variable is in accord with the fact that, as distance from the college increases, the proportion of the students commuting will decrease. One can expect that the proportion of students commuting from a sector would relate to the distance of that sector from the college. Regression analysis in this case allows us to predict the proportion of students who commute from a sector. It is, therefore, a good tool for planning related to commutation. Of course, it depends on the accuracy with which local enrollment from a sector can be predicted.

144   THE COLLEGE AND COMMUNITY DEVELOPMENT

TABLE 5.7

Data for Regression Equation for Student Commutation
at the State University of New York at Cortland and
Alfred Agricultural and Technical College

**Percent of Local Students Commuting
vs. Distance to College**

Dependent variable	%-CMUTE		
Independent variable	Dist-R	Significance level	0.005
		Standard error of	
R squared	0.93	estimate	9.680
Constant	90.50	Beta	—0.965

Note: See Table 5.5 for description of code
names for variables.

Alfred Technical College draws most of its local
enrollment from outside Alfred Village. The presence
of the City of Hornell and the Village of Wellsville
(population 5,967 in 1960) in the second- and third-
residence rings increases both the student enrollment
and commuter potential for the college, as shown in
Table 5.6. In the fifth and seventh rings, Dansville
and Olean, respectively, supply a good proportion of
the local student enrollment. But large gaps in both
enrollment and commutation are noticeable in the
northeast and the southwest channels radiating from
the college.

These areas of high and low local enrollment can
again be related to high school attendance (ADA,
grades 7-12), in various sectors, and a regression
analysis was used to determine this relationship.
To obtain direction for this analysis, a scatter
diagram was first made. The diagram indicated a relationship closer to a second-degree curve rather
than to lineal form. Therefore, the independent
variable (ADA) was squared, and a multiple-regression
equation was sought.

The results of this analysis are listed in Table 5.8, and 63 percent of the variance in the dependent variable (local enrollment) is accounted for. The multiple-regression equation takes the following form:

$$Y_{24} = 3.34 + 2 \times 10^{-5} \, x_{26}^2$$

where Y_{24} is the local student enrollment at Alfred Technical College by sector, and X_{26} is as defined in Table 5.5. The above regression analysis is valid only to ring 7, which coincides approximately with the commutation limit line. A satisfactory analysis could not be obtained when the rings beyond the seventh were included.

The fact that the regression equation is nonlinear and the ratios of local student enrollment to ADA are high for rings 2 and 3 in Table 5.6 suggests the high influence of Alfred Technical College on nearby localities in its area. Hornell and Wellsville appear to bend what might have been a straight line of regression so that local college attendance from these locations is above the usual situation encountered.

TABLE 5.8

Data for Regression Equation for Local Student Enrollment at the State University of New York at Alfred Agricultural and Technical College

College Enrollment (multisector analysis, curvilinear regression)		
Dependent variable	ALF-NROLL-S	Significance
Independent		level 0.001
variable	$(ADA-S)^2$	Standard error
R squared	0.68	of estimate 10.52
Constant	3.34	Beta 2×10^{-5}

Note: See Table 5.5 for description of code names for variables.

With a total local enrollment of 856 students and an enrollment of close to 2,300 students, Alfred Technical College compares well with SUNY Cortland in its service to local students.

Some clues as to the effect of college-town size on local student enrollment and commutation are obtained by juxtapositioning of information on SUNY Cortland and Alfred Technical College and by analysis of cumulative data by ring as shown in Table 5.9. SUNY Cortland starts with high college-town enrollment and commutation. Alfred Technical College is low in this regard. However, with small villages in ring 2 about SUNY Cortland, and a large draw from Hornell in ring 2 for Alfred Technical College, cumulative scores for both colleges approach each other. By ring 3, the cumulative totals for Alfred Technical College have spurted ahead, and those for SUNY Cortland lag. The two-year college maintains its high in commutation to the end of the local student range. However, in the enrollment category, SUNY Cortland, with heavy Syracuse and Binghamton contingents in rings 6 and 7, draws ahead of Alfred Technical College. Although Elmira and Olean are within Alfred's local range, as defined, the former is over 45 miles away, and the latter is not a large city.

Comparison of the above colleges may not be justified. They are substantially different in many ways. Both well serve their local area; the two-year college perhaps provides for a more local situation. But small or large size of the college town is only a part of the factor that determines local student enrollment and commutation.

When similar data for Auburn Community College is examined, it is noted that in 1967 close to 80 percent of the students enrolled at this college came from permanent residences within a 25-mile radius of the college.[12] A college located in a small town near large cities could have a large local enrollment; one located in a fairly large rural city, surrounded only by small towns for a 25-radial-mile range, may have a small local enrollment. The point

TABLE 5.9

Local Student Enrollment and Commutation at the
State University of New York at Cortland and
Alfred Agricultural and Technical College, 1967

	Enrollment				Commutation			
	Cortland		Alfred Ag. & Tech.		Cortland		Alfred Ag. & Tech.	
Ring	To-tal	Cu-mu-la-tive	To-tal	Cu-mu-la-tive	To-tal	Cu-mu-la-tive	To-tal	Cu-mu-la-tive
C-T	157	157	26	26	138	138	23	23
1	26	183	18	44	23	161	18	41
2	23	206	151	195	12	173	112	153
3	26	232	115	3.0	14	187	75	228
4	64	296	29	339	20	207	12	240
5	25	321	119	458	6	213	31	271
6	171	492	33	491	15	228	0	271
7	256	748	97	588	10	238	3	274
8	80	828	72	660	0	238	1	275
9	75	903	65	725	0	238	1	276
10	47	950	131	856	1	239	0	276

Note: Refer to average distances for rings in
Tables 5.3 and 5.6; they differ slightly for SUNY
Cortland and the Alfred Agricultural and Technical
College.

is that colleges cannot be located on the basis of
college-town size alone. Although college-town size
is a factor in local student enrollment and commutation, this factor is primary if we define only college-town inhabitants as local students. If the
local student is defined as coming from a broader
area, such as the 54-mile circle, it is necessary to
analyze the condition in the broader area and to
seek additional parameters. In light of the above
data, the broader definition appears more justifiable.

SUMMARY

At the colleges studied, enrollment from a sector within a 50-mile circle about the college town
varies with the ADA in grades 7-12 in that sector.
The proportion of students who commute from these
sectors varies with their distances from the college
town and drops to 0 near 35 miles from the college
town.   Local area enrollment and commutation may be
estimated by regression analysis.

Of further interest is the fact that although
the larger college community (Cortland) itself indicates far greater enrollment than the smaller
(Alfred Village), the enrollment of students from
Hornell, Wellsville, and other towns in the Alfred
area brings the cumulative local enrollment at Alfred Technical College close to that at Cortland
College at the 30-mile circle.

Similar regression equations can be developed
for other public colleges in the same manner.   The
findings can be used in long-range planning for college dormitories and other housing, parking areas,
locally oriented curriculum, shopping facilities,
transportation facilities, and related needs.

NOTES

1.   Albert T. Skinner, "Auburn Community College,
Report of the President for the Year July 1, 1965 to
June 30, 1966" (Auburn, N.Y.:   Board of Education of
the Auburn City School District, 1966), pp. 7-8.

2.   State University of New York, The Regents
Tentative Statewide Plan for the Expansion and De-
velopment of Higher Education, 1964 (Albany: State
Education Department, 1965), p. 127.

3.   State of New York, Report of the Temporary
Commission on the Need for a State University (Albany: Williams Press, Inc., 1948), pp. 21-22.

4. Of 1,481 students living offcampus and away
from home, only 181 (12.2 percent) set up accommodations outside the city. The great number of nonlocal,
offcampus students (1,148, or 86.4 percent) found
lodging at boarding houses, residence hotels, and
other rentals within the city limits; of those living
outside the city and away from home, 37 (20.4 percent) commuted from Homer, the Syracuse area, Ithaca,
and other locations.

5. The source for this information was the
Bureau of Statistical Services, State Education Department, <u>Annual Educational Summary, New York State,</u>
<u>1964-65</u> (Albany: State Education Department, 1966),
pp. 84-95. School-district data supplied in this
study were fitted to sectors in the 54-mile circle
about Cortland College.

6. The ADA pattern in Figure 4 was obtained by
graphing channel totals and by using the rings as
a scale. The rings graduate from the center at intervals of 5,000 up to 30,000 ADA for ring 10. For
example, channel B has a total ADA value of 8,371,
and its coordinate lies a bit beyond ring 3.

7. A number of attempts were made to set up
regression equations for college enrollment. The
smaller the unit areas (sectors) used in the evaluation, the lower were the R-squared values; thus,
high multiple correlation can be obtained for county-
based regression equations, but prediction becomes
more difficult as minor civil divisions and smaller
areas are examined.

8. Exact data on Alfred's ADA and university
enrollment by local students was not obtained. Alfred's ADA is combined with Almond in one school
district and can only be approximated, and the university's local enrollment was not obtained in the
limited time.

9. See Walter Christaller, <u>Central Places in</u>
<u>Southern Germany,</u> Carlisle W. Baskin, trans. (Engle-
wood Cliffs, N.J.: Prentice Hall, 1966), pp. 43-58;
Christaller's work in central-place theory indicates

that on a theoretical basis the size of the central
city will relate to the size of the cities and towns
in its surrounding area. The large city would tend
to be surrounded by localities decreasing in size
with distance up to a point of minimum central-city
influence. Also see August Losch, The Economics of
Location (New Haven, Conn.: Yale University Press,
1954), pp. 109-34 and 389-451.

10. Only New York State residents are included
within the local student grouping in this reference.
Students from nearby Pennsylvania locations enrolled
as follows: 4 in dorms, 1 commuting from home, and
2 in offcampus housing, totaling 7. Twenty-four additional students came from more distant locations
outside commuting range in the State of Pennsylvania.
Twenty-two of these lived in dormitories. The in-
hibition of the state boundary and college tuition
rates is quite evident here, as Alfred is well within
20 miles of the Pennsylvania border.

11. Unfortunately, time, resources, and limited
access to private college computer facilities restricted the work in this area to SUNY Cortland and
Alfred Agricultural and Technical College. Local
student enrollment and commutation at private colleges probably differ from these patterns. Private
colleges tend to draw many more students from out of
state and lesser components from the local area, depending on tuition, admission requirements, curriculum, and other factors.

12. Based on data obtained from the president's
office at Auburn Community College.

6

COLLEGE-STUDENT
INTERACTION
IN THE COMMUNITY:
ECONOMIC IMPACT
AND SOCIAL FACTORS

The economic inpact of a student on the college community appears small when compared to that of a staff member. However, when the large number of students is multiplied by the relatively low per capita expenditure level, the student total approaches local staff expenditures. Again, spillout is an important factor, and although total dollar volume may be large, the place of its incidence is important to the college community. Students may be limited in their travel and, consequently, limited in their ability to buy outside the college community. On the other hand, travel by bus and car pool, especially in obtaining recreational and amusement services, can effect considerable spillout from the town that lacks these amenities. This is also true relative to social factors. Localization of student contact to on-campus activities limits contact with people in the community. However, although the college student patronizes or deals with few local residents, in aggregate the contact becomes substantial.

This chapter is concerned with the student side of spillout and student interaction with people in the college community. Data obtained at four- and two-year colleges are contrasted, as in the staff analysis, and some consideration is given to the influence of city size.

SELECTED ECONOMIC CHARACTERISTICS

For the college communities studied, the major economic impact of the student occurs through his retail purchases. Student impact and spillout relative to retail expenditures are examined in this section.

Impact on Retail Trade

In studying economic impact of the student, it was felt that the volume of his local purchases might possibly relate to proximity of the shopping district or his frequency of visitation to this area. However, at the colleges studied, neither of these is an important factor.

The great majority of students at both Alfred Technical College (70 percent) and Cortland College (77 percent) are in the shopping district of their respective college towns two days or less during the week. (See Table 6.1.) At Alfred University, the situation is quite different; most Alfred University students (64 percent) are in the shopping area five or more days during the week, and close to 80 percent of the students pass through this district on at least four out of seven days. A major reason for the difference between Alfred Technical College and Alfred University in this regard is that several classrooms and administrative offices of the latter are actually in the commercial district. (See Map 1.) Some Alfred Technical students live in this area, and, although the college campus adjoins the shopping district, it is clearly separate from this area. Short distances are involved in all cases.

As for Auburn Community College, although its campus is about a mile from the main shopping area, 50 percent of its students are in the shopping district five or more days of the week. In Cazenovia, 32 percent of the college students are in nearby shopping areas for the same number of days.

The question is: How much does frequency of visitation (spillin) to the shopping district affect

TABLE 6.1

Number of Days During the Week Student is in
Shopping District in the College Town

Number of Days	Alfred Tech.	Cortland	Alfred University	Cazenovia	Auburn	Total
0	4.0	5.0	1.1	2.1	7.7	4.1
1	33.6	42.9	3.2	2.1	10.3	23.3
2	32.2	28.6	7.5	25.5	14.1	23.1
3	9.9	7.6	9.7	23.4	14.1	11.3
4	5.9	3.4	15.1	14.9	3.9	7.6
5	6.6	5.0	8.6	14.9	26.9	10.6
6	4.0	2.5	14.0	8.5	7.7	6.5
7	4.0	5.0	40.9	8.5	15.4	13.5
Total	100.0	100.0	100.0	100.0	100.0	100.0
N	152	119	93	47	78	489

Note: Details may not add up to totals because
of rounding

purchasing volume by students at the various colleges?
This can be examined by using Tables 6.2 to 6.4.

Food Purchases

As depicted in Table 6.2, about half (48 percent) of the Alfred University students buy 10 percent or less of their groceries in town, compared to
38 percent of the Alfred Technical College students
buying at this low level.[1] From another view, 48
percent of the Alfred Technical College students indicated they made over half their food purchases in
the college town, compared to 42 percent in this
category at Alfred University. Thus, other things
being equal, it would appear that, at Alfred, the
frequent presence of students in the shopping district

TABLE 6.2

Students' Food Purchases in the College Town,
in Percent

Percent Purchased in College Town	Alfred Tech.	Cortland	Alfred University	Cazenovia	Auburn	Total
0-10	37.5	28.1	47.8	33.4	26.6	35.3
20-40	14.8	10.4	9.8	4.2	8.0	10.5
50-80	16.3	17.7	10.9	20.8	20.0	16.6
90-100	31.2	43.8	31.5	41.7	45.3	37.6
Total	100.0	100.0	100.0	100.0	100.0	100.0
N	128	96	92	48	75	439

Note: Details may not add up to totals because
of rounding.

does not necessarily cause greater food purchasing
in the college town. More important, the food dollar, especially of the Alfred University student, is
attracted to other localities during the school year;
the Alfred Technical student shows a slightly greater
tendency than the Alfred University student to make
his food purchases in the village.

At Cortland, well over half (61.5 percent) of
the students purchase more than 50 percent of their
groceries locally; however, on the low side, 28 percent indicated that they made only 10 percent or less
of their purchases in this city. From additional
data on other colleges presented in Table 6.2, one
can conclude that the proportion of food purchased
locally by students is at about the same level as in
Cortland, Auburn, and Cazenovia; leakage in these
college communities is not unusual, but it is not as
severe as in Alfred. The data indicate that the

larger cities (Auburn and Cortland) do well in retaining food-purchasing dollars and that the small town (Cazenovia) with adequate and attractive retail facilities can do comparatively well in this regard, especially when it is somewhat remote from competing centers.[2]

Clothing Purchases

Data on clothing purchases indicate that college students buy only a small proportion of these items in the college town (Table 6.3). Alfred University is particularly low in this category. Close to 90 percent of its students indicated that only 10 percent or less of their clothing purchases were made in the college town. Alfred Technical College students show a slightly better local purchasing record. Local

TABLE 6.3

Students' Clothing Purchases in the College Town, in Percent

Percent Purchased in College Town	Alfred Tech.	Cortland	Alfred University	Cazenovia	Auburn	Total
0-10	80.4	62.0	87.4	68.8	43.6	70.2
20-40	10.2	21.5	8.5	20.9	16.7	14.7
50-80	4.8	10.8	3.2	8.4	19.3	8.5
90-100	4.7	5.8	1.1	2.1	20.5	6.6
Total	100.0	100.0	100.0	100.0	100.0	100.0
N	148	121	95	48	78	490

Note: Details may not add up to totals because of rounding.

clothing purchases increase somewhat from a low to a
medium level in Cazenovia, Cortland, and Auburn,
where 10 percent, 17 percent, and 40 percent of the
college students make half (or more) of their clothing purchases in the respective college towns. Of
course, the latter two colleges have the greatest
number of students coming from permanent residences
in the college community itself. The record for
clothing purchases in Auburn is not particularly high
because, as indicated in Chapter 5, well over 30 percent of the full-time student enrollment comes from
the Auburn School District. However, as mentioned
previously, although clothing purchases in the college community are low, when multiplied by the large
number of students a fairly substantial sales volume
can result.

Expenditures for Amusement

In a study of Le Moyne College, in Syracuse,
Roy Gerard indicated that the largest single, continuous expense by students was for amusement and
recreation.[3] A significant difference exists between
the five colleges examined here in regard to incidence of this expenditure in their college towns.
This difference relates, in some degree, to town
size and to the number of retail trade and service
facilities. However, examinations of more college
communities would be necessary to confirm this.

Cortland and Auburn absorb a far greater proportion of student expenditures for amusement services than Alfred and Cazenovia. At Auburn and
Cortland, 50 and 58 percent of the students, respectively, obtain 50 percent or more of these services
in the college town; this is the case for only 23
percent of the students at Cazenovia; at Alfred, only
7.6 percent of the university and 11.2 percent of
the technical college students obtain 50 percent or
more of their amusement services locally. (See
Table 6.4.)

When we look at the lower end of the scale and
the situation in the small towns, the great majority
of students at Alfred University (74 percent) and

TABLE 6.4

Students' Amusement Services in the College Town,
in Percent

Percent Purchased in College Town	Al- fred Tech.	Cort- land	Al- fred Uni- ver- sity	Caze- novia	Au- burn	Total
0-10	65.9	20.4	73.7	43.8	35.5	49.3
20-40	22.9	22.0	19.0	33.4	14.6	21.6
50-80	8.4	45.8	5.4	23.0	32.9	22.3
90-100	2.8	11.8	2.2	0.0	17.1	6.9
Total	100.0	100.0	100.0	100.0	100.0	100.0
N	144	118	95	48	76	481

Note: Details may not add up to totals because of rounding.

Alfred Technical College (66 percent) obtain 10 percent or less of their amusement services locally,
compared to 44 percent of the students at Cazenovia.
In this expenditure category, an opportunity loss by
Alfred Village is quite evident.[4] Furthermore, the
large cities appear better able to provide amusement
services for students. This is not only owing to
their greater choice of these services but also to a
less limiting environment.

Other retail-trade categories exhibit similar
patterns to those presented earlier. Undergraduate
students do not make substantial purchases of clothing and durable items in the college community. The
small town with an attractive and ample shopping area
can retain a considerable proportion of student purchases in food, toiletries, and impulse items. However, an inadequate shopping area can lose substantial

trade to more distant but attractive competing centers. The large cities exhibit the least spillout
of purchases. As previously mentioned, student purchases are not large on an individual basis but become substantial when multiplied by their volume.

SELECTED SOCIAL CHARACTERISTICS

Alfred and Cortland each absorb well over 3,000
students every year. These and other college communities draw young men and women from diverse and distant areas of the state. Along with the economic
impact owing to the student presence, the community
receives an array of student attitudes and characteristics. Although most students leave after graduation, their impact is retained and repeated through
constant replacement. Thus, a continuity in impact
is established, and this depends on the range of student sociopolitical characteristics and the extent
of their exposure to community residents, social
institutions, and on the proportion of students who
remain in the county or college community after graduation.

A substantial body of research exists on characteristics and attitudes of the college student.[5]
However, only a small fraction of this touches on
his relationship to college-community elements. This
section of the study is primarily concerned with the
student's social interaction with local institutions
and residents. The latter include businessmen,
farmers, and workers living in the college community
and surrounding area.

Social Contact with
Local Residents

Student social interaction with local residents
was measured on a qualitative and quantitative basis
(as was discussed previously for college-staff members). The results offer insight into the extent of
this relationship.

At Alfred, Cortland, and Cazenovia, from 70 to 80 percent of the students indicated frequent contact with only a few (one or none) of the local residents, as shown in Table 6.5. Close to 20 percent of the students at Alfred University, Cortland, and Cazenovia, and only 12 percent at Alfred Technical College, were in frequent contact and discussion with a moderate number (two to three) of the local residents, and about 10 percent of the students at these colleges indicated frequent contact and discussion with a substantial number (four or more) of these individuals.[6]

As depicted in Table 6.5, there is a significant difference in this situation between the above colleges and the Auburn Community College. At the latter

TABLE 6.5

Number of Local Residents Contacted Fairly Frequently by College Students, in Percent

Number Contacted	Alfred Tech.	Cortland	Alfred University	Cazenovia	Auburn	Total
None	63.8	60.0	60.6	56.5	21.8	54.8
1	14.1	10.0	9.6	13.0	3.9	10.5
2-3	12.1	20.0	17.0	19.6	30.8	18.7
4-5	6.0	6.7	9.6	4.4	20.5	9.0
6 or more	4.0	3.3	3.2	6.5	23.1	7.0
Total	100.0	100.0	100.0	100.0	100.0	100.0
N	149	120	94	46	78	487

Note: Details may not add up to totals because of rounding

college, only 26 percent of the students indicated low contacts with local residents; 31 percent of the

Auburn students showed frequent contact and discussion with a moderate number (two to three) of these individuals and 44 percent denoted frequent contact with four or more residents in the area.

One can readily anticipate this difference as about one third of the students at Auburn Community College have permanent residence within the city, compared to less than 10 percent of the students with such residence at the other colleges.[7] As of this study, Auburn Community College had no dormitories. Many students at Auburn live in offcampus rental housing, and under this condition, more extended contact with local residents seems likely.[8] College-community size has little influence on this interaction for the colleges studied (note data on Cortland, Alfred, and Cazenovia). However, dormitory living is probably associated with spillout in this category.

A qualitative indication of the association between students and permanent residents in the college community was obtained through student assessment of their social ties with these individuals. The resulting data, shown in Table 6.6, parallel that on student contact with local residents, except for Cazenovia, where a higher proportion of students at the all-girl college show close social relationships.

At Alfred Technical College, Cortland, and Alfred University, only from 5 to 10 percent of the students indicated strong social relationships with local residents in the area; 20 to 25 percent showed moderate ties and 65 to 75 percent depicted relationships as weak or nonexistent. At Cazenovia, students at the all-girl college indicated somewhat closer social relationships with local people, with 17 percent, 29 percent, and 54 percent showing strong, moderate, and weak or nonexistent social ties, respectively. It is possible that female students tend toward closer social relationships with community residents; however, more data are necessary to corroborate this.

TABLE 6.6

Strength of Social Relationships Between College
Students and Local Residents in the Area, in Percent

Social Relation- ships	Al- fred Tech.	Cort- land	Al- fred Uni- ver- sity	Caze- novia	Au- burn	Total
Very strong	1.3	2.5	2.1	2.1	6.4	2.6
Fairly strong	6.0	2.5	7.4	14.6	23.1	8.9
Moderate	25.2	19.8	25.3	29.2	37.2	26.2
Fairly weak	27.2	26.5	27.4	20.8	19.2	25.2
None	40.4	48.8	37.9	33.3	14.1	37.1
Total	100.0	100.0	100.0	100.0	100.0	100.0
N	151	121	95	48	78	493

Note: Details may not add up to totals because
of rounding.

Again, students at Auburn Community College
indicate closer association with local residents
than at other colleges. Here, about one third each
had strong, moderate, and weak or nonexistent relationships with local residents. College-community
size shows little bearing on the situation.[9] Offcampus housing may relate to stronger social relationships with community residents, but more evidence
is needed to corroborate this.

Student Attitudes Toward Local Residents

The degree of social contact between students
and local residents relates to student attitudes

toward the latter. An assessment of these attitudes is given in Table 6.7. The great majority (63 percent) of students are neutral in attitude (or show little reaction) toward community residents. This neutrality is highest in Alfred, as indicated by about 68 percent of the students. However, close to half (about 43 percent) of the students at Auburn and Cazenovia indicated that attitudes in these localities were more accurately described as "friendly."[10] Cortland students showed a more distant attitude toward local people; only 18 percent

TABLE 6.7

Attitude of Students Toward Local Residents,
in Percent

Attitude	Al-fred Tech.	Cort-land	Al-fred Uni-ver-sity	Caze-novia	Au-burn	Total
Very friendly	0.7	1.6	2.1	6.3	3.8	2.2
Fairly friendly	24.5	16.4	25.3	37.5	39.2	26.3
Neutral	68.2	65.6	67.4	52.1	50.6	63.0
Fairly un-friendly	6.6	14.8	3.2	4.2	5.1	7.5
Very un-friendly	0.0	1.6	2.1	0.0	1.3	1.0
Total	100.0	100.0	100.0	100.0	100.0	100.0
N	151	122	95	48	79	495

Note: Details may not add up to totals because of rounding.

designated friendliness and 16 percent indicated
unfriendliness between students and community residents. However, the relationship between community
size and student attitude is not apparent from the
information at hand. The data for Auburn are influ-
enced by the large contingent of local students.

Attitudes of Shopkeepers Toward Students

Students at the five colleges assessed the attitudes of shopkeepers toward college students, as
shown in Table 6.8. Shopkeepers in the college communities were found "friendly" by the highest proportion of students at Cazenovia (83 percent) and

TABLE 6.8

Attitude of Shopkeepers Toward College Students,
in Percent

Attitude	Alfred Tech.	Cortland	Alfred University	Cazenovia	Auburn	Total
Very friendly	19.7	27.3	24.2	27.1	28.2	24.5
Fairly friendly	44.1	41.3	55.8	56.3	43.6	46.8
Neutral	25.7	24.0	12.6	10.4	23.1	20.9
Fairly unfriendly	9.9	5.8	6.3	6.3	3.9	6.9
Very unfriendly	0.7	1.7	1.1	0.0	1.3	1.0
Total	100.0	100.0	100.0	100.0	100.0	100.0
N	152	121	95	48	78	494

Note: Details may not add up to totals because
of rounding.

lowest in Alfred (at the technical college, at 64 percent). Other student responses indicating friendliness by shopkeepers were 80 percent for Alfred University, 72 percent at Auburn, and 69 percent at Cortland. The differences of opinion at Alfred Technical College and Alfred University appear primarily to center on the larger group of students at the former institution who indicated a neutral attitude on the part of shopkeepers. It is interesting to note that more students at the two private colleges (Alfred University and Cazenovia) found the shopkeepers friendly than at the other colleges.

One can conclude that, in most cases, nonlocal students have few social relationships with people in the college community. A neutral or friendly attitude is the rule, but not many strong relationships are established. Community size does not appear to affect the situation. Most students seek solely to develop college ties and are rather isolated in their campus environment. It would seem that more interaction between local residents and students would be mutually advantageous; however, this may be difficult to achieve under the circumstances.

BACKGROUND INFORMATION

Although many students do not frequently contact and establish social ties with community residents, there can be a substantial amount of induced or indirect contact owing to the presence of the college and the student body. Student interaction with local people may occur through business and social routine and visitations to the shopping district. Student political activity and social behavior generally evoke community comment. A group of college professional staff and students may seek community involvement, or the college itself may function as a unit in community relationships. This study has previously discussed college influence on local government, school-district policy, and other factors; it can only consider a few related elements in its limited scope.

Political Views Contrasted with
Those of the Community

Table 6.9 indicates that, generally, the political views of students at the five colleges are less
conservative than those of the local residents in
the respective areas. However, their effect on change
in the college community would depend on the extent
of their exposure, interaction, and involvement with
the local population.

Students at the baccalaureate institutions show
less conservatism than those at the junior colleges.
Community size (population) bears little upon the
situation, especially as noted in the data on the two
colleges in Alfred. Almost three fourths of the students at Alfred University (73 percent) and Cortland
(72 percent) indicated less conservative political
attitudes than local people. The large influx of
undergraduates to these colleges from New York City
and other metropolitan areas in New York State (see
Table 5.2) probably has considerable effect in this
regard. Close to half of the students at Cazenovia
(51 percent), Auburn (49 percent), and Alfred Technical College (44 percent) declared less conservative
political attitudes than local residents. Further
study is needed in this category with control variables that use curriculum or major study area, age,
and other factors. A comparison of political views
of local and nonlocal students would also be of value
but is beyond the scope of this study. As indicated
previously, the two-year college generally draws more
of the local-area students than the four-year college.

It is possible to state that the four-year colleges surveyed are input devices for focusing or
assembling students with less conservative political
views and that the two-year colleges tend toward a
more mixed situation. Students at the four-year college in the small town (Alfred) are quite a bit
less conservative than those at the junior college.

TABLE 6.9

Political Views of College Students Compared to Local Residents, in Percent

Political Views	Alfred Tech.	Cortland	Alfred University	Cazenovia	Auburn	Total
Far more conservative	3.6	0.0	1.1	2.1	3.9	2.1
Fairly more conservative	7.9	5.9	2.1	10.6	6.4	6.3
At same level of opinion	44.6	22.0	23.4	36.2	41.0	33.4
Fairly less conservative	25.2	41.5	36.2	29.8	26.9	32.1
Far less conservative	18.7	30.5	37.2	21.3	21.8	26.1
Total	100.0	100.0	100.0	100.0	100.0	100.0
N	139	118	94	47	78	476

Note: Details may not add up to totals because of rounding.

Student Attitudes Toward
Political Demonstrations

Student demonstrations for political and social causes have made front-page news in the last several years. This action has taken place at public and private colleges of all sizes and in both urban and rural locations. Demonstrations have been most often confined to the college campus. However, local police and other municipal officials frequently become involved in related administrative and operational problems, and local residents are at least peripherally affected by this type of student action.

Our survey found that students at the four-year colleges and at the two-year college at Auburn were more favorable toward demonstrations on political affairs than those at two-year colleges; however, substantial numbers at all the colleges studied favored demonstrations in this category. The actual percentages of students favoring this political action were 59 percent at Cortland, 58 percent at Alfred University, 55 percent at Auburn, 42 percent at Cazenovia, and 39 percent at Alfred Technical College. About one student in five at these colleges was neutral or undecided, as indicated in Table 6.10; opposition to this action was highest for students at Alfred Technical College (37 percent) and lowest for those at Cortland College (17 percent). Comparison of the two colleges in Alfred indicates considerably more opposition to political demonstrations at the technical college than at the university.

Student Attitudes Toward College
Policy Demonstrations

Student opinion is most emphatic in attitude toward demonstrations on college policy, as indicated in Table 6.11. Of the students at Cortland College, 80 percent favored student demonstrations on college policy. Even at Alfred Technical College, where students were demonstrably more conservative in attitude, 63 percent favored this type of action and set a higher percentage in this category than students at Alfred University (59 percent), Auburn (56 percent),

TABLE 6.10

Student Attitudes Toward Political Demonstrations,
in Percent

Attitude	Al-fred Tech.	Cort-land	Al-fred Uni-ver-sity	Caze-novia	Au-burn	Total
Very much in favor	10.0	19.8	19.2	18.8	19.2	16.5
Somewhat in favor	29.3	38.8	38.3	22.9	35.9	33.8
Neutral or not de-cided	23.3	24.0	17.0	25.0	19.2	21.8
Somewhat opposed	21.3	13.2	16.0	12.5	18.0	16.9
Very much opposed	16.0	4.1	9.6	20.8	7.7	11.0
Total	100.0	100.0	100.0	100.0	100.0	100.0
N	150	121	94	48	78	491

Note: Details may not add up to totals because
of rounding.

and Cazenovia (56 percent). The desire to influence
college policy thus appeared rather strong at all
colleges studied.[11]

Student Attitudes Toward
the Use of Drugs

College students at the public two-year colleges
studied were more opposed to use of such drugs as
marijuana and LSD than students at the four-year colleges and the private two-year girls' college at
Cazenovia (Table 6.12). This opposition was

TABLE 6.11

Student Attitudes Toward Demonstrations
on College Policy, in Percent

Attitude	Al-fred Tech.	Cort-land	Al-fred Uni-ver-sity	Caze-novia	Au-burn	Total
Very much in favor	33.3	39.7	22.6	25.0	21.8	30.2
Somewhat in favor	30.0	40.5	36.6	31.2	34.6	34.7
Neutral or not de-cided	15.3	5.8	15.1	20.8	26.9	15.3
Somewhat opposed	14.0	8.3	18.3	6.3	9.0	11.8
Very much opposed	7.3	5.8	7.5	16.7	7.7	8.0
Total	100.0	100.0	100.0	100.0	100.0	100.0
N	150	121	93	48	78	490

Note: Details may not add up to totals because of rounding.

indicated by 70 percent of the students at Alfred
Technical College, 66 percent at Auburn, 55 percent
at Cortland, 54 percent at Cazenovia, and 52 percent
at Alfred University. Students "very much in favor"
of the use of these drugs ranged from 2 percent at
Alfred Technical College to 10 percent at Cazenovia
College.

The exact effect on the community residents of
the above student attitudes is difficult to assess.
Differences in political views, opinions on student

TABLE 6.12

Student Attitudes Toward Use of Drugs,
in Percent

Attitudes	Al-fred Tech.	Cort-land	Al-fred Uni-ver-sity	Caze-novia	Au-burn	Total
Very much in favor	2.0	8.3	7.4	10.4	6.3	6.1
Somewhat in favor	12.0	9.1	11.6	12.5	13.9	11.6
Neutral or not de-cided	16.0	28.1	24.5	22.9	13.9	21.9
Somewhat opposed	15.3	21.5	16.8	8.3	8.9	15.4
Very much opposed	54.7	33.1	34.7	45.8	57.0	45.0
Total	100.0	100.0	100.0	100.0	100.0	100.0
N	150	121	95	48	79	493

Note: Details may not add up to totals because of rounding.

demonstrations, and the use of drugs may have high or low impact on the lives of local businessmen, farmers, or workers. Much depends on the rate of student contact with area residents and indirect effects. Data obtained at the five colleges studied indicate that student-townspeople relationships present very minor problems.

ADDITIONAL FACTORS

The public colleges studied have substantial impact in that they offer education to students from

lower-income groups. Some of these students cannot
afford the high tuition of the private institution,
but they can earn their room and board by part-time
or summer work while attending the low tuition public college. Students may attend a college out of
commutation range by choice or by necessity. Others
can only afford to commute to the nearest public college. (See Appendix Table F.1.)

Student Employment

At the five colleges studied, about one fourth
to half of the college students were employed while
attending college. (See Appendix Table F.3.) Except for Auburn and Cortland, students who were
employed most frequently worked for the college.
Maximum student unemployment (at 74 percent) was evident in Cortland and minimum (at 45 percent) in Auburn. In the latter city, over one fourth (26 percent)
of the students found jobs at companies in the college community; at Cortland, only a small percentage
(6.6 percent) were so engaged. Thus, student employment shows high deviation for two- and four-year
colleges examined in the larger cities. Of interest
is the fact that at Alfred Technical College few if
any of the working students found jobs with village
firms, and a relatively high proportion (8.5 percent)
worked for out-of-town organizations. Notable also
is the relatively high employment of students by the
private colleges. These data suggest that more work
opportunity is available in the larger communities
and that students at the two-year college in the
city (Auburn) are more likely to be employed than
students at the other colleges. Additional data indicate that a considerable number (49 percent) of
employed Auburn students work longer hours (15 or
more) per week than students at the other colleges
and that students at each of the two-year public colleges (Alfred Technical and Auburn) work longer hours
than those at the four-year public institution
(Cortland).

Parental Income

Data obtained indicate that a significant difference exists in parental annual income for college

students at the five institutions studied.   (See
Table 6.13.)   A rather high proportion of the parents
of students at the private colleges are in the highest income brackets; about 68 percent of the students
at Cazenovia and 42 percent at Alfred University indicated parental income at the $15,000 level or
higher.   This proportion drops at the public colleges
to 35, 13, and 12 percent for Cortland, Auburn, and
Alfred Technical, respectively.   Students at the two-
year public colleges denoted the lowest levels for
parental income; however, about 12 percent declared
a $15,000 or higher parental-income level.

Insight into the services that public colleges
perform for students with parents at lower-income
levels can be obtained from Table 6.13 as well.   Data
for Alfred Technical College, Auburn, and Cortland,

TABLE 6.13

Parents' Total Income in 1968, as Indicated by
College Students, in Percent

Annual Income (in dollars)	Al- fred Tech.	Cort- land	Al- fred Uni- ver- sity	Caze- novia	Au- burn	Total
Less than 6,000	17.8	10.5	14.1	2.3	22.4	14.6
6-7,999	21.2	15.7	5.4	2.3	10.5	13.3
8-9,999	17.1	14.8	13.0	6.8	29.0	16.7
10-14,999	31.5	24.4	25.0	20.5	25.0	26.4
15-19,999	5.5	20.0	19.6	25.0	7.9	14.0
20,000 or more	6.8	14.8	22.8	43.2	5.2	15.0
Total	100.0	100.0	100.0	100.0	100.0	100.0
N	146	115	92	44	76	473

Note: Details may not add up to totals because
of rounding

respectively, indicate that 39, 33, and 26 percent of the students stated that parental annual income was below $8,000. At Alfred University, 20 percent of the students are also in this category. Thus, this private institution serves a substantial number of students with families in the low-income group.

Student Choice of College

Although low cost of attendance is an important factor for many students at the colleges studied, most students give high priority to the reputation of the college. As depicted in Table 6.14, about half the students at Alfred Technical College and Alfred University (52 and 50 percent, respectively) and about one third of those at Cortland and Cazenovia (36 and 35 percent, respectively) consider reputation of the college a primary requirement. However, low cost of education is first in importance for the largest group of respondents (29 percent) at Auburn Community College. In addition, if the proportion of students who chose the college because it was "within commuting distance" (16.5 percent) were added to low cost, these combined categories apply to almost half (46 percent) of the students surveyed at Auburn. Residence in or near the college community helps many of these individuals who are seeking low college costs in the City of Auburn.

Appendix Table F.2 depicts second major reasons for attending the colleges studied and their percentage distribution. Here, low cost is the predominant reason for 18 percent of the total group of students examined; however, none of the students at Cazenovia attend that college for reasons of economy. At Alfred Technical College, Cortland, and Auburn, 13, 27, and 34 percent of the students, respectively, cite the importance of low cost for their education, and, if commutation possibility is added to this proportion the percentages increase to 20, 30, and 52 percent, respectively. However, any conclusion in this regard should be qualified by data in Appendix Table F.1, which indicates that a high percentage of students favor attending a college outside the commuter range.

TABLE 6.14

Students' Primary Reason for Attending a Particular College, in Percent

Reason	Alfred Tech.	Cortland	Alfred University	Cazenovia	Auburn	Total
Reputation	52.0	36.4	50.0	35.4	25.3	41.9
Commutation	3.3	3.3	1.1	4.2	16.5	5.1
Near home	8.0	6.6	5.3	8.3	8.9	7.3
Low cost	6.7	17.4	4.3	0.0	29.1	11.8
Away from home	9.3	12.4	5.3	4.2	1.3	7.5
Parent	2.7	5.8	9.6	12.5	3.8	5.9
Councelor	8.7	3.3	11.7	10.4	0.0	6.7
Other	9.4	15.0	12.9	25.0	15.3	13.8
Total	100.0	100.0	100.0	100.0	100.0	100.0
N	150	121	94	48	79	492

Note: The following question was asked: "Underline your two major reasons for attending this college, then enter 1 and 2 (in order of importance) below: (1) reputation of the college and curriculum, (2) within commuting distance, (3) can't commute, but fairly near home, (4) low cost, (5) location away from home, (6) athletic program, (7) advice of high school counselor, (8) parents or relatives, (9) counselor at college, (10) social reasons, (11) I like this area and climate, (12) other [specify]." Parts 6, 9, 10, 11, and 12 were combined in the above table. See also Appendix Tables F.1 and F.2.

Student Location After Graduation

Although the local college benefits the surrounding area by serving a considerable number of local students, comparatively few of the students surveyed planned to remain in the general area of their college after graduation, except for a sizable segment of those in attendance at the Auburn Community College (Table 6.15). Plans for settling outside the county and adjacent counties were indicated by a very high percentage of students at Alfred University (97 percent), Cortland (92 percent), Cazenovia (92 percent), Alfred Technical College (88 percent), and Auburn (64 percent). This high spillout reflects the fact that most undergraduates come from outside the area and also that a substantial number of local students leave the area of the college after receiving their education. Although 15 percent of the Auburn students intend to settle in the college community, this is considerably less than those attending the college from the Auburn School District.

Close to three fourths of the graduates from the public colleges studied planned to remain in New York State. Data indicated that 25 percent of the students at Alfred Technical College and Cortland, 33 percent at Auburn, 41 percent at Alfred University, and 50 percent at Cazenovia intended to leave New York State after graduation. This again reflects the place of permanent residence of the undergraduate student at the private colleges. However, although enrollment of New York State residents at State University colleges in the area studied has been well above 90 percent of the total student body in past years (see Table 5.2), outmigration of a considerable proportion of New Yorkers is probable, especially at Auburn, if eventual student action in this regard matches current plans.

SUMMARY

This chapter further substantiates earlier findings of economic and social spillout. Small

TABLE 6.15

Students' Choice of Residence after Graduation, in Percent

Area	Alfred Tech.	Cortland	Alfred University	Cazenovia	Auburn	Total
College town	0.0	1.7	0.0	0.0	15.4	2.8
County[a]	3.3	1.7	2.1	2.1	5.1	2.8
Adjacent county	8.5	5.0	1.1	6.3	15.4	7.1
New York State[b]	63.4	66.9	55.8	41.7	30.8	55.6
Outside New York State[c]	20.3	23.1	34.7	47.9	33.3	28.5
Outside United States	4.6	1.7	6.3	2.1	0.0	3.2
Total	100.0	100.0	100.0	100.0	100.0	100.0
N	153	121	95	48	78	495

[a]In county but not in college town.
[b]In New York State but not in college town, county, or adjacent county.
[c]Outside New York State but in the United States.

Note: Details may not add up to totals because of rounding.

college communities examined attracted student expenditures for food, accessories, and amusements to a lesser degree than the larger cities. Student purchases become substantial when multiplied by their volume and can aid in expansion of the college communities' retail trade and economic base.

To the decisionmaker in college planning, social factors related to student input are also of high importance. Although nonlocal students do not frequently contact and establish social ties with community residents, student behavior and activity generally evoke community concern. College students are less conservative politically and socially than local people. A high percentage of students at all the colleges contacted indicated strong motivation in political and college affairs. Those at the two-year public colleges were generally more conservative than other college students. However, at all of the colleges studied, substantial numbers favored political action. If we consider these views and similar expressions by the professional staff, it seems that to successfully accommodate the college, the small college community, especially, would have to show adaptability toward change. Substantial benefits come to the college community through local education of its young. The public colleges studied indicated that a considerable number of students came from low-income families. However, the college community must be prepared to lose a large proportion of its college graduates. As data indicate, many local students leave the area after receiving their education.

NOTES

1. In all cases cited, the purchases made do not include items paid for by college contract or fees for room and board. In interpreting Table 6.2, it should be understood that the colleges at Alfred and Cortland have a high proportion of dormitory students, Cazenovia College has only dormitory students, and Auburn Community College has no dormitories. Additional data on Alfred and Cortland

indicate that nondorm students tend to buy considerably more of their food in the college town than do
dormitory students.

2. Village boundaries and market locations
affect the situation.

3. Roy Gerard, Impact 1, Economic Impact of Le
Moyne College on the Syracuse, New York Community
(Syracuse: Le Moyne College, 1962), p. 35; and
Frances S. Doody, The Immediate Economic Impact of
Higher Education in New England (Boston: Boston
University Bureau of Business Research, 1961); both
detailed or listed various goods and services by
students.

4. The population of Cazenovia in 1960 was
2,584, compared to an Alfred population of 2,807;
however, the latter village housed many more students
than did Cazenovia in that year, as indicated in
Table 3.1A. Although the villages are not far apart
in the number of permanent residents, this difference
has a considerable effect. Cazenovia had a greater
retail-trade operation in 1963 than did Alfred and
also indicated more people engaged in entertainment
and recreational services in 1960.

5. Rose K. Goldsen, Morris Rosenberg, Robin M.
Williams, Jr., and Edward A. Suchman, What College
Students Think (Princeton, N.J.: Van Nostrand Company,
Inc., 1960); Philip E. Jacob, Changing Values in
College: An Exploratory Study of the Impact of Col-
lege Teaching (New York: Harper & Bros., 1957);
Kaoru Yamamoto, comp., The College Student and His
Culture: An Analysis (Boston: Houghton Mifflin,
1968); Richard E. Peterson, The Scope of Organized
Student Protest in 1964-65 (Princeton, N.J.: Edu-
cational Testing Service, 1966); Peter H. Armacost,
"The Student and His Public Image, The Dean Speaks
Out," Bulletin No. 2, (Champaign, Ill.: National
Association of Student Personnel Administrators,
April, 1967); Burton R. Clark, Educating the Expert
Society (San Francisco: Chandler Publishing Company,
1962), pp. 202-43. In a poll of middle-income groups
in the United States, 84 percent said campus

demonstrators were treated too leniently and 60 percent said demonstrations had little or not justification; this was reported in "The Troubled American, A Special Report on the White Majority," Newsweek, October 6, 1969, pp. 35 and 46. For selected references and current papers, see also "Student Protest," The Annals, CCCSCV (Philadelphia: American Academy of Political and Social Science, May, 1971).

6. See Delbert C. Miller, Handbook of Research Design and Social Measurement (New York: David McKay Company, Inc., 1964), pp. 220-21, for a related measurement.

7. This is based on data previously cited. The proportion changes somewhat over a period of time.

8. Higher contact with local residents by nondormitory college students is indicated in limited data obtained in this survey.

9. This statement applies to nonlocal students and their social relationships with local people. The City of Auburn, with a nondormitory community college, shows higher interaction and can provide for more offcampus accommodations for students. However, in late 1969, the Auburn Community College indicated that dormitory accommodations would be available for a small number of students.

10. Miller, loc. cit.

11. See The Alfred Reporter, XLV, 13 (Alfred, N.Y.: Alfred University, December, 1969); a major incident of campus unrest occurred at Alfred University on December 10, 1969. This was about one year after the questionnaire survey for this study was made. Students staged a sit-in in one of the university's buildings and presented demands relating to college regulations.

CHAPTER

7

IMPACT

OF

COLLEGE PURCHASES

ON THE COLLEGE

COMMUNITY

AND THE REGION

In addition to impact of staff and students on the college community, important considerations in analysis of the college's economic effect on its area are its local and regional expenditures for supplies, utilities, maintenance, and related items.[1] For example, as shown in Table 7.1, in the 1967-68 fiscal year, SUNY Cortland made $343,903 in selected operational and maintenance expenditures in the City of Cortland. In addition, out of a total of $2.6 million in purchases by its Faculty-Student Association (FSA), $1.3 million were made in the college community, as indicated in Table 7.4. This had a substantial effect on retail trade, selected services, and payrolls in the area.[2]

Our purpose in this phase of the discussion is not to generalize a proportionate relationship between local purchases and college-community size. This would be a formidable undertaking and would require detailed analysis of the accounting records of many colleges.[3] However, a study of the purchasing characteristics of SUNY Alfred Technical College and Cortland College can yield additional insight into economic impact of the institution on the small and

TABLE 7.1

Location of Selected Operational and Maintenance Expenditures, State University of New York at Cortland, 1967-68

Expenditure Category	City of Cortland ($)	(%)	Town of Cortland ($)	(%)	Cortland County ($)	(%)	Outside Cortland County ($)	(%)	Total Expenditure in Category ($)	(%)	Category Percent of Overall Expenditure
Educational supplies	9,441	12.06	931	1.19	10,372	13.25	67,927	86.75	78,299	100.00	11.00
Utilities	229,143	100.00	--	--	229,143	100.00	--	0.00	229,143	100.00	32.19
Rentals	79	0.25	--	--	79	.25	31,755	99.75	31,834	100.00	4.47
Repairs and maintenance	30,999	19.79	3,487	2.23	34,486	22.02	122,151	77.98	156,637	100.00	22.00
Equipment	12,529	13.93	375	0.42	12,904	14.35	77,026	85.65	89,930	100.00	12.63
Telephone and telegraph	61,712	100.00	--	--	61,712	100.00	--	0.00	61,712	100.00	8.67
Travel	--	--	--	--	--	--	64,243	100.00	64,243	100.00	9.03
Totals	343,903	48.31	4,793	0.67	348,696	48.99	363,102	51.01	711,798	100.00	100.00

large college community. This analysis also considers spillout. It distinguishes between categories
of college expenditures that are typically local and
nonlocal in character and examines the effect of college location on purchasing in and out of the county.
Hypothesis V is tested to determine if major cities
within the region attract the college's purchasing
dollar in accordance with a gravity model.

COLLEGE EXPENDITURES AT
THE STATE UNIVERSITY OF
NEW YORK AT CORTLAND

Expenditures at SUNY Cortland fall into two
broad categories: first, operational expenditures
made by the college, and, second, expenditures made
by its FSA. The former may be divided into payroll
(personnel) and costs for goods and services used in
maintenance and operations.[4] The latter involves expenditures by auxiliary enterprises and includes the
college store, the cafeteria, and student activities.

In its 1967-68 budget, New York State allocated
about $7 million to support the operation at Cortland;
during the same period, computerized records indicated an expenditure of well over $2.5 million by
the FSA. These amounts represented a relatively
high money inflow to the City of Cortland. However,
due to the large proportion of college purchases made
in other localities, many dollars received by the
college left Cortland in a first round of expenditure.
The major operational and maintenance expenditures
by SUNY Cortland for the fiscal year 1967-68 are
listed in Table 7.1 by amount, percentage distribution, and location of purchase.[5]

As with other colleges, utilities generally take
a high proportion (32.2 percent) of SUNY Cortland's
expenditures for operation and maintenance. As
shown, these are purchased only from firms and agencies within the City of Cortland.[6] This factor is
most responsible for the boosting of local purchases
to 48 percent of the total. Repairs and maintenance
form another relatively large block (22 percent) of

the total expenditure. Close to 80 percent of these
goods and services are obtained outside the city.
This would appear to represent an opportunity loss
for local companies. However, much of this expenditure relates to equipment and products maintained
by contractors who did the original installation.

Although Cortland is one of the larger communities studied, it supplies relatively little (12 percent of the total) in educational supplies to the
college. The bulk of these (86.8 percent) also come
from outside the county. Rentals of equipment indicate a similar situation and are almost totally
(99.8 percent) purchased beyond the county line.
Thus, in fact, only utilities and communication services show a high local expenditure; supplies, rentals, and equipment purchases are primarily made
outside the City of Cortland and the county.

COLLEGE EXPENDITURES AT THE STATE
UNIVERSITY OF NEW YORK AT ALFRED
AGRICULTURAL AND TECHNICAL COLLEGE

An interesting comparison with the situation at
Cortland can be made by examination of data on selected operational and maintenance expenditures at
SUNY Alfred Agricultural and Technical College. As
exhibited in Tables 7.2 and 7.3, expenditures for
utilities again represent a high proportion (30.2
percent) of total expenditures ($718,504). However,
in the case of SUNY Alfred, only 19.5 percent of
these purchases were made locally, 41.2 percent in
Wellsville (in the county) and 37.9 percent in
Hornell (outside the county). The fact that Alfred
is a small village with little industrial and commercial development causes this basic expenditure to be
made largely outside the village. However, in the
category of rentals the reverse occurs. Although
Cortland indicated rentals as its lowest expenditure
in the college area, this item constitutes the highest community purchase for SUNY Alfred. Both Alfred
University and Alfred Village supply the technical
college in this regard and are instrumental in bringing this figure to its relatively high point.

TABLE 7.2

Selected Expenditures at Various Locations by the State University of New York, Agricultural and Technical Institute at Alfred, 1967-68, in Dollars

Expense Category	Alfred Village	Wellsville	Allegany County	Hornell	Steuben County	Buffalo	Elmira	Rochester	Syracuse	Remainder	New York State Total
Educational supplies	3,223	6,441	10,595	6,066	6,066	6,142	2,685	8,214	951	18,477	53,130
Utilities	42,065	89,423	121,488	82,103	82,103	--	--	--	--	3,029	216,620
Rentals	28,860	--	28,860	--	--	--	42,581	2,340	--	8,032	81,813
Repair and maintenance	5,139	12,632	21,519	49,631	52,952	9,934	4,996	2,553	2,197	34,869	129,020
Equipment	1,036	2,996	5,854	5,247	8,857	12,147	16,709	8,859	3,228	124,359	180,013
Telephone and telegraph	5,666	--	5,666	--	--	4,965	--	--	47,277	--	57,908
Total	85,989	111,492	203,982	143,047	149,978	33,188	66,971	21,966	53,653	188,766	718,504

Source: State University of New York, Agricultural and Technical College at Alfred, Finance Office, 1968.

TABLE 7.3

Distribution of Selected Expenditures by the State University of New York, Agricultural and Technical Institute at Alfred, 1967-68, in Percent

Expense Category	Alfred Village	Wells- ville	Alle- gany County	Hor- nell	Steu- ben County	Buf- falo	Elmira	Roch- ester	Syra- cuse	Re- main- der	Total	Cate- gory Per- cent of Over- all Total
Educational supplies	6.1	12.1	19.9	11.4	11.4	11.6	5.1	15.5	1.8	34.7	100.0	7.4
Utilities	19.5	41.2	60.7	37.9	37.0	0.0	0.0	0.0	0.0	1.4	100.0	30.2
Rentals	35.3	0.0	35.3	0.0	0.0	0.0	52.1	2.9	0.0	9.8	100.0	11.4
Repair and mainte- nance	4.0	9.8	16.7	38.4	41.0	7.7	3.9	2.0	1.7	27.1	100.0	18.0
Equipment	0.6	1.7	3.3	2.9	4.9	6.8	9.3	4.9	1.8	69.1	100.0	25.0
Telephone and tele- graph	9.8	0.0	9.8	0.0	0.0	8.6	0.0	0.0	81.6	0.0	100.0	8.1
Total	12.0	15.5	28.4	20.0	20.9	4.6	9.3	3.1	7.5	26.2	100.0	100.0

Note: Details may not add up to totals because of rounding.

Source: State University of New York, Agricultural and Technical College at Alfred, Finance Office, 1968.

In all, 28.4 percent of the college's expenditures for goods and services are made in Allegany
County, compared with 48.3 percent in the case of
Cortland. A basic reason for this difference is college-community size and location. Alfred, among the
smallest of the towns studied, possesses few commercial, repair, and utility services, in contrast with
Cortland, a relatively large-sized city. As for location, Alfred Village is about 3 miles from the
Allegany-Steuben county line and within 10 miles of
the City of Hornell (population 13,907 in 1960).
This city, in Steuben County, formerly a rail center
for the area but on the downgrade since 1940, has
begun to reassert its centrality in the region. It
now takes 20 percent of Alfred Technical College's
expenditures and a good slice of professional- and
auxiliary-staff purchases, as previously shown.

Wellsville Village, in Allegany County, benefits
by receiving 15.5 percent of Alfred Technical College's expenditures, largely through its supply of
utilities, educational supplies, and repair and
maintenance services. This village supports two
good-sized manufacturing plants and adequate commercial facilities. But it is more distant than Hornell
and less successful in attracting college expenditures, as noted in Table 7.3.

If purchases in Allegany and Steuben counties
are summed, they add to 49.3 percent of the total
expenditures and are similar to the total amount for
Cortland County, in Table 7.1. Perhaps this represents an area-purchasing probability for colleges
located remotely from metropolitan areas and with at
least one small city close at hand. More cases would
have to be examined to verify this supposition.

Gravity Model of Expenditures for Maintenance and Operation

Alfred Technical College appears to be a regional purchaser, especially when items with a broad
choice of vendors are considered. Purchases depend
on distance to the vendor's city and its size. A
regression analysis utilizing a gravity model was

applied to Alfred Technical College's expenditures
after utilities (including telephone) and rentals
were excluded. The results were very good, in spite
of the low number of observations.

Table 7.4 indicates the input data for the regression analysis. Adjusted college expenditures
(for educational supplies, repair and maintenance,
and equipment) in six cities are listed, along with
the 1960 population and radial distances of the localities from Alfred Village. The dependent and independent variables are, respectively, the percent
of total adjusted expenditures and the locality's

TABLE 7.4

Input Data for Regression Analysis of Alfred
Technical College, Adjusted Expenditures

Location	Population 1960, P_2	Radial Distance from Alfred in Miles d_{1-2}	P_2/d_{1-2}^2	Percent of Total Adjusted Expenditures	Adjusted Expenditures ($)
Wells-ville	5,967	12.0	41.0	14.2	22,069
Hornell	13,907	7.5	295.0	39.0	60,944
Buffalo	532,759	62.0	138.0	18.1	28,223
Elmira	46,517	49.0	19.4	6.0	9,390
Rochester	318,611	58.0	93.0	12.6	19,626
Syracuse	216,038	95.0	24.0	4.1	6,376

Note: Expenditures for utilities (including
telephone) and rentals are not included; only those
for educational supplies, repairs and maintenance,
and equipment are considered in the gravity model.

population (P_c) in 1960 divided by the radial distance squared.

The results of the regression analysis are depicted in Table 7.5. The value of R is 0.97. When the gravity model is used, 95 percent of the possible variance in the dependent variable is explainable.

The beta value and the constant term can be used to form the following multiple-regression equation:

$$Y_{31} = 386.7 + 1.16X_{32}$$

TABLE 7.5

Data for Regression Equation for Alfred Technical College, Adjusted Operational and Maintenance Expenditures

Dependent variable	%-EXPEND
Independent variable	P/D^2
R squared	0.950
Constant	386.700
Significance level	0.005
Standard error of estimate	338.500
Beta coefficient	1.160

Variable Code Names and Descriptions

Variable Number		Code Names
31	Dependent variable	
	Percent of total adjusted expenditures made in a major locality in the region	%-EXPEND
32	Independent variable	
	1960 population of the city observed, divided by the square of its radial distance from Alfred Village	P/D^2

where Y_{31} and X_{32} are the dependent and independent variables described above and in Table 7.5.

As noted in the equation for Alfred Technical College, when there is a wide choice of vendors, the proportion of college purchases made at a major locality in the region increases directly with the population of the locality and inversely with the square of its distance from the college community.

FACULTY-STUDENT ASSOCIATION
PURCHASES AT CORTLAND

The SUNY College at Cortland maintains records of its FSA purchasing in an IBM card file. This presents a great advantage for a locational analysis of expenditures, as zip codes of vendors may readily be used and data processed by zones, as previously described. In this analysis, purchasing data for the FSA were compartmentalized by civil divisions (village, city, and county) and by zip-code area rather than by sector, ring, or channel techniques previously used; this was considered more applicable for the desired exposition.[7]

As indicated in Table 7.6, purchases from 2,631 vendors in Cortland County amounted to $1.35 million, or 60.2 percent of total purchases made by the FSA. Almost all of these expenditures were made in the City of Cortland: Homer Village, probably by virtue of its proximity to the college, supplied $39,692 in purchases (1.8 percent).

As is the case with operational and maintenance expenditures for SUNY Cortland and Alfred Technical College, although a substantial amount of first-round expenditures is made within Cortland County, close to 40 percent of the purchasing dollar leaves the immediate area of the college in the initial stage and benefits other areas in the state.

Expenditures made in all of New York State amount to $2.03 million, and the state accounts for 90.3 percent of all purchases made by the association.

TABLE 7.6

Purchases at Various Locations by the Faculty-Student
Association, New York State University at Cortland, 1967-68

Location[a]	Number of Vendors	Net Purchases[b] (in dollars)	Percent of Total Net Purchases	Percent of Total New York State Purchases
1. New York State				
Cortland	2,501	1,311,851.04	58.37	64.61
McGraw	8	292.87	0.01	0.01
Homer	118	39,692.76	1.76	1.95
Cortland County, other selected locations	4	25.38	c	c
Subtotal, Cortland County	2,631	1,351,862.05	60.15	66.58
Tompkins County, selected locations	72	4,274.31	0.19	0.21
Adjacent counties and other selected locations	36	5,889.08	0.26	0.29
Rome	11	118.80	c	c
New York City				
Manhattan	1,532	232,980.97	10.37	11.47
Other	140	12,469.65	0.55	0.61
Total	1,672	245,450.62	10.92	12.09
Westchester area	94	6,764.13	0.30	0.33
Hicksville area	209	15,446.37	0.69	0.76
Albany (city)	59	28,542.50	1.27	1.41
Albany area	19	1,505.79	0.06	0.07
Schenectady	5	527.40	0.02	0.03
Kingston area	10	1,108.81	0.05	0.05
Glens Falls-Plattsburgh	19	3,503.38	0.16	0.17
Syracuse (city)	940	106,403.33	4.73	5.24
Syracuse area	348	44,736.43	1.99	2.20
Utica (city)	111	6,942.49	0.31	0.34
Utica area	145	5,820.83	0.26	0.29
Watertown	17	2,793.92	0.12	0.14
Binghamton (city)	242	66,741.09	2.97	3.29
Binghamton area	59	5,046.49	0.22	0.49
Buffalo (city)	63	10,057.57	0.45	0.49
Buffalo area	14	942.18	0.04	0.05
Niagara Falls	1	345.00	0.02	0.02
Rochester (city	301	57,707.71	2.57	2.84

(Continued)

TABLE 7.6 Continued

Location[a]	Number of Vendors	Net Purchases[b] (in dollars)	Percent of Total Net Purchases	Percent of Total New York State Purchases
Rochester area	35	2,745.58	0.12	0.14
Jamestown	7	708.25	0.03	0.03
Elmira (city)	81	20,066.08	0.89	0.99
Elmira area[e]	102	34,321.09	1.53	1.69
Total New York State	--	2,030,372.28	90.34	100.00
2. Outside New York State, in the United States				
New England area	796	88,107.34	3.92	
Pennsylvania	311	25,935.79	1.15	
Virginia-Carolina area	147	5,373.26	0.24	
Florida-Tennessee area	47	2,641.42	0.12	
Michigan-Kentucky area	351	24,601.66	1.09	
Montana-Iowa area	218	25,906.76	1.15	
Kansas-Illinois area	416	29,161.80	1.30	
Texas-Arkansas area	29	5,276.94	0.23	
Idaho-Arizona area	9	351.80	0.02	
California-Washington area	189	9,266.54	0.41	
Total outside New York State in United States	--	216,623.91	9.64	
3. Foreign Countries	13	401.42	--	
Over-all total	--	2,247,397.01	100.00	

[a]See National Zip Code Directory (Washington, D.C.: Zip Code Publishing Company, 1971), for area definitions in part 2 of this table.

[b]Net purchases include gross purchase price, discount, and transportation costs.

[c]Less than 0.01 percent.

[d]Syracuse area data do not include previously listed areas such as Cortland.

[e]Elmira area data do not include previously listed areas such as Tompkins County selected locations.

Note: Details may not add up to totals because of rounding.

Principal points of expenditure outside the Cortland area are New York City (10.4 percent), Syracuse (4.7 percent), Binghamton (3 percent), and Rochester (2.6 percent); a host of small expenditures are made from numerous vendors at diverse locations throughout the state.

Gravity Model of Purchases

A gravity model was applied to purchases made at various locations by the FSA of SUNY Cortland. Major cities in New York State outside of Cortland are major points for expenditure and were included in this analysis. (See Table 7.7)

TABLE 7.7

Input Data for Regression Analysis of Cortland College Faculty-Student Association Purchases

City	Population, 1960, P_2	Radial Distance from Cortland in miles, d_{1-2}	P_2/d_{1-2}^2	Percent of Total New York State Purchases by SUNY Cortland
Albany	129,726	112.0	10.3	1.27
Binghamton	75,941	32.4	72.3	2.97
Buffalo	532,759	130.0	31.5	0.45
Elmira	46,517	43.2	25.0	0.89
Jamestown	41,818	154.0	1.8	0.03
New York	7,781,984	162.0	296.3	10.92
Niagara Falls	102,394	140.0	5.2	0.02
Rochester	318,611	75.5	42.3	2.57
Rome	51,646	52.6	18.7	0.00
Schenectady	81,682	109.0	6.8	0.02
Syracuse	216,038	26.0	319.8	4.73
Utica	100,410	53.4	35.1	0.31
Watertown	33,306	91.8	3.9	0.12

TABLE 7.8

Data for Regression Equation for Cortland College
Faculty-Student Association Purchases

Dependent variable	%-NY-EXPEND
Independent variable	P/D
R squared	0.750
Constant	22.200
Significance level	0.001
Standard error of estimate	159.200
Beta coefficient	0.246

Variable Code Names and Descriptions

Variable Number		Code Names
33	Dependent variable	
	Percent of total New York State purchases made by college in city observed	%-NY-EXPEND
34	Independent variable	
	1960 population of city observed, divided by the square of its radial distance from Cortland	P/D

A regression analysis was used with percent of
total purchases at a locality as the dependent variable; the locality's population in 1960 divided by
the square of its radial distance from the college
town was used as the independent variable. The results of this analysis are indicated in Table 7.8.
The value of R is 0.86, and the independent variable
in the form of a gravity model accounts for 75 percent of the possible variance in the dependent variable.

The beta value and the constant term can be used to form the following multiple-regression equation:

$$Y_{33} = 22.2 + 0.25X_{34}$$

where Y_{33} and X_{34} are the dependent and independent variables, respectively, as described above.

Because a positive relationship exists for the variables, the proportion of college purchases made in a major locality in the region will tend to increase directly with its population and inversely with the square of its distance from the college, other things being equal.

SUMMARY

The evidence as displayed in this chapter was limited to SUNY Cortland and Alfred Technical College, but some generalizations are possible because of the large number of vendors considered. A substantial part of rural-college expenditures tends to diffuse into the surrounding region. This applies to the relatively large, as well as the small, college community.[8] The larger rural college town will supply some of the needed repair and maintenance services, equipment, and educational supplies, but much of this will come from outside the county. Utilities and communications expenditures constitute a large part of the total operational and maintenance budget and will be made locally. However, in the case of the small college community, especially when utility installations are limited or nonexistent, there is the possibility that college purchases for operational and maintenance needs will be made almost totally from outside sources. When an item is available from a large number of vendors, major cities within the region attract the purchasing dollar of the college substantially in accordance with a gravity model. If a small college community is located near the county boundary, there is the probability that much of the purchasing dollar will leave the county. This is especially the case when a relatively large out-of-county central place is near enough to attract expenditures by the college, its staff, and students.

A difference in economic impact can be anticipated for colleges located in large cities such as
Syracuse and Rochester. Out-of-town purchasing by
these colleges is sharply diminished since cities of
this size can supply many of the needs for college
operation. However, when the economic development of
a city district is planned, and includes utilization
of a college input and similar means, it can be assumed that spillout of the purchasing dollar will be
substantial, and will depend on the economy of the
district and other factors previously discussed.

NOTES

1. The economic impact of a college on its local area relates to its social and political impacts.
The college purchasing from local firms concomitantly
establishes a social and political bond that can effect its acceptance and influence in the locality.

2. See New York State Department of Commerce,
Business Fact Book, 1967-68 (Albany: Part I, Business and Manufacturing, Syracuse Area, 1968), p. 16;
in 1963, retail sales for the City of Cortland were
$38.9 million, and selected services amounted to
$3.5 million.

3. If purchasing records at colleges are accessible and computerized, a rigorous statistical study
may be feasible.

4. New York State Division of the Budget, "The
Executive Budget, Fiscal Year April 1, 1968 to March
31, 1969," submitted by Nelson A. Rockefeller, Governor (Albany: New York State Division of the Budget, 1968), pp. 429-590, shows a program-planning-
budgeting arrangement; the 1959-60 budget, pp. 241-306,
shows the type of breakdown discussed in the text.

5. Expense items in the categories listed are
as follows: (1) educational supplies--books, charts,
chemicals, slides, art supplies, scientific supplies,
paper supplies, and duplication expenses; (2) utili-
ties--gas, water, electricity, heating oil, and

propane gas; (3) rentals--duplicating equipment
(Xerox), data-processing equipment, sewer, etc.; (4)
repairs and maintenance--lumber, gravel, sand, plas-
ter, plumbing materials, electrical supplies, heating
and ventilating supplies, maintenance contracts on
elevators and air-conditioning equipment, repairs to
state vehicles, gasoline, oil, etc.; and (5) equip-
ment--classroom, office, and maintenance.

6.   See also New York State Division of the
Budget, 1959-60, loc. cit.

7.   See Appendix Tables D.1 and D.3.

8.   Auburn Community College indicated that in
the fiscal year 1967-68 only about 5 percent of its
purchases in educational supplies were made in Auburn; its proximity to Syracuse appears to be an important factor in this regard.

8

CONCLUSIONS
AND
RECOMMENDATIONS

This study has sought to present information of value to decisionmakers who seek to predict impact of the college on the rural community. In so doing, we have made a critical analysis of the spillout of economic and social benefits from existing college communities. Our broad purpose has been to initiate a procedure for assessing actual benefits accrued to these localities owing to the college presence, to point up opportunity losses due to spillout, and to indicate some of the burdens incurred. The locality prone to high spillout will experience difficulty in supporting college-related services, and a location and development decision should consider this possibility.[1]

Impact on the college community may be examined in two phases. The first includes an analysis of data to predict input of the college population and dollars into the locality. The second considers interaction and incidence of this input relative to community components. In both phases, spillout is an important consideration. High spillout in one phase may be counterbalanced by low spillout in the other. When spillout is high in both phases, difficulties arise, and their extent depends on the size of the college burden.

COLLEGE INPUT, INTERACTION,
AND SPILLOUT

In Phase I of this study, the input of staff, local students, and purchasing dollars into the college community was considered. It was found that professional-staff residence (input) ratings for private and public colleges taken as a group varied little with the size (population) of the community in which the college was situated. This was also true for private colleges examined as a group. However, when four-year public colleges alone were considered, a definite pattern was noted. Residence ratings for four-year public colleges varied closely with community size. They were higher in the cities and lower in villages. It is important to note that the public colleges examined has considerably larger enrollments (1,998 to 3,573 students), and professional-staff sizes (308 to 498 employees), than the private colleges (with enrollments from 909 to 1,837, and staff sizes from 96 to 293). The relatively large State University colleges in small towns exhibited lower professional-staff residence (input) ratings. This may be due to either new staff coming from distant points and settling outside the small college community or new staff commuting from residences previously established in nearby towns or cities. Both factors were probably operative to varying degrees in the cases studied.

With regard to Hypothesis I, we can say that the proportion of professional staff residing in a college town is a function of community size (population) for the four-year State University colleges studied, but this is not so for the private colleges examined or for all four-year colleges taken as a group. The proportion of professional staff living in the smaller college communities will increase with an increase in the number of Ph.D's on the teaching staff, and the age of the institution.

Generally, professional-staff residence (input) ratings for established four-year colleges of moderate size were higher (70-95 percent) than those for

two-year colleges (52-84 percent). The attractive
small town may receive a high professional-staff
input and fully be able to carry a small college
without difficulty. However, a critical point in
town size may exist below which staff input and interaction may be sharply reduced. This is especially
possible for small communities that are low in centrality or entrepreneurial capacity and that experience high competition from attractive locations in
the area, or where village boundaries, topography,
and other limitations severely restrict town growth
and development. The city may also experience substantial residential spillout, particularly when the
college is located in its outskirts; however, in most
cases, its centrality yields payoff in the interaction
phase, and its existing infrastructure is capable of
carrying the college without excessive burden. The
small town is less able to take high spillout with a
sizable college in its midst. The ideal situation is
one of balanced growth for the college and the college community.

     The proportion of auxiliary staff residing in
the college community showed fair correlation with
town size (Hypothesis II) when all the colleges were
grouped. The proportion varied between 53 and 89
percent for cities and between 25 and 63 percent for
villages. The extremely low input in a number of
small towns reflects their small labor force and indicates high commutation for auxiliary staff from
neighboring rural areas. The statistical argument
relative to auxiliary-staff input is strengthened by
the fact that in the City of Poughkeepsie, auxiliary-
staff residence ratings were almost identical (near
78 percent) for two- and four-year colleges. At
Canton, a small town, the two colleges also had
similar ratings (both near 55 percent). Also at
Oneonta and Potsdam, similarity in college-staff
input for two colleges in each of these localities
was indicated. Private colleges drew slightly more
upon college-area population for auxiliary staff than
did public colleges.

     In metropolitan areas, professional staff fre-
quently settle in the suburbs. If a college is

located in the suburbs, faculty clustering in residences near the campus can result in a high input of
social and economic benefits to the community, as
previously discussed. If the college is located in
the central core of the large city and a major proportion of the faculty reside in the suburbs, a
lowered input of college-related benefits accrues to
the college community. However, needed educational
goals may require inner-city location. Also auxiliary staff for secretarial, custodial, and other services are generally drawn from within the neighborhood of the college, and the influx of jobs can aid
in development of the urban district.

     A device was designed for the analysis of local
student enrollment at SUNY Alfred Technical College
and SUNY Cortland. There are indications that the
techniques involved and conclusions derived are applicable to the other public colleges in our study.
This device permitted the locational analysis of
computer-based information on enrollment and commutation. Local students were divided into two groups:
first, those with permanent residences within the
college town, and, second, those with homes within
a 50-mile radius (approximately) of the college town.
The number of local college students enrolled with
permanent residences in the college town showed definite variation with town size at three colleges
studied (Auburn, 399; Cortland, 157; and Alfred, 26
students).[2] Generally, two-year colleges show greater
draw from the local student population than do baccalaureate institutions. To substantiate these conclusions and to obtain a regression equation on the
relationships, data from additional colleges should
be examined. However, statistical analysis of the
variation in enrollment with grades 7-12 ADA in a
50-mile ring for both SUNY Cortland and SUNY Alfred
Technical College indicated an association between
town size and local enrollment and also provided a
regression equation for predicting local enrollment
from outside the college town. The detailed analysis
of local enrollment at SUNY Alfred Technical College
and SUNY Cortland showed that although the latter
drew by far the greater number of students from the
college community, at about 10 miles out, the

cumulative total of "local" students at both colleges
was about the same (Hypothesis III). This was due to
the large Hornell and Wellsville enrollment at Alfred.
Cortland eventually regains the lead at the 35-mile
radial distance because of its Syracuse and Binghamton
enrollments. The marginal number of commuting students at these colleges provides little basis for
college locations in Alfred and Cortland. Reasons
relating to city and regional development are more
compelling. Also, the large proportion of local students in the 50-mile ring is of importance.

    Regression analysis permits high prediction of
student commutation among local students enrolled.
Most local students live in dormitories at both SUNY
Alfred Technical College and SUNY Cortland. Only
about one third and one fourth, respectively, commute.
Commutation drops to about 50 percent for SUNY Cortland students about 8 miles out of the city; for SUNY
Alfred Technical students, it drops at about 15 miles
from the village. It is close to zero from sectors
35-40 miles distant (Hypothesis IV). The form in
which the regression analysis for enrollment and
commutation is couched makes it applicable to the
other public colleges studied.

    As discussed previously, the college is a sup-
plier of jobs, education, salaries, purchasing dollars, and other benefits that go to individuals in
the college community and in the region. However,
except for utilities and other special purchases
(rentals, in the case of Alfred Technical College),
about 80-100 percent of the goods and services needed
for operational and maintenance purposes (educational
supplies, equipment, repairs, and maintenance services) were purchased outside the county by both
Cortland College and Alfred Technical College. Data
on Cortland College's FSA purchases for auxiliary
enterprises (the college store, cafeteria, and student activities) indicate a different situation.
About two thirds of these purchases were made in
Cortland County.

    To analyze location of vendors for FSA purchases,
a gravity model was used. Relatively high predictability of expenditure location was found possible

for items purchasable from a broad spectrum of vendors
in major cities of the region. The purchases made
varied directly with city size and inversely with the
distance squared (Hypothesis V).

   In considering the second phase of this study
of college impact on a locality, social and economic
input and spillout relative to the college population
was demonstrated.[3] Staff and students at Alfred Technical College and Alfred University indicated relatively low retail purchases in the village. Cazenovia,
only slightly larger than Alfred Village, exhibited
comparatively high retail sales in all categories but
furniture and clothing. The cities of Cortland and
Auburn benefit by good retaining power in retail
sales to staff and students. However, low retail
sales were noted in a few categories. (Students
make comparatively minor clothing expenditures in the
college community unless it is their place of permanent residence.) Even the larger rural city experiences a degree of spillout.

   Social input and interaction are considerable
factors in college impact. The institutional population newly entering the college community brings a
potential for social change and development.[4] In
addition to the educational program and the usual set
of student and staff characteristics, the college input of human and social capital includes measurable
units of community-service potential and a battery
of political attitudes. Impact on the community may
be considerably diluted by virtue of the isolation
of the campus, spillout of residence location, and
low levels of interaction with local residents. However, interaction by even a small fraction of the
college professional staff and the sizable student
body may add up to a substantial contact with local
people. College influence on school-district policy
and local government depends on the involvement of
the college population in these matters and their
weight in the decisionmaking process.

   The public colleges examined denoted close to
one third of their student population in the lower
family income groups (below $8,000 per year), and

Alfred University indicated about one fifth in this category. These colleges thus represent opportunity for the less affluent local student as well as those from distant locations. However, upon graduation, only a small percentage of even the local students plan to stay in the area of the college community, and at least one in five of all students questioned indicated plans to leave New York State.

REGIONAL CONSIDERATIONS

In evaluating the affect of the college on the college community, it is also necessary to consider regional factors. These were discussed in considerable detail at the beginning of this study. A three-way interaction occurs between the college, the community, and the region. The college has impact on the community, the community on the region, and, conversely, regional development affects the community and the college. Consequently, the college should be located in a growth center that will greatly benefit regional development and that will be capable of absorbing needed economic and social benefits for its own growth.

RECOMMENDATIONS

This research is intended to provide data for college planning, urban and regional development policy, and public and private investment decisions. The information obtained relates to the work of the community, county, regional, and educational planner and is best utilized in a coordinated effort.

A policy matrix based upon college impact on the area is illustrated in Figure 5. As indicated in the diagram, Hypothesis I, which involves the input and spillout of professional staff, is the concern of the educational planner, the village, city, and county planner, and, to a lesser extent, the regional planner. These individuals can use information on professional-staff input in the planning of parking, space utilization, housing, community services, transportation, and

FIGURE 5

Policy Matrix Based on College Impact on an Area

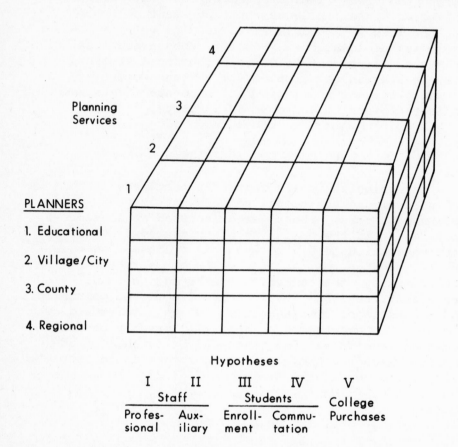

Planning
Services

4

3

2

1

PLANNERS

1. Educational

2. Village/City

3. County

4. Regional

Hypotheses

I	II	III	IV	V
Staff		Students		College
Profes-	Aux-	Enroll-	Commu-	Purchases
sional	iliary	ment	tation	

Planning Services

1. Campus planning: dorms, parking, circulation, enrollment
   space utilization, and so forth.

2. Town planning: housing, transportation, services (water,
   waste, police, and so forth), industry, land use, commercial
   facilities, education, and so forth.

3. County planning: recreation, transportation, industry,
   environmental health, and so forth.

4. Regional planning: recreation, transportation, rural development,
   and so forth.

recreation. The other hypotheses feed into policymaking in a similar manner.

Costs and benefits relative to college impact on
property values, retail sales, education, family income, social interaction, and other categories related to community development should be investigated
at the town, city, county, and regional levels.
Adaptability of an area to the change imposed by the
college input is also an important consideration for
study.

Recommendations for additional research include
the refining of techniques and the variables considered as well as the development of additional
procedures that, in sum, will contribute toward effective planning.

The system developed in this study to facilitate
locational analysis of student enrollment, commutation,
and college purchases can also be used to analyze
alumni location, employee and payroll incidence, and
other college-related factors. Utilization of grid
and zip code numbers for locational identification
permits closeup analysis and mapping of economic and
social interaction in sectors, channels, and rings
immediately surrounding the college community. It
also provides data for regression analyses and long-
range planning and relates the college matrix to
local and regional elements. The combination of a
detailed locational analysis and sharper definitions
of spillout leads to improved estimates of the local
impact of the college population and its activities,
and it also delineates the tie-in between educational
planning and local and regional development.

Further research in several of the above areas
could lead to fruitful results. The grid-ADA locational analysis lends itself to a procedure for maximization of local enrollment in college-location
planning. A radarlike sweep to obtain local ADA
totals for a multiple of college locations could be
obtained with computer aid. Standard centrographic
techniques would be helpful in this connection.[5] A
locational analysis of State University purchases

that utilize IBM records would also be informative. This would aid in assessing and forecasting money flow from institutional purchases throughout the state.

In a broader vein, the application of a format for the accounting of city, village, county, and regional input and spillout for colleges in various locations would yield additional insight to planners. Our concern was with the impact of the college on the community and region. Other impact tools and simulation models can be developed for urban and rural areas with varying characteristics.

Longitudinal studies of community change owing to the college presence and its impact would help in yielding additional insight into the input needed to transform an area. These studies could utilize social and political indicators, as previously described, to analyze interaction and input of human and social capital.

With college communities currently absorbing and integrating a wide segment of key societal characteristics and undergoing relatively rapid social change, the possibility for broad application of research results is enhanced. Assessment of college impact in the economic and social spheres can give considerable insight into the costs and benefits of other forms of public and private investment.

With application of the above research approaches, the college may yet serve in one of its most important functions--to develop models, guides, and leadership for planned community change in a rapidly changing society.

NOTES

1. If a college community is located near the county boundary, spillout may remove much of the college purchasing dollar from the county. This is a likelihood when a relatively large city in the adjacent county is near enough to attract expenditures by the college, its staff, and students. When

college-community spillout goes to other localities, the latter show benefit.

2. Albert T. Skinner, "Auburn Community College, Report of the President for the Year July 1, 1965 to June 30, 1966" (Auburn, N. Y.: Board of Education of the Auburn City School District, 1966), p. 8; this number of students came from the Auburn Enlarged City School District in 1965. Data for Cortland and Alfred are for Fall, 1967. For the public colleges studied, the proportion of local students enrolled is about 0.01-0.03 percent of the 1960 college community permanent population, and 10-20 percent of the 1964 grades 7-12 ADA. The higher fractions occur in Alfred. Only full-time enrollments at the colleges were analyzed. If part-time and night-school enrollments are considered, colleges in cities such as Auburn and Cortland would indicate considerably more extensive programs and attendance than those in the smaller towns.

3. The auxiliary staff by and large reflect the opinion of community residents. Although in Alfred several secretaries were faculty wives, the samples of auxiliary-staff members primarily included maintenance crew, food-service employees, and others not related to the professional staff.

4. For pertinent discussions of social and cultural change, see Harry M. Johnson, Sociology, A Systematic Introduction (New York: Harcourt, Brace, and World, Inc., 1960), pp. 625-49; and Lowell D. Holmes, Anthropology, An Introduction (New York: Ronald Press Company, 1965), pp. 279-98.

5. See Douglass B. Lee, Jr., Analysis and Description of Residential Segregation: An application of Centrographic Techniques to the Study of the Spatial Distribution of Ethnic Groups in Cities (Ithaca, N. Y.: Cornell University, Center for Housing and Environmental Studies, Division of Urban Studies, 1968).

APPENDIXES

This study is divided into two phases. The first considers the input of the college staff and student population into college communities in New York State. The second analyzes interaction of the college population with regard to selected social and economic factors operating within these communities. Community size is evaluated as an influence in population input and spillout.

Investigation of the hypothesis that the proportion of college-staff input to a community varies with the size (population) of the community required a multicollege analysis.[1] To determine parameters for the influx of the local student population, extensive data from two public colleges were analyzed, and this analysis provided the basis for a general statement applicable to other public colleges. Lastly, interaction of the college population was determined by use of questionnaires submitted to random samples of both staff and students at the colleges. The above phases were supplemented by interviews with college and community officials.

DETERMINATION OF STAFF INPUT
VIA THE MULTICOLLEGE STUDY

The multicollege study included data obtained from a survey of thirty-nine colleges. These colleges were selected on the basis of college and community size (minimum undergraduate student enrollment and community population), as previously discussed, and therefore constitute an exclusive set. All were outside of designated metropolitan areas (SMSAs) as of the 1960 census.[2]

Letters were sent to college presidents and college research directors to request their cooperation in obtaining data on staff place of residence in 1967-68. Special forms were made up for orderly and consistent accounting of these data.

On a multicolumn sheet, the numbers of full-time and part-time professional- and auxiliary-staff members residing in each city or village in the college

215

area were to be indicated. A sample form, partially
completed and with instructions, was included in the
mailing. Professional- and auxiliary-staff member-
ship characteristics were clearly defined for sep-
arate-column entry. These broad categories included
faculty, administrators, and other professional staff
in one group, and secretarial, clerical, maintenance,
and food-service personnel in the other. Laboratory
technicians, housemothers, and individuals in part-
time employment were included under separate columns.
The primary reason for including a part-time column
was to provide for noncontamination of data on full-
time staff members. Data received on laboratory
technicians and housemothers were later included
with auxiliary-staff group data. In this way, two
major sets were formed, one for the professional and
another for the auxiliary or service staff.

Information required in this survey was obtained
from all thirty-nine colleges contacted. The colleges are listed (in Tables 3.1A and 3.1B) along
with a summary of the data received. More complete
data on the colleges are in Appendix B. Returns
from SUNY Oswego and Potsdam were incomplete; only
professional-staff data were submitted by the former,
and only grouped or total data were submitted by the
latter college.

Although thirty-nine colleges were included in
the multicollege survey and are reported upon (see
Appendix Tables B.1, B.2, and B.3), not all of these
were included in a regression analysis that sought
to determine the relationship between staff input to
the college community, community size (population),
and other variables. Several colleges were ruled
out of this part of the analysis because of their
small staff size (below 80 professionals), recency
of establishment in the college community (after
1964), low enrollment as of 1964, absence of data in
the U.S. Census of Population, 1960, location in a
metropolitan area (SMSA), or incomplete data on
staff. The omitted colleges are listed in Appendix
Table A.1, and the reason for omission is indicated.
The relationship between these colleges and those
included in the regression analysis is discussed in

Colleges Omitted from the Regression Analysis on Staff Residence Location

Colleges	Low Enrollment, 1964	Small Staff, 1964	Recency in Town	No Town Data[a]	in SMSA	Staff Data Incomplete
			Reasons for Omission			
Four-Year Colleges						
SUNY Potsdam						X
SUNY Oswego (in part)						X
Houghton				X		
Two-Year Colleges						
Adirondack C.C.		X				
Fulton-Montgomery C.C.		X				
Genesee C.C.		X	b			
Jamestown C.C.		X				
Jefferson C.C.		X				
Paul Smiths				X		
Rockland C.C.					X	
Sullivan C.C.	X					
Ulster C.C.			c			

[a]There is no population information on these localities in the U.S. Census of Population, 1960.

[b]Genesee Community College was established after 1964.

[c]"The Summary Bulletin" of the State University of New York listed the location of the Ulster County Community College as at Kingston, New York, in Spring, 1966, and as at Stone Ridge, in Fall, 1967.

[d]Reasons for omission are detailed in the text.

Chapter 3.   Their inclusion would not have appreciably changed the results.

For the regression analysis, college-community
population data and related information were obtained
from such standard sources as the U.S. Census of
Population and Housing.   In some cases, settlement
around the college is more accurately represented
by a combination of the population of two villages
or a city and a village in close proximity.   This
occurs when the populations are neighboring or tend
toward agglomeration.   On a map, the village or city
locations are shown as within 2 miles of each other.
This situation occurs in the Alfred-Alfred Station
area, the Cortland-Homer area, and others.   These
situations are indicated in the tables in Chapter 3.
Population and staff input data obtained are indicated for the agglomeration as well as for the single
village or city (college community) in Appendix
Tables B.1, B.2, and B.3.   The regression analysis
treats data on the agglomeration only because this
is the more appropriate basis for predictability.

DETERMINATION OF LOCAL STUDENT
POPULATION INPUT

As indicated in previous research, a student's
economic impact on the college community depends on
whether he is a local or nonlocal student and also
on his type of residence while at college.   Education
of the nonlocal student component is an "export"
product.   Education of the local student provides the
area with usable skills and other benefits, as discussed in Chapter 1.[3]   Home commuters' expense budgets generally differ from those of dormitory
students, and both differ from those of offcampus
commuters who live away from home.[4]

Study of student economic input is, first, a
problem of determining the expectation of local student enrollment (the remainder being nonlocal).
Second, it is a problem of determining home-commuter
expectation; the remainder includes the set of dormitory and offcampus residents.   The number of dormitory

residents is a matter of college policy, construction, and regulation. Other things being equal, the remaining set of offcampus students is fixed by establishing the level of total enrollment. Consequently, the only variables that are not arbitrarily determined and that lend themselves to prediction are local student enrollment and home commutation. An attempt was made to explain their occurrence through regression analysis.

Local student enrollment and commutation were defined as occurring within a 50-mile radius (approximately) of the college campus. A framework for study of both local enrollment and commutation was set up by fixing sectoral boundaries on a map of the locality, as described below and in Figure 6.

A sheet of Keuffel and Esser Company's polar coordinate graph paper was Xeroxed to obtain a copy of the circular grid on transparent acetate. For our purposes, concentric rings on the acetate, one-half inch apart, were used to set distance boundaries at regular intervals. Beginning at the 0-degree line, radii at 30-degree intervals were marked. The area on the sheet within a circle of a 5-inch radius was thus delineated by 10 rings, 12 channels, and 120 sectors. The inmost ring was also marked off to delineate the immediate area at the center of the circles (the college community). This added one additional sector.

This grid was then imposed on a map of the area to be studied. It was anchored by fixing the center of the circle on the college's map location and by passing the 0, 180-degree, or other radius through a village or other point on the map. In this manner, cities and towns on the map could be grouped into a framework of rings, channels, or sectors as desired for analysis. Channels and rings were labeled A through L and 1 through 10, respectively, and sectors or zones were then described by number and letter. For example, sector 2A is in channel A and between rings 2 and 1, and this sector contains within its boundaries the towns on the map on which it is imposed.

FIGURE 6
Grid for Locational Impact Analysis

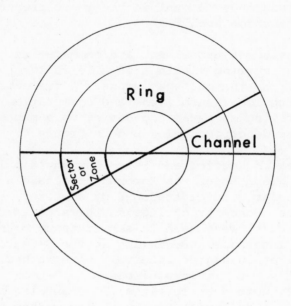

The basic framework can be used in the analysis
of many different types of data relative to locational properties and factors. It is applied here
for analysis of local events occurring within a few
miles of the campus, and it can be expanded in application to any distance from a campus. Generally,
higher-correlation coefficients are obtained when
data are analyzed for a larger area. Thus, channel
analysis offers higher predictive value than sectoral
analysis, but the information obtained is less detailed.

Our objective was to use IBM-card data on students' permanent residence locations by cities and
towns, in conjunction with the above grid, to analyze
local student enrollment and commutation. However,
city and town data on computer cards at SUNY Cortland
and Alfred are not readily used in analysis. This
is because city and town names are inconsistently
registered. Zip codes on student IBM cards can be
applied readily, and these were used to identify location of students' permanent residences and other
locational phenomena.

The National Zip Code Directory was used to obtain zip codes of localities in each designated
zone, as listed in Appendix Tables D.1, D.2, and
D.3.[5] Outside the 50-mile circle and within New York
State, zip code data for sectional center facilities
of the U.S. Post Office were applied, and national
zip code areas as listed on a standard U.S. zip code
map were used for locations outside New York State.
Zip codes assigned to each sector or zone were then
matched against those on the student's IBM card (for
location of permanent residence).[6] The computer
printout supplied zone and ring totals. In effect,
a student-input map was obtained indicating the source
(or permanent-residence location) of dormitory, home-
commuter, and other offcampus students.[7]

Our next step was to use the resulting data in
a regression analysis to predict enrollment and commutation of local students. Dependent variables
were set up on a basis of the enrollment and commutation data obtained, and these were run in regression

analysis against zone variables such as distance and
high school attendance. Once it is possible to predict the number of local students enrolled and local
students commuting from home, we can make a statement about the set of local students living in
dormitories and offcampus. The total number of nonlocal students is arbitrarily decided on, as previously discussed, and these students either live in
dormitories (again arbitrarily decided on), or in
offcampus housing. This information can be used to
determine the potential economic impact of the student body when modified by spillout considerations.
The demonstration of spillout and local student enrollment are of primary interest in this study.
However, the data derived are additionally useful in
predicting how many local students will benefit by
establishment and expansion of a college in a certain
locality and in facilities planning.[8]

DETERMINATION OF INTERACTION
OF THE COLLEGE POPULATION

    In Part II of this study, an investigation of
interaction of the college population with city or
town elements was made by use of staff and student
questionnaires. The questionnaires were pretested
with undergraduate students and staff on the Cornell
campus. They were revised, pretested again, and
then found satisfactory for field use. Cooperating
colleges were Alfred Agricultural and Technical College, SUNY College at Cortland, Cazenovia College,
Auburn Community College, and Alfred University.
The data were obtained by survey in Fall, 1968. Random samples of students were taken at the various
colleges. Only sophomore students were examined at
the four-year colleges (SUNY Cortland College and
Alfred University). The random sample for each college was based on limited resources available and
the need to determine the economic and social characteristics of interest for each college. Details of
the random sample taken at the various colleges are
displayed in Appendix Table A.2.

TABLE A.2

Random Samples for Colleges Studied

College	Staff Population	Final Staff Sample Size	Percent of Coverage	Under-graduate Full-Time Student Enrollment (head count)	Final Student Sample Size	Percent of Coverage
Alfred Ag. & Tech.	512	156	32.3	2,699	153	5.7
Cortland	720	101	14.0	909[a]	122	13.4
Alfred Univ.	403	84	20.8	317[a]	95	30.0
Auburn	114	97	85.1	1,445	79	5.5
Cazenovia	156	73	46.8	563	48	8.5

[a]Sophomores.

Note: Student enrollment and staff-size information was provided by the respective college offices. Staff size includes both professional and auxiliary staff. Staff on leave for the year are not included. This study was made in Fall, 1968.

Generally, excellent cooperation was obtained in administering the questionnaires. Our initial approach at each college was through the president's office for his recommendations and guidance. The individuals involved in administering the questionnaires to staff and students were deans or directors of institutional research. Lists of names of staff and students to be included in the random samples were submitted to their offices, and returns on the questionnaires were between 72 and 86 percent of the staff and between 73 and 80 percent of the students at the various colleges.

The questionnaires were introduced by lead information that indicated their purpose and the college's interest in the survey. Questionnaires were mailed to offcampus students who could not be contacted directly; stamped, return envelopes addressed to the project's Cornell University office were included. Returns from these mailings were not at the level of those obtained through direct contact with the student by the administration, and a bias with underrepresentation of offcampus students can be expected because of this. Returns from professional- and auxiliary-staff members were good, and both groups were well represented.

Because of the personal nature of some of the questions, respondents were instructed not to enter their names on the questionnaire. Faculty and administrative groups consulted were of the opinion that this would result in a higher number of returns and more representative answers.

Information on each of the returned questionnaires was coded and punched on IBM cards. The coding was done by students in the Sociology and Rural Sociology departments and checked for accuracy. Key punching was done at the Warren Hall computer center and included a verification run.[9]

The printout for the staff questionnaire used the professional- and auxiliary-staff breakdown as major categories. A more detailed analysis could have used other control variables, such as age, rank,

salary, sex, education, and others, but this was beyond the scope of our resources, time, and purposes.
Additional research is recommended with the data on
hand to obtain further insight into related areas.
A like situation applies to the output from student
questionnaires.

Our basic effort in this phase of the study was
to demonstrate the following for different college
communities: first, economic and social impact of
the college population in respect to selected factors, and, second, spillout of selected activities
or characteristics of the college population.

Analysis was made of pertinent economic and social factors. The questionnaire was not analyzed in
its entirety, as some of the questions served for
orientation and other purposes. Also, our intent
was to help develop a methodology for a system of
spillover accounting rather than coverage of the
full range of social and economic factors involved.
Chi-square tests were applied when useful for the
exposition, and percentage distributions were used
to display the total output.

NOTES

1. See Lachlan Blair, "College and Community,
A Study of Interaction in Chicago" (Chicago: Department of Urban Planning, University of Illinois, 1967),
p. 54. (Mimeographed.) Blair briefly suggests a
study of staff input in determining job input to a
community. Our study sought a predictive factor
relative to input to cities and towns and therefore
required a multicollege analysis. The input may
also be considered to be the number of jobs added to
the college-community labor force by the college
work force or table of organization.

2. Data on the Rockland County Community College (within the New York City SMSA) were also obtained to gain some insight into the effect of a
large city on a small town relative to college-staff
input.

3. From another viewpoint, the input may be analyzed in terms of educational units accrued to local students.

4. In some categories of social activity, the impact of the student also will vary on a basis of his being local or nonlocal and with his type of college residency.

5. National Zip Code Directory (Washington, D.C.: Zip Code Publishing Company, 1967).

6. Zone zip codes can be matched in this way against numerous other variables stored on IBM cards to display distribution of college purchases, staff payroll, part-time and evening student sources, alumni data, and other factors of interest. In this study, the input of college purchases to the college community and region also is evaluated by utilizing this technique.

7. The system of combining zip code designations into sectors was checked for accuracy by obtaining a printout of addresses of all students in channel I (randomly selected) for SUNY Cortland College. The results were identical when either individual addresses or the zip code technique was used for sectoral assignment.

An original program for the computer processing of all data used in the zip code analysis was developed and written by Eugene R. Krause, Manager of the Computer Center at the State University of New York College at Cortland. Data from both the Alfred Technical College and SUNY Cortland were processed on the Univac 9300 magnetic-tape system at the latter institution.

8. The information obtained can be used as a basis for planning of parking and transportation facilities, campus and village roads, locally oriented educational programs, and other factors, all having impact on the community.

9.   The CONTAB 8 program (written in Fortran G) was used for analysis of college staff and student interaction.   This program was obtained through the Computer Office at Warren Hall, Cornell University, and was run on the IBM 360/65 computer.

B

**DATA
FOR
THE
MULTICOLLEGE
STUDY**

Places of Staff Residence at Various Public Four-Year Colleges and Universities, 1967-68

College	City or Village	Professional Staff		Auxiliary Staff		Total Staff	
		Num-ber	Per-cent	Num-ber	Per-cent	Num-ber	Per-cent
Brockport	Brockport	317	70.3	137	45.2	454	61.2
	Albion	5	1.1	43	14.2		
	Batavia	2	0.4	1	0.3		
	Bergen	3	0.7	12	4.0		
	Hamlin	6	1.3	14	4.6		
	Holley	7	1.5	47	15.5		
	Rochester	66	14.6	6	2.0		
	Spencerport	16	3.6	9	3.0		
	14 other locations	29	6.4	--	--		
	10 other locations	--	--	22	7.6		
	Total	451	100.0	291	100.0	742	100.0
Cortland	Cortland	296	75.1	225	69.5	521	72.6
	Groton	2	0.1	8	2.5		
	Homer	27	6.9	36	11.1		
	Ithaca	19	4.8	2	0.7		
	McGraw	5	1.3	11	3.4		
	Syracuse	13	3.3	0	0.0		
	23 other locations	30	7.6	--	--		
	19 other locations	--	--	42	13.0		
	Total	394	100.0	324	100.0	718	100.0
	Cortland-Homer	323	82.0	261	80.6	584	81.3
Fredonia	Fredonia	224	72.7	150	46.7	374	59.5
	Brocton	7	2.3	8	2.5		
	Buffalo	2	0.6	0	0.0		
	Dunkirk	52	16.9	132	41.0		
	Jamestown	3	1.0	0	0.0		
	Silver Creek	6	2.0	7	2.2		
	13 other locations	14	4.5	--	--		
	9 other locations	--	--	24	7.5		
	Total	308	100.0	321	100.0	629	100.0
	Fredonia-Dunkirk	276	89.6	282	87.8	558	88.6

(Continued)

College	City or Village	Professional Staff		Auxiliary Staff		Total Staff	
		Number	Percent	Number	Percent	Number	Percent
Geneseo	Geneseo	238	71.5	93	25.6	331	47.5
	Avon	5	1.5	9	2.5		
	Batavia	1	.3	1	0.3		
	Conesus Lake	7	2.1	3	0.8		
	Dansville	1	0.3	44	12.1		
	Groveland	2	0.6	11	3.0		
	Leicester	6	1.8	17	4.7		
	Livonia	2	0.6	11	3.0		
	Mount Morris	15	4.5	69	19.0		
	Nunda	2	0.6	16	4.4		
	Perry	4	1.2	20	5.5		
	Piffard	3	0.9	10	2.8		
	Rochester	15	4.5	0	0.0		
	York	7	2.1	3	0.8		
	17 other locations	21	6.3	--	--		
	26 other locations	--	--	67	18.5		
	Total	333	100.0	363	100.0	696	100.0
New Paltz	New Paltz	334	75.5	171	43.8	505	60.6
	Beacon	2	0.5	1	0.3		
	Gardiner	7	1.6	22	5.6		
	Highland	18	4.1	42	10.7		
	Kingston	6	1.4	24	6.4		
	Newburgh	5	1.1	6	1.5		
	Poughkeepsie	17	3.8	2	0.5		
	Walden	1	0.2	21	5.4		
	Middletown	2	0.5	0	0.0		
	35 other locations	--	--	--	--		
	26 other locations	--	--	--	--		
	Total	442	100.0	391	100.0	833	
Oneonta	Oneonta	319	82.6	218	66.7	537	75.3
	Cooperstown	11	2.9	1	0.0		
	Franklin	6	1.5	2	0.1		
	Maryland	4	1.0	8	2.4		
	Schenectady	3	0.8	0	0.0		
	Unadilla	6	1.5	2	0.1		
	West Oneonta	4	1.0	10	3.1		
	Worcester	1	0.3	14	4.3		

College	City or Village	Professional Staff		Auxiliary Staff		Total Staff	
		Num-ber	Per-cent	Num-ber	Per-cent	Num-ber	Per-cent
Oneonta (con-tinued)	19 other locations	32	8.3	--	--		
	27 other locations	--	--	72	22.0		
	Total	386	100.0	327	100.0	713	
Oswego	Oswego	435	87.4	N.A.	N.A.	N.A.	N.A.
	Camillus	2	0.4				
	Fulton	12	2.4	N.A.	N.A.	N.A.	N.A.
	Liverpool	5	1.0	N.A.	N.A.	N.A.	N.A.
	Minetto	8	1.6	N.A.	N.A.	N.A.	N.A.
	Syracuse	14	2.8	N.A.	N.A.	N.A.	N.A.
	14 other locations	22	4.4	N.A.	N.A.	N.A.	N.A.
	Total	498	100.0	N.A.	N.A.	N.A.	N.A.
Platts-burgh	Plattsburgh	289	85.3	224	52.6	513	67.0
	Cadyville	1	0.3	17	4.0		
	Dannemora	0	0.0	19	4.5		
	Ellenburg Depot	0	0.0	17	4.0		
	Keeseville	2	0.6	13	3.0		
	Montreal	3	0.9	0	0.0		
	Morrisonville	9	2.7	34	8.0		
	Peru	8	2.4	24	5.6		
	15 other locations	27	8.0	--	--		
	23 other locations	--	--	78	18.3		
	Total	339	100.0	426	100.0	765	100.0
Potsdam	Potsdam					447	66.4
	Canton					21	3.1
	Colton					15	2.2
	Massena	N.A.	N.A.	N.A.	N.A.	35	5.2
	Norwood					35	5.2
	Winthrop					17	2.5
	33 other locations					103	15.3
	Total					673	100.0

TABLE B.2

Places of Staff Residence at Various Private Four-Year Colleges
in New York State, 1967–68

College	City or Village	Professional Staff		Auxiliary Staff		Total Staff	
		Number	Percent	Number	Percent	Number	Percent
Alfred University[a]	Alfred	133	63.4	45	23.2	178	44.3
	Alfred Station	28	13.4	34	17.6		
	Almond	18	8.6	33	17.1		
	Andover	8	3.8	26	13.5		
	Canisteo	1	0.5	0	0.0		
	Hornell	13	6.2	28	14.5		
	Wellsville	2	1.0	7	3.6		
	4 other locations	7	3.3	--	--		
	7 other locations	--	--	20	10.4		
	Total	210	100.0	193	100.0	403	100.0
	Alfred-Alfred Station	161	76.6	79	40.9	240	59.5
Clarkson	Potsdam	167	86.1	82	51.3	249	70.3
	Canton	5	2.6	3	1.9		
	Colton	1	0.5	9	5.6		
	Massena	1	0.5	3	1.9		
	Norwood	4	2.1	10	6.2		
	Parishville	2	1.0	9	5.6		
	West Potsdam	3	1.5	0	0.0		
	Winthrop	2	1.0	4	2.5		
	5 other locations	9	4.6	--	--		
	12 other locations	--	--	40	25.0		
	Total	194	100.0	160	100.0	354	100.0
Colgate	Hamilton	231	94.6	93	63.3	324	82.9
	Bouckville	0	0.0	4	2.7		
	Eaton	2	0.9	6	4.1		
	Earlville	0	0.0	7	4.8		
	Madison	1	0.4	7	4.8		
	Poolville	3	1.3	5	3.4		
	Oneida	0	0.0	2	1.4		
	Utica	2	0.9	0	0.0		
	Syracuse	1	0.4	0	0.0		
	3 other locations	4	1.6	--	--		

College	City or Village	Professional Staff Number	Professional Staff Per-cent	Auxiliary Staff Number	Auxiliary Staff Per-cent	Total Staff Number	Total Staff Per-cent
Colgate (con-tinued)	14 other loca-tions	--	--	23	15.6		
	Total	244	100.0	147	100.0	391	100.0
Hartwick	Oneonta	101	88.6	81	72.3	182	80.5
	Binghamton	2	1.8	0	0.0		
	Morris	0	0.0	5	4.5		
	Otego	1	0.9	5	4.5		
	West Oneonta	1	0.9	8	7.1		
	8 other loca-tions	9	7.9	--	--		
	9 other loca-tions	--	--	13	11.6		
	Total	114	100.0	112	100.0	226	100.0
Hobart and William Smith	Geneva	136	88.8	132	81.9	268	85.4
	Ithaca	3	2.0	0	0.0		
	Penn Yan	4	2.6	1	0.6		
	Rochester	2	1.3	0	0.0		
	Seneca Falls	1	0.6	4	2.5		
	Stanley	2	1.3	3	1.9		
	Waterloo	2	1.3	7	4.4		
	2 other loca-tions	3	2.0	--	--		
	6 other loca-tions	--	--	14	8.7		
	Total	153	100.0	161	100.0	314	100.0
Houghton	Houghton	89	92.7	79	80.6	168	86.6
	Belfast	0	0.0	3	3.1		
	Caneadea	1	1.0	1	1.0		
	Centerville	2	2.1	0	0.0		
	Fillmore	4	4.2	9	9.2		
	Rushford	0	0.0	2	2.0		
	0 other loca--tions	0	0.0	--	--		
	4 other loca-tions	--	--	4	4.1		
	Total	96	100.0	98	100.0	194	100.0

(Continued)

College	City or Village	Professional Staff		Auxiliary Staff		Total Staff	
		Number	Percent	Number	Percent	Number	Percent
Ithaca	Ithaca	220	87.3	123	69.5	343	79.9
	Brooktondale	6	2.4	3	1.7		
	Candor	1	0.4	6	3.4		
	Dryden	3	1.2	2	1.1		
	Freeville	3	1.2	5	2.8		
	Newfield	2	0.8	8	4.5		
	Trumansburg	6	2.4	8	4.5		
	10 other locations	11	4.4	--	--		
	10 other locations	--	--	22	12.4		
	Total	252	100.0	177	100.0	429	100.0
St. Bona- venture	St. Bonaventure	73	31.6	0	0.0	73	15.9
	Allegany	54	23.4	52	22.7	106	23.0
	Bradford, Pa.	5	2.2	0	0.0		
	Derrick, Pa.	1	0.4	0	0.0		
	Olean	79	34.2	151	65.9	230	50.0
	Portville	8	3.5	10	4.4		
	Rixford, Pa.	3	1.3	2	0.9		
	8 other locations	8	3.5	--	--		
	9 other locations	--	--	14	6.1		
	Total	231	100.0	229	100.0	460	100.0
	St. Bonaventure- Allegany-Olean	206	89.2	203	88.6	409	89.0
	St. Bonaventure- Olean	152	65.8	151	65.9	303	65.9
St. Law- rence	Canton	187	93.9	168	55.3	355	70.6
	Colton	0	0.0	12	3.9		100.0
	DeKalb Junction	0	0.0	18	5.9		
	Herman	1	0.5	12	3.9		
	Madrid	0	0.0	10	3.3		
	Massena	0	0.0	1	0.3		
	Ogdensburg	1	0.5	4	1.3		
	Potsdam	4	2.0	13	4.3		
	Pyrites	0	0.0	15	4.9		
	Russell	0	0.0	15	4.9		
	5 other locations	6	3.0	--	--		

College	City or Village	Professional Staff		Auxiliary Staff		Total Staff	
		Number	Percent	Number	Percent	Number	Percent
St. Lawrence (continued)	20 other locations	--	--	36	11.8		
	Total	199	100.0	304	99.8	503	100.0
Skidmore	Saratoga Springs	156	79.9	97	77.0	253	78.8
	Albany	1	0.5	1	0.8		
	Ballston Spa	5	2.6	9	7.1		
	Delmar	1	0.5	0	0.0		
	Gansevoort	5	2.6	2	1.6		
	Greenfield Center	7	3.6	6	4.8		
	Schenectady	2	1.0	1	0.8		
	Troy	2	1.0	0	0.0		
	16 other locations	16	8.2	--	--		
	8 other locations	--	--	10	7.9		
	Total	195	100.0	126	100.0	321	100.0
Vassar	Poughkeepsie	268	91.4	407	76.2	675	81.6
	Beacon	1	0.3	2	0.4		
	Hopewell Junction	4	1.4	14	2.6		
	Hyde Park	1	0.3	15	2.8		
	Kingston	0	0.0	2	0.4		
	New Paltz	3	1.0	3	1.0		
	Newburgh	0	0.0	1	0.2		
	Pleasant Valley	5	1.7	17	3.2		
	Wappingers Falls	1	0.3	32	5.9		
	8 other locations	10	3.4	--	--		
	19 other locations	--	--				
	Total	293	--	534	--	827	100.0
	Poughkeepsie-Hyde Park	269	91.7	422	79.0		

[a]Alfred University data are for Fall, 1968.

Places of Staff Residence at Various Two-Year Colleges in
New York State, 1967-68

College	City or Village	Professional Staff		Auxiliary Staff		Total Staff	
		Number	Percent	Number	Percent	Number	Percent
Adiron-dack C.C.	Glens Falls	30	45.5	14	38.9	44	43.1
	Ft. Edward	2	3.0	3	8.3		
	Hudson Falls	14	21.2	9	25.0		
	Lake George	5	7.6	0	0.0		
	Saratoga Springs	0	0.0	0	0.0		
	South Glens Falls	2	3.0	3	8.3		
	10 other locations	13	19.7	--	--		
	5 other locations	--	--	7	19.4		
	Total	66	100.0	36	100.0	102	100.0
	Glens Falls-South Glens Falls-Hudson Falls-Ft. Edward	48	72.8	29	80.5	77	75.5
Auburn C.C. (Fall, 1968)	Auburn	53	64.6	24	75.0	77	67.6
	Cayuga	2	2.5	0	0.0		
	Camillus	3	3.7	1	3.1		
	Sennett	2	2.5	0	0.0		
	Skaneateles	11	13.6	0	0.0		
	Syracuse	2	2.5	0	0.0		
	7 other locations	9	11.1	--	--		
	6 other locations	--	--	7	21.9		
	Total	82	100.0	32	100.0	114	100.0
Corning C.C.	Corning	73	57.5	70	69.3	143	62.7
	Big Flats	7	5.5	2	2.0		
	Elmira	9	7.1	5	4.9		
	Horseheads	17	13.4	1	1.0		
	Nelson, Pa.	0	0.0	1	1.0		

College	City or Village	Professional Staff		Auxiliary Staff		Total Staff	
		Number	Per-cent	Number	Per-cent	Number	Per-cent
	Painted Post	11	8.6	8	7.9		
	7 other locations	10	7.9	--	--		
	7 other locations	--	--	14	13.9		
	Total	127	100.0	101	100.0	228	100.0
	Corning-Painted Post	84	66.1	78	77.1	162	71.1
Dutchess C.C.	Poughkeepsie	74	49.3	73	67.0	147	56.8
	Beacon	0	0.0	3	2.8		
	Hyde Park	32	21.3	12	11.0		
	Hopewell Junction	4	2.7	3	2.8		
	Middletown	1	0.7	0	0.0		
	New Paltz	3	2.0	0	0.0		
	Staatsburg	5	3.3	1	0.9		
	Wappingers Falls	5	3.3	4	3.7		
	20 other locations	26	17.3	--	--		
	10 other locations	--	--	13	11.9		
	Total	150	100.0	109	100.0	359	100.0
	Poughkeepsie-Hyde Park	106	70.6	85	78.0	191	73.7
Fulton-Mont-gomery C.C.	Johnstown	30	47.6	12	46.1	42	47.2
	Amsterdam	14	22.2	3	11.5		
	Fultonville	2	3.2	0	0.0		
	Gloversville	12	19.1	8	30.0		
	5 other locations	5	7.9	--	--		
	3 other locations	--	--	3	11.5		
	Total	63	100.0	26	100.0	89	100.0
	Johnstown-Gloversville	42	66.7	20	76.9	62	70.0

(Continued)

College	City or Village	Professional Staff		Auxiliary Staff		Total Staff	
		Number	Per-cent	Number	Per-cent	Number	Per-cent
Genesee C.C.	Batavia	27	42.9	15	75.0	42	50.6
	Attica	3	4.8	0	0.0		
	Buffalo	1	0.0	0	0.0		
	Corfu	3	4.8	1	5.0		
	LeRoy	5	7.9	0	0.0		
	Rochester	2	3.2	0	0.0		
	16 other locations	22	34.9	--	--		
	4 other locations	--	--	4	20.0		
	Total	63	100.0	20	100.0	83	100.0
Herkimer C.C.	Ilion	9	29.0	1	8.3	10	23.3
	Frankfort	1	3.2	2	16.7		
	Herkimer	3	9.7	4	33.3		
	Little Falls	1	3.2	4	33.3		
	Mohawk	3	9.7	1	8.3		
	Utica	7	22.6	0	0.0		
	6 other locations	7	22.6	--	--		
	0 other locations	--	--	0	0.0		
	Total	31	100.0	12	100.0	43	100.0
Jamestown C.C.	Jamestown	42	61.8	17	62.9	59	62.1
	Ashville	4	5.9	0	0.0		
	Bemus Point	2	2.9	1	3.7		
	Chautauqua	2	2.9	0	0.0		
	Falconer	4	5.9	1	3.7		
	Lakewood	5	7.4	1	3.7		
	7 other locations	9	13.2	--	--		
	4 other locations	--	--	7	25.9		
	Total	68	100.0	27	100.0	95	
	Jamestown-Falconer	46	67.6	18	66.6	64	67.4
Jefferson C.C.	Watertown	43	76.8	24	77.4	67	77.0
	Adams Center	3	5.4	2	6.7		
	Sackets Harbor	2	3.6	1	3.3		

College	City or Village	Professional Staff		Auxiliary Staff		Total Staff	
		Num-ber	Per-cent	Num-ber	Per-cent	Num-ber	Per-cent
Jefferson C.C. (con-tinued)	8 other loca-tions	8	14.3	--	--		
	4 other loca-tions	--	--	4	12.9		
	Total	56		31		87	100.0
Orange C.C.	Middletown	80	60.6	57	70.4	137	64.3
	Chester	5	3.8	1	1.2		
	Goshen	18	13.6	3	3.7		
	Kingston	1	0.8	0	0.0		
	Newburgh	3	2.3	0	0.0		
	New Hampton	1	0.8	5	6.2		
	Pine Bush	3	2.3	3	3.7		
	Slate Hill	3	2.3	1	1.2		
	16 other loca-tions	18	13.6	--	--		
	10 other loca-tions	--	--	11	13.6		
	Total	132	100.0	81	100.0	213	100.0
Rockland C.C.	Suffern	27	14.8	4	5.3	31	12.0
	Haverstraw	6	3.3	9	11.8		
	Monsey	16	8.8	14	18.4		
	Nanuet	2	1.1	2	2.6		
	New City	11	6.0	10	13.2		
	New York	47	25.9	6	7.8	53	21.0
	Nyack	10	5.5	5	6.6		
	Pearl River	11	6.0	6	7.8		
	Spring Valley	21	11.6	18	23.7		
	New Jersey	23	12.6	1	1.3		
	1 other loca-tion	8	4.4	--	--		
	1 other loca-tion	--	--	1	1.3		
	Total	182	100.0	76	100.0	258	100.0
SUNY Alfred	Alfred Village	81	41.5	42	14.2	123	25.1
	Alfred Station	36	18.5	36	12.2		
	Almond	15	7.7	27	9.2		
	Andover	5	2.6	53	18.0		
	Belmont	4	2.1	12	4.1		

(Continued)

College	City or Village	Professional Staff		Auxiliary Staff		Total Staff	
		Number	Percent	Number	Percent	Number	Percent
	Hornell	21	10.8	59	20.0		
	Scio	3	1.5	9	3.1		
	Wellsville	18	9.2	28	9.5		
	Whitesville	0	0.0	11	3.7		
	9 other locations	12	6.2	--	--		
	14 other locations	--	--	18	6.1		
	Total	195	100.0	295	100.0	490	100.0
	Alfred-Alfred Station	117	60.0	78	26.4	195	40.0
SUNY Canton	Canton	118	79.2	111	56.1	729	66.0
	Governeur	3	2.0	7	3.5		
	Massena	1	0.7	4	2.0		
	Norwood	3	2.0	2	1.0		
	Ogdensburg	11	7.4	23	11.6		
	Potsdam	12	8.0	5	2.5		
	1 other locations	1	0.7	--	--		
	7 other locations	--	--	46	23.2		
	Total	149	100.0	198	100.0	347	100.0
SUNY Cobleskill	Cobleskill	95	72.0	127	54.0	232	60.5
	Albany	4	3.0	0	0.0		
	Amsterdam	1	0.8	1	4.3		
	East Worcester	2	1.5	4	1.7		
	Middleburgh	0	0.0	11	4.7		
	Richmondville	13	9.9	19	8.1		
	Schoharie	4	3.0	4	1.7		
	Sharon Springs	1	0.8	11	4.7		
	Warnerville	4	3.0	12	5.1		
	7 other locations	8	6.1	--	--		
	20 other locations	--	--	46	19.6		
	Total	132	100.0	235	100.0	367	100.0
SUNY Delhi	Delhi	102	83.5	144	60.0	246	68.0
	Bovina	1	0.8	10	4.2		
	DeLancey	0	0.0	4	1.7		

College	City or Village	Professional Staff		Auxiliary Staff		Total Staff	
		Num-ber	Per-cent	Num-ber	Per-cent	Num-ber	Per-cent
SUNY	Franklin	3	2.5	11	4.6		
Delhi	Hamden	1	0.8	12	5.0		
(con-	Margaretville	2	1.6	19	7.9		
tinued)	Oneonta	6	4.9	7	2.9		
	Walton	1	0.8	17	7.1		
	6 other locations	6	4.9	--	--		
	7 other locations	--	--	16	6.7		
	Total	122	100.0	240	100.0	362	100.0
SUNY	Morrisville	47	51.7	50	32.5	97	40.0
Morris-	Bouckville	3	3.3	3	1.9		
ville	Canastota	3	3.3	12	7.8		
	Cazenovia	4	4.4	10	6.5		
	Eaton	3	3.3	19	12.3		
	Erieville	0	0.0	10	6.5		
	Hamilton	8	8.8	9	5.8		
	Manlius	1	1.1	0	0.0		
	Oneida	2	2.2	0	0.0		
	Syracuse	2	2.2	1	0.7		
	Utica	2	2.2	0	0.0		
	12 other locations	16	17.6	--	--		
	20 other locations	--	--	40	26.0		
	Total	91	100.0	154	100.0	244	100.0
Sullivan	South Fallsburg	5	5,4	7	15.2	12	8.6
C.C.	Ellenville	2	2.2	0	0.0		
	Fallsburg	2	2.2	0	0.0		
	Grahamsville	9	9.7	8	17.4		
	Hurleyville	6	6.5	3	6.5		
	Liberty	9	9.7	5	10.9		
	Middletown	2	2.2	1	2.2		
	Monticello	34	36.6	4	8.7	38	27.3
	Woodbourne	0	0.0	6	13.1		
	16 other locations	24	25.8	--	--		
	11 other locations	--	--	12	26.1		
	Total	93	100.0	46	100.0	139	100.0

(Continued)

College	City or Village	Professional Staff		Auxiliary Staff		Total Staff	
		Number	Percent	Number	Percent	Number	Percent
Ulster C.C.	Stone Ridge	9	11.1	10	21.8	19	15.0
	Albany	1	1.2	0	0.0		
	Kingston	33	40.7	24	52.1	57	45.0
	New Paltz	5	6.2	0	0.0		
	West Hurley	4	4.9	0	0.0		
	Woodstock	9	11.1	0	0.0		
	14 other locations	20	24.7	--	--		
	6 other locations	--	--	12	26.1		
	Total	81	100.0	46	100.0	127	100.0
Cazenovia	Cazenovia	63	75.0	39	54.2	102	65.4
	Auburn	0	0.0	1	1.4		
	Canastota	0	0.0	4	5.5		
	Delphi Falls	0	0.0	1	1.4		
	Erieville	2	2.8	9	12.5		
	Fayetteville	5	5.9	0	0.0		
	Manlius	4	4.8	3	4.2		
	Syracuse	6	7.1	2	2.8		
	4 other locations	4	4.8	--	--		
	9 other locations	--	--	13	18.1		
	Total	84	100.0	72	100.0	156	100.0
Paul Smiths	Paul Smiths	28	50.0	28	41.1	56	45.2
	Gabriels	7	12.5	3	4.4		
	Saranac Lake	15	26.8	37	54.5		
	4 other locations	6	10.7	--	--		
	0 other locations	--	--	0	0.0		
	Total	56	100.0	68	100.0	124	100.0

Note: All of the above are part of the State University of New York, except for the last two, Cazenovia and Paul Smiths, which are private colleges.

TABLE B.4

Correlation Matrix of Variables Used in Determining
the Relationship Between Percent of Staff Living
in the College Community and Size of the
College Community, Multicollege Analysis

Large and Small College Communities (combined)

		1	2	4	6	8	9
SQM	1	--					
DEN	2	−09	--				
%-PROF-IN	4	13	02	--			
$-AUXIL-IN	6	51	40	42	--		
TOWN-CTY-POP	8	28	85	11	63	--	
POPUL-60	9	43	73	11	74	92	--
POPUL-40[a]	18	40	74	06	73	93	99

Small College Communities Only

		1	2	4	6	8	9
SQM	1	--					
DEN	2	−49	--				
%-PROF-IN	4	03	36	--			
%-AUXIL-IN	6	02	22	72	--		
TOWN-CTY-POP	8	15	53	34	59	--	
POPUL-60	9	14	75	40	18	60	--
POPUL-40	18	44	47	36	38	72	84

Large College Communities Only

		1	2	4	6	8
SQM	1	--				
DEN	2	−51	--			
%-PROF-IN	4	04	−25	--		
%-AUXIL-IN	6	22	−11	15	--	
TOWN-CTY-POP	8	−17	84	−07	19	--
POPUL-60	9	−11	70	−17	23	90

[a]The POPUL-40 variable was not run for college communities, as low correlation was assumed from the data at hand.

Note: See Table 3.3 for definitions of code names.

TABLE B.5

Correlation Matrixes of Independent Variables for Staff Regressions, Multicollege Analysis, in Percent

College Professionals Living in Large and Small College Communities

Variables		7	11
%-PHD	7	--	
DEGREE-YRS	11	65	--
POPUL-40	18	12	—03

College Professionals Living in the Larger College Communities

Variables		3	7	8
PROSTAF	3	--		
%-PHD	7	49	--	
TOWN-CTY	8	—04	01	--
DEGREE-YRS	11	21	61	27

College Auxiliary Staff Living in Large and Small College Communities

Variables		1	5	9
SQM	1	--		
AUXSTAF	5	—16	--	
POPUL-60	9	43	—01	--
DEGREE-YRS	11	—01	14	—02

TABLE C.1

Local Student Enrollment and Commutation by Sectors, the State University of New York at Cortland, 1967-68

Ring	A	B	C	D	E	F	G	H	I	J	K	L	Totals
1	24-21	--	--	2-2	--	--	--	--	--	--	--	--	26-23
2	2-2	--	--	--	--	--	--	6-1	5-3	10-6	--	--	23-12
3	--	10-6	1-1	2-1	--	4-2	1-1	--	1-0	--	7-3	--	26-14
4	2-0	2-1	4-4	1-0	--	8-2	4-2	--	41-11	2-0	--	--	64-20
5	2-0	--	1-1	--	--	--	2-0	4-1	4-0	5-1	--	7-3	25-6
6	114-10	12-2	1-0	--	8-0	--	1-0	3-0	--	--	3-1	29-2	171-15
7	13-1	8-0	5-0	16-0	1-0	157-9	26-0	--	12-0	1-0	14-0	3-0	256-10
8	16-0	7-0	4-0	2-0	5-0	8-0	5-0	2-0	14-0	7-0	7-0	3-0	80-0
9	4-0	3-0	5-0	--	6-0	3-0	--	46-0	3-0	--	5-0	--	75-0
10	--	--	4-0	--	2-0	--	--	4-1	21-0	1-0	12-0	3-0	47-1
Totals	177-34	42-9	25-6	23-3	22-0	180-13	39-3	65-3	101-14	26-7	48-4	45-5	793-101

Note: In the above table, for each sector, the number of local students enrolled is first indicated, and this is followed by the number commuting. For example, for sector 2H, six students are enrolled and one commutes. Sectors without numbers have zero enrollment and commutation. The commutation limit line is indicated on the above table and based on at least one commuter present in a sector.

The one commuter in sector 10H is omitted from consideration because the preceding three sectors are zero for channel H. If two commuters per sector is made the basis for the limit line, a considerably smaller commutation area results. See Figure 4.

TABLE C.2

Local Student Enrollment and Commutation by Sectors, the State University of New York, Agricultural and Technical College at Alfred, 1967-68

Ring	A	B	C	D	E	F	G	H	I	J	K	L
1	--	18-18	--	--	--	--	--	--	--	--	--	--
2	14-12	104-83	19-6	--	--	14-11	--	--	--	--	--	--
3	14-12	--	--	--	1-0	3-1	--	75-49	11-9	7-3	--	4-1
4	--	--	--	7-4	1-0	--	--	--	7-1	8-5	--	3-1
5	47-12	17-3	9-4	3-1	--	P	P	13-4	15-5	3-0	4-0	8-2
6	4-0	--	10-0	5-0	--	P	P	--	1-0	2-0	2-0	9-0
7	2-0	9-0	--	2-0	--	P	P	4-0	46-2	12-0	8-1	11-0
8	11-0	3-0	--	4-0	P	P	P	P	19-1	14-0	11-0	7-0
9	3-0	23-1	P	P	P	P	P	P	P	P	12-0	16-0
10	21-0	3-0	P	P	P	P	P	P	P	P	17-0	16-0

CHANNEL

Note: Sectors labeled P are predominately in the State of Pennsylvania; for explanation, see note for Table C.1.

D

ZIP CODE
AND
AVERAGE
DAILY ATTENDANCE

Zone, Location, Average Daily Attendance, and Zip Code Data for Cortland

Zone or Sector	Location	Grades 7-12, ADA	Zip Code	Zone or Sector	Location	Grades 7-12, ADA	Zip Code
099	Cortland	1,464	13045	11A	Fulton	1,761	13069
01A	Homer	1,011	13077	12A	Syracuse	11,105	13200
01D	McGraw	319	13101		Colvin	--	13205
01H	South Cortland	--	--		Eastwood	--	13206
02A	Little York	--	13087		Elmwood	--	13207
	Preble	--	13141		Hancock Field	--	13225
03A	Vesper	--	--		Mattydale	--	13211
	Otisco Valley	--	--		Onondaga	567	13215
04A	Otisco	--	--		Salina	--	13208
	Cardiff	--	--		University	--	13210
	Lafayette	469	13084		Veterans'		
05A	Cedarvale	--	--		Hospital	--	13210
	Navarino	--	--	02B	East Homer	--	13056
	Nedrow	--	13120	03B	Truxton	148	13158
06A	Onondaga Hill	954	--		Tully	430	13159
	Split Rock	--	--	04B	Keeney	--	--
	Camillus	2,541	13031		Apulia	--	--
	Fairmount	--	13219		Apulia Station	--	13020
	Amboy	--	--		Fabius	399	--
	Solvay	936	13209	05B	New Woodstock	--	--
	Jamesville	--	13078		Delphi Falls	--	13051
	DeWitt	1,400	13214		Pompey	--	13138
	East Syracuse	1,902	13057		Pompey Center	--	--
07A	Minoa	--	13116		Watervale	--	--
	Collamer	--	--	06B	Nelson	--	--
	North Syracuse	4,206	13212		Cazenovia	858	13035
	Liverpool	2,363	13088		Chittenango		
	Warners	--	13164		Falls	--	--
08A	Bridgeport	--	13030		Oran	--	13125
	Cicero	--	13039		Manlius	1,836	13104
	Brewerton	--	13029		Fayetteville	--	13066
	Euclid	--	--		Manlius Center	--	--
	Belgium	--	--	07B	Peterboro	--	13134
	Phoenix	1,023	13135		Siloam	--	--
	Three Rivers	--	--		Perryville	--	13133
	Baldwinsville	1,922	13027		Chittenango	980	13037
	Lamson	--	--		Chittenango		
09A	Constantia	--	13044		Station	--	13038
	West Monroe	--	--		Clockville	--	13042
	Central Square	1,342	13036		Sullivan	--	--
	Pennellville	--	13132		North Manlius	--	--
	Caughdenoy	--	--		Mycenal	--	--
	Hinmansville	--	--		Kirkville	--	13082
10A	Amboy Center	--	--	08B	Valley Mills	--	--
	West Amboy	--	--		Merrillsville	--	--
	North Constantia	--	--		Wampsville	--	13163
	Mallory	--	13103		Oneida Castle	--	--
	Hastings	--	13076		Oneida Lake	--	--
	Hastings Center	--	--		Lenox	--	--
	Clifford	--	--		Canastota	876	13032
	Palermo	--	--		Lakeport	--	--
	Volney	--	--				

(Continued)

Zone or Sector	Location	Grades 7-12, ADA	Zip Code	Zone or Sector	Location	Grades 7-12, ADA	Zip Code
09B	Verona	--	13478	10C	Hella	--	--
	Bernhards Bay	--	13028		Westmoreland	580	13490
	Durhamville	--	13054		Clark Mills	--	13321
	Cleveland	--	13042		Kirkland	--	--
	State Bridge	--	--		Clinton	860	13323
	Jewell	--	--		Hamilton		
	North Bay	--	13123		College	--	--
	Vernon	--	13476		Franklin		
	Sylvan Beach	--	13157		Springs	--	13341
	Sherrill	60	13461		Chadwicks	151	13319
	South Bay	1,357	--		Sauquoit	--	13456
	Oneida Valley	--	--		Paris	--	13429
	Verona Beach	--	13162		Clayville	--	--
	Higginsville	--	--		Cassville	--	13318
10B	Vienna	--	--		Bridgewater	84	13313
	McConnellsville	--	13401		West Winfield	446	13491
	Stacy Basin	--	--		Unadilla Forks	--	13474
	Greenway	--	--		Leonardsville	96	13364
	Lowell	--	--		West Exeter	--	13487
11B	Rome	4,201	13440	11C	Utica		{13500
12B	Oneida	1,467	13421				{13502
02C	Cheningo	--	--	02D	Solon	--	--
03C	Cuyler	--	13050	03D	Union Valley	--	--
04C	Lincklaen	--	--		Taylor	--	--
	DeRuyter	298	13052		Pitcher	--	13136
05C	Sheds	--	13151		Cincinnatus	334	13040
	Georgetown	88	13072	04D	South Otselic	146	13155
	Otselic	--	13129		North Pitcher	--	13124
06C	Erieville	--	13061		Pharsalia	--	--
	West Eaton	--	13484	05D	Beaver Meadow	--	13735
	Lebanon	--	13085		North Pharsalia	--	--
07C	Earlville	234	13332		East Pharsalia	--	13758
	Poolville	--	13432	06D	Smyrna	--	--
	Randallsville	--	--		Sherburne Four		
	Hamilton	367	13346		Corners	--	--
	Eaton	--	13334		Plymouth	--	13832
	Bouckville	--	13310		South Plymouth	--	13844
	Morrisville	398	13408		Preston	--	--
	Pratts Hollow	--	13434	07D	Sherburne	640	13460
08C	Stockbridge	231	--		North Norwich	--	13814
	Knoxboro	--	13362		Chenango Lake	--	--
	Munnsville	--	13409		Norwich	1,456	13815
	Augusta	--	--	08D	Columbus	--	--
	Oriskany Falls	149	13425		New Berlin	334	13411
	Solsville	--	13465		South New		
	Madison	284	13402		Berlin	168	13843
	North Brookfield	--	13418		Holmesville	--	13789
	Hubbardsville	--	13355		Rockwell Mills	--	--
	East Hamilton	--	--		Mt. Upton	139	13809
90C	Vernon Center	--	13477	09D	Edmeston	290	13335
	Deansboro	--	13328		South		
	Waterville	463	13480		Edmeston	--	13466
	Sangerfield	--	13455		Pittsfield	--	--
	Brookfield	156	13314		Morris	225	13808
	West Edmeston	--	13485		Gilbertsville	137	13776

Zone or Sector	Location	Grades 7-12, ADA	Zip Code	Zone or Sector	Location	Grades 7-12, ADA	Zip Code
10D	Burlington			03F	Marathon	398	13803
	Flats	--	13315		Hunt's Corners	--	--
	Burlington	--	--		Killaway	--	13794
	West Burlington	--	13482	04F	Upper Lisle	--	--
	Garrattsville	--	13342		Lisle	--	13797
	West Laurens	--	--		Center Lisle	--	--
	Otsdawa	--	--		Whitney Point	696	13862
	Otego	687	13825	05F	Triangle	--	--
11D	Oneonta	1,514	13820		Itaska	--	--
02E	East Freetown	--	13055		Nanticoke	--	--
03E	Texas Valley	--	--		Glen Aubrey	--	13777
04E	Willet	--	13863	06F	North Fenton	--	--
05E	McDonough	--	13801		Chenango Forks	2,282	13746
	Smithville				Castle Creek	--	13744
	Flats	--	13841		West Chenango	--	--
06E	Oxford	495	13830		Glen Castle	--	--
	Tyner	--	--	07F	Chenango
	Brisben	--	13741		Branch	--	13745
	Greene	692	13778		Port Crane	--	13833
07E	Guilford	--	13780		Sanitaria
	Coventryville	--	--		Springs	8	13836
	Coventry	--	--		West
	North				Colesville	--	--
	Colesville	--	--		Port Dickinson	--	--
	Belden	--	--		Stella	--	--
08E	Rockdale	--	--		Westover	--	--
	East Guilford	--	--		Willot Point	--	--
	Bainbridge	522	13733	08F	Ouaquaga	--	13826
	North Afton	--	--		West Windsor	--	--
	Afton	338	13730		Kirkwood	--	13793
	Vallonia				Conklin	1,108	13748
	Springs	--	--		Hawleyton	--	--
	Nineveh	--	13813	09F	East Windsor	--	--
	Harpursville	423	13787		Windsor	937	13865
	Center Village	--	--		Damascus	--	--
	Doraville	--	--		Great Bend	--	13643
09E	Unadilla	--	13849		Corbettsville	--	13749
	Sidney	948	13838	10F	McClure	--	--
	Youngs	--	--		Oquaga Lake	--	--
	Bennettsville	--	--		Gulf Summit	--	--
	Masonville	--	13804	11F	Binghamton	5,653	13900
	North Stanford	--	--	12F	Johnson City	1,191	13790
	Sanford	--	--	02G	Virgil	174	--
10E	Franklin	205	13775	03G	Harford	--	13784
	Bartlett				Harford Mills	--	13785
	Hollow	--	--		Richford	--	13835
	Sidney Center	--	13839	04G	East Berkshire	--	--
	Trout Creek	--	13847		Berkshire	--	13736
	Rockroyal	--	--		Speedsville	--	--
	Deposit	491	13754	05G	Jenksville	--	--
	Hambletville	--	--		Newark Valley	650	13811
	Stilesville	--	--		Weltonville	--	--
02F	Messengerville	--	--		Hubbardtown	--	--

(Continued)

Zone or Sector	Location	Grades 7-12, ADA	Zip Code	Zone or Sector	Location	Grades 7-12, ADA	Zip Code
6G	Maine	--	13802	05I	Jacksonville	--	14854
	Gaskill	--	--		Perry City	--	--
	Flemingsville	--	--		Enfield	--	--
07G	Tioga Center	481	13845		Newfield	370	14867
	Lounsberry	--	--	06I	Reynoldsville	--	--
	Owego	1,440	13827		Mecklenburg	--	14863
	Apalachin	--	13732		Cayutaville	--	--
	Campville	--	--		Alpine	--	14805
	Vestal	2,624	13850		Pony Hollow	--	--
08G	Smithboro	--	13840	07I	Bennettsburg	--	--
	Nichols	--	13812		Burdett	--	14818
	Vestal Center	--	--		Watkins Glen	745	14891
11G	Endicott	2,652	13760		Montour Falls	--	14865
02H	Dryden	661	13053		Odessa	619	14869
03H	Ellis	--	--		Catharine	--	--
	Slaterville Springs	--	14881		Cayuta	--	14824
	Caroline	--	--	08I	Altay	--	--
04H	Brooktondale	--	14817		Reading Center	--	14876
	Caroline Center	--	--		Townsend	--	--
05H	Danby	--	--		Millport	--	14864
	Willseyville	--	13864		Pine Valley	--	14872
	Candor	400	13743		Horseheads	2,311	14845
	West Danby	--	14896		Sullivanville	--	--
06H	Spencer	259	14883	09I	Weston	--	--
	Van Ettin	270	14889		Post Creek	--	--
	Straits Corners	--	--		Tyrone	--	14887
07H	Halsey Valley	--	--		Bradford	146	14815
	Erin	--	14838		Hornby	--	--
	Swartwood	--	--		Monterey	--	--
08H	Barton	--	13734		Beaver Dams	--	14812
	Lockwood	--	14859		Chambers	--	--
	Chemung Center	--	--		Big Flats	--	14814
	Hicks	--	--		Catlin	--	--
	North Chemung	--	--	10I	North Urbana	--	--
	Breesport	--	14816		Sonora	--	--
09H	Waverly	944	14892		South Corning	--	14830
	Chemung	--	14825		Gibson	--	--
	Lowman	--	14861		Painted Post	--	14870
	Wellsburg	--	14894	11I	Corning	3,809	14830
	East Elmira	--	--	12I	Ithaca	3,346	14850
	Elmira Heights	981	14903	02J	Groton	562	13073
	Southport	--	--	03J	West Groton	--	--
11H	Elmira	5,666	14900		North Lansing	--	--
02I	McLean	--	13102	04J	King Ferry	--	13081
	Freeville	--	13068		Goodyears	--	--
	Peruville	--	13073		Five Corners	--	--
03I	Varna	--	14850		Lake Ridge	--	--
	Etna	--	13062		Lansingville	--	--
	West Dryden	--	13068		Ludlowville	--	14862
	South Lansing	590	14882		Myers	--	14866
04I	Cayuga Heights (Ithaca)	--	--	05J	Sheldrake	--	--
					Interlaken	313	14847
					Covert	--	--
					Trumansburg	637	14886

Zone or Sector	Location	Grades 7-12, ADA	Zip Code	Zone or Sector	Location	Grades 7-12, ADA	Zip Code
06J	Hayts Corners	--	14465	06K	Half Acre	--	--
	Ovid	338	14521		Oakwood	--	--
	Lodi	--	--		Union		
	East				Springs	565	13160
	Steamburg	--	--		Levanna	--	13086
	Logan	--	--		Aurora	--	13026
07J	Willard	--	14588	07K	Cayuga	--	13034
	Caywood	--	--		Seneca Falls	986	13148
	Valdis	--	--		Canoga	--	--
	Hector	--	14841		Fayette	--	13065
	Himrod	--	14842		MacDougall	--	14501
	Glenora	--	--		Romulus	296	14541
	Rock Stream	--	14878	08K	Tyre	--	--
	Lakemont	--	14857		Magee	--	--
	Starkey	--	--		Waterloo	994	13165
08J	Bellona	--	14415	09K	Clyde	422	14433
	Dresden	--	14441		Marengo	--	--
	Penn Yan	1,224	14527		Alloway	--	--
	Milo Center	--	--		Oaks		
	Dundee	507	14837		Corners	--	14518
09J	Benton Center	--	--		Seneca		
	Bluff Point	--	14417		Castle	--	14547
	Keuka Park	--	14478		Flint	--	--
	Branchport	--	14418		Stanley	--	14561
	Crosby	--	--		Gorham	401	14461
	Keuka	--	--		Hall	--	14463
	Wayne	--	14893	10K	Wayne Center	--	--
	Catawba	--	--		Lock Berlin	--	--
10J	Rushville	--	14544		Lyons	651	14489
	Potter	--	--		Phelps	574	14532
	Middlesex	337	14507		Clifton		
	Italy Hill	--	--		Springs	553	14432
	Pulteney	--	14874		Orleans	--	--
	South				Reeds		
	Pulteney	--	--		Corners	--	--
	Urbana	--	--	11K	Geneva	1,369	14456
	Hammondsport	470	14840	12K	Newark	1,177	14513
02K	Summer Hill	--	--	13K	Canandaigua	1,460	14424
03K	Montville	--	--	02L	Scott	--	--
	Moravia	623	13118		Dresserville	--	--
	Locke	--	13092	03L	Sempronius	--	--
04K	Genoa	591	13071		Spafford	--	--
	Venice				New Hope	--	--
	Center	--	13161		Kelloggsville	--	--
	Cascade	--	--	04L	Amber	--	--
05K	Poplar Ridge	--	13139		Borodino	--	--
	Sherwood	--	--		Mandana	--	--
	Ledyard	--	--		Niles	--	--
	Scipioville	--	--	05L	Marcellus	903	13108
	Scipio	--	--		Rose Hill	--	--
	Owasco Lake	--	--		Marietta	--	13110
	Mapleton	--	--		Skaneateles	915	13152
	Fleming	--	--		Owasco	--	13130

(Continued)

Zone or Sector	Location	Grades 7-12, ADA	Zip Code	Zone or Sector	Location	Grades 7-12, ADA	Zip Code
06L	Sennett	--	13150	09L	Hannibal		
	Hartlot	--	13075		Center	--	--
	Skaneateles				South		
	Falls	--	13153		Hannibal	--	--
	Mottville	--	13119		Bowens		
	Marcellus Falls	--	--		Corners	--	--
	Elbridge	--	13060		Ira	--	--
07L	Ionia	--	14475		Victory	--	--
	Weedsport	478	13166		South Butler	--	13154
	Port Byron	650	13140	10L	North		
	Throopsville	--	--		Hannibal	--	--
	Jordan	710	13080		Hannibal	627	13074
	Memphis	--	13112		Crocketts	--	--
08L	Savannah	--	13146		Sterling	--	13156
	Spring Lake	--	--		Martville	--	13111
	Montezuma	--	13117		Westbury	--	--
	Lysander	--	13094		Red Creek	--	13143
	Plainville	--	13137		Wolcott	--	14590
	Cato	548	13033		Rose	--	14542
	Meridian	--	13113		North Rose	289	14516
	Conquest	--	--	11L	Auburn	2,643	13021

Zone, Location, and Zip Code Data for Cortland, by Village and City

Zone or Sector	Location	Zip Code	Zone or Sector	Location	Zip Code
CO1	Cortland	13045	CO5	(continued)	
CO2	McGraw	13101		Brooktondale	14817
	South			Caroline	--
	Cortland	--		Caroline	
CO3	Homer			Center	--
CO4	Cortland County			Speedsville	--
	Scott	--		Danby	--
	Preble	13141		West Danby	14896
	Little York	13087		Pony Hollow	--
	Keeney	00		Newfield	14867
	Cuyler	13050		Enfield	--
	Truxton	13158		Jacksonville	14854
	East Homer	13056		Trumansburg	14886
	Cheningo	--	CO6	Cortland Area Out-	
	Union Valley	--		side the County; Ad-	
	Solon	--		jacent Counties;	
	Taylor	--		Just Beyond County	
	Cincinnatus	13040		Border	
	Willet	13863		Pitcher	13136
	Texas Valley	--		Locke	13092
	East Freetown	13055		Tully	13159
	Marathon	13803		Moravia	13118
	Hunt's Corners	--		DeRuyter	13052
	Messengerville	--		Genoa	13071
	Virgil	--	CO7	Syracuse	13200
	South Cortland	--		DeWitt	13214
	Harford	13784		Syracuse Vicinity	
	Harford			Marietta	13110
	Mills	13785		Skaneateles	13152
CO5	Tompkins County			Camillus	13031
	Groton	13073		Fayetteville	13066
	West Groton	--		Liverpool	13088
	North Lansing	--		Clay	13041
	Lake Ridge	--		North Syracuse	13212
	Lansingville	--	CO8	Cortland Area, More	
	Ludlowville	14862		Distant, Outside-	
	Peruville	--		County Towns	
	McLean	13102		Raquette Lake	13436
	Myers	14866		Hamilton County	
	South Lansing	14882		Afton (Chenango)	13730
	West Dryden	--		Interlaken	
	Freeville	13068		(Seneca)	14847
	Dryden	13053		Watkins Glen	
	Etna	13062		(Schuyler)	14891
	Cayuga Heights	--	CO9	Corning	14830
	Varna	--	C10	Ilion	13357
	Ellis	--	C11	Rome	13440
	Slaterville		C12	Ithaca	14850
	Springs	14881	C13	Auburn	13021

Zone, Location, Average Daily Attendance, and Zip Code Data for
Alfred Agricultural and Technical College (SUNY)

Zone or Sector	Location	Grades 7-12, ADA	Zip Code	Zone or Sector	Location	Grades 7-12, ADA	Zip Code
99A	Alfred	218	14802	14A	(continued)		
02A	Almond	182	14804		Henrietta	--	14467
	Bishopville	--	--		East Rochester	--	14445
03A	Arkport	261	14807		Fairport	--	14450
	Burns	--	--	01B	Alfred Station	--	14803
04A	Beachville	--	--	02B	Hornell	1,611	14843
	South Dansville	--	--		North Hornell	--	--
05A	Cumminsville	--	--	03B	Big Creek	--	--
	Dansville	955	14437		Stephen Mills	--	--
	Perkinsville	--	14529	04B	Haskinville	--	--
	Wayland	617	14572		Howard	--	--
06A	Scottsburg	--	14545	05B	Atlanta	--	14808
	Websters Crossing	--	14584		Cohocton	149	14826
	Springwater	--	14560		Wallace	--	14890
	Tabor Corners	--	--		Avoca	337	14809
07A	South Livonia	--	--	06B	North Cohocton	--	14868
	Conesus	--	14435		Ingleside	--	--
	Canadice	--	--		Beens	--	--
08A	Lakeville	--	14480		Wheeler	--	--
	South Lima	--	14558	07B	Woodville	--	--
	Livonia	596	14487		Naples	358	14512
	Hemlock	--	14466		Italy	--	--
	Bristol Springs	--	--		Italy Hill	--	--
09A	East Avon	--	--		Prattsburg	240	14873
	Lima	216	14485		South Pulteney	--	--
	West Bloomfield	481	14585		Urbana	--	--
	Allens Hill	--	--	08B	Vine Valley	--	--
	Vincent	--	--		Middlesex	337	14507
	Bristol Center	--	--		Guyanoga	--	--
	Cheshire	--	--		Branchport	--	14418
10A	Rush	469	14543		Crosby	--	--
	Honeyoye Falls	570	14472		Pulteney	--	14874
	Mendon	--	14506		Keuka	--	--
	North Bloomfield	--	--	09B	Cottage City	--	--
	Ionia	--	14475		Rushville	--	14544
	Bloomfield	--	14443		Potter	--	--
	Holcomb	--	14469		Yatesville	--	--
	West Rush	--	14587		Penn Yan	1,224	14527
11A	Canandaigua	1,460	19424		Keuka Park	--	14478
12A	Rochester	--	14600		Second Milo	--	--
	Rochester	--	14609 to 19	10B	Reeds Corners	--	--
					Gorham	401	14461
	Rochester	--	14622 to 27		Fergusons Corners	--	--
					Benton	--	--
	Newark	--	14513		Milo Center	--	--
	Pittsford	--	14534		Dresden	--	14441
					Himrod	--	14842
					Caywood	--	--

Zone or Sector	Location	Grades 7-12, ADA	Zip Code	Zone or Sector	Location	Grades 7-12, ADA	Zip Code
11B	Geneva	--	14456	11C	Ithaca	--	14850
12B	Auburn	--	13021	01D	Purdy Creek	--	--
13B	Syracuse	--	13201 to 25	03D	South Canisteo	--	--
02C	Canisteo	567	14823	04D	Cameron	--	14819
03C	Adrian	--	--		Hegesville	--	--
	Buena Vista	--	--		Jasper	182	14855
05C	Unionville	--	--	05D	Cameron Mills	--	14820
	Bath	996	14810		Rathbone	--	14875
	Kanona	--	14856		Woodhull	61	14898
	Risingville	--	--	06D	Addison	624	14801
06C	Hammondsport	470	14840		Freeman	--	--
	Pleasant Valley	--	--		Van Fleet	--	--
	Savona	181	14879		Borden	--	--
	Thurston	--	--	07D	Coopers Plains	--	14827
	Campbell	266	14821		Painted Post	--	14870
07C	Weston	--	--		Gang Mills	--	--
	Bradford	146	14815		Erwins	--	--
	Sonora	--	--		Presho	--	--
	East Campbell	--	--	08D	Lindley	--	14858
08C	Wayne	--	14893		South Corning	--	--
	Altay	--	--		East Corning	--	--
	Tyrone	--	14887		Riverside	--	--
	Monterey	--	--		Caton	--	--
	Hornby	--	--	09D	Big Flats	--	14814
09C	Dundee	507	14837		Sagetown	--	--
	Lakemont	--	--	10D	Horseheads	2,311	14845
	Rock Stream	--	14878		Elmira Heights	981	14903
	Reading Center	--	14876		West Elmira	--	--
	Post Creek	--	--		Southport	--	--
	Townsend	--	--		Webb Mills	--	--
	Moreland	--	--		Pine City	--	14871
	Beaver Dams	--	14812		Seeley Creek	--	--
	Chambers	--	--	11D	Corning	3,809	14830
10C	Logan	--	--	12D	Elmira	5,666	14900
	Sullivanville	--	--	03E	Greenwood	128	
	Hector	--	14841		Rexville	--	14877
	Pine Valley	--	14872	04E	Troupsburg	113	14885
	Valois	--	14888	02F	Andover	235	14806
	Millport	--	14864	03F	Independence	--	--
	Catharine	--	--		West Union	--	--
	Odessa	619	14869		Whitesville	123	14897
	Montour Falls	--	14865	02G	Elm Valley	--	--
	Watkins Glen	745	14891	03G	Hallsport	--	--
	Burdett	--	14818	04G	York Corners	--	--
	Bennettsburg	--	--		Shongo	--	--
				03H	Scio	255	14880
				04H	Pikeville	--	--
					Allentown	--	14707

(Continued)

Zone or Sector	Location	Grades 7-12, ADA	Zip Code	Zone or Sector	Location	Grades 7-12, ADA	Zip Code
05H	Richburg	190	14774	05J	Rushford	183	14777
	Bolivar	342	14715		Houghton	--	14744
	Little Genesee	--	14754	06J	Freedom	--	14065
	Alma	--	14708		Centerville	--	14029
06H	Ceres	--	14721		Fairview	--	--
	Obi	--	--		Farmersville	--	--
	Myrtle	--	--		Farmersville		
07H	Portville	--	14770		Station	--	14060
	Milldrove	--	--		Rawson	--	--
	Carroll	--	--	07J	Sandusky	--	14133
12H	Wellsville	1,042	14895		Elton	--	--
01I	Five Corners	--	--		Lime Lake	--	--
	Phillips				Machias	404	14101
	Creek	--	--		Franklin-		
03I	Belmont	217	14813		ville	--	14737
	Belvidere	--	--		Capiz	--	--
04I	Friendship	239	14739	08J	Chaffee	--	14030
	Nile	--	--		Yorkshire	--	14173
05I	Abbotts	--	--		Arcade	666	14009
	Black Creek	--	14714		Sardinia	--	14134
	North Cuba	--	--		Delevan	346	14042
	Cuba	452	14727		Devereaux	--	--
	West				Ashford	--	--
	Clarksville	--	14785	09J	Riceville	--	--
06I	Ischua	--	14746		West Valley	194	14171
	Hinsdale	275	14743		Ashford		
07I	Westons				Hollow	--	--
	Mills	--	14788		Plato	--	--
08I	Four Mile	--	--	10J	Eddyville	--	--
	Allegany	644	14706		Maples	--	--
	Humphrey				East Otto	--	14729
	Center	--	--		Springville	1,150	--
	Humphrey	--	--		East Concord	--	14055
	Sugartown	--	--		Glenwood	--	14069
09I	Ellicottville	374	14731	11J	Dunkirk	--	14048
	Great Valley	--	14741		Fredonia	--	14063
	Peth	--	--	03K	Allen		
	Orlando	--	--		Center	--	--
	Carrollton	--	--		Birdsall	--	14713
	Limestone	148	14753	04K	Short Tract	--	--
	Chipmunk	--	--	05K	Higgins	--	--
10I	Little Valley	250	14755		Hume	--	14745
	Elkdale	--	--		Fillmore	385	14735
	Salamanca	970	14779		Wisby	--	14789
11I	Olean	1,816	14760		Rossburg	--	14776
12I	Jamestown	--	14701		East Koy	--	--
02J	West Almond	--	--		Portageville	--	14536
03J	Angelica	162	14709		Hunt	--	14846
04J	Caneadea	--	14717	06K	Pike	--	14130
	Oramel	--	14765		Lamon	--	--
	Belfast	197	14711		Silver		
	Rockville	--	--		Springs	--	14550

Zone or Sec- tor	Location	Grades 7-12, ADA	Zip Code	Zone or Sec- tor	Location	Grades 7-12, ADA	Zip Code
07K	Eagle	--	--	06L	Brooks Grove	--	--
	Bliss	--	14024		Letchworth	605	--
	Wethersfield				Castile	--	14427
	Center	--	--		Ridge	--	--
	Wethersfield				Groveland		
	Springs	--	--		Station	--	--
	Gainesville	--	14066		Tuscarora	--	14562
	Hermitage	--	--		Groveland	--	14462
	Rock Glen	--	14540		Sonyea	--	14556
	South Warsaw	--	--	07L	East		
08K	Orangeville				Groveland	--	--
	Center	--	--		Cuylerville	--	14436
	Warsaw	561	14569		Leicester	--	14481
	North Java	--	14113		Mount Morris	366	14510
	Java Center	--	14082		Perry	731	14530
	Curriers	--	--		Perry Center	--	--
09K	Attica Center	--	--		Silver Lake	--	14549
	Dale	--	14039	08L	Geneseo	493	14454
	Varysburg	--	14167		Retsof	--	14539
	Johnsonburg	--	14084		Piffard	--	14533
	Strykersville	--	14145		Greigsville	--	--
	Java Village	--	14083		Peoria	--	--
	Holland	--	14080		Lagrange	--	--
	Protection	525	--	09L	Avon	428	14414
10K	Alexander	478	14005		Fowlersville	--	--
	Attica	787	14011		Ashantee	--	--
	Bennington	--	--		York	416	14592
	Folsomdale	--	--		Linwood	--	14486
	Wales Center	--	14169		Covington	--	--
	Blakeley	--	--		Pavilion		
	South Wales	--	14139		Center	--	--
11K	Buffalo	--	14200		Pavilion	462	14525
			to 26		Pearl Creek	--	--
12K	Lancaster	--	14086		West		
13K	Depew	--	14043		Middleburg	--	--
14K	North Tonawanda	--	14120		Verna	--	--
15K	Tonawanda	--	14150		Linden	--	--
16K	Lockport	--	14094		Wyoming	188	--
17K	Hamburg	--	14075	10L	North Rush	--	--
18K	Niagara Falls	--	14301		Garbutt	--	--
			to 03		Mumford	--	14511
03L	Garwoods	--	--		Caledonia	468	14423
	Canaseraga	194	14822		Lime Rock	--	--
04L	Swain	--	14884		LeRoy	728	14482
	Ossian	--	--		Stafford	--	14143
05L	Dalton	70	14836		East Bethany	--	14054
	Oakland	--	--		Bethany	--	--
	Nunda	392	14517	11L	Batavia	--	14020
	Byersville	--	--	12L	Brockport	--	14420
	West Sparta	--	--		Albion	--	14411

Zone, Location, and Zip Code Data for the State University of New
York, Alfred Agricultural and Technical College,
by Village and City

Zone or Sector	Location	Zip Code	Zone or Sector	Location	Zip Code
A01	Alfred	14802	A09	(continued)	
A02	Wells-ville	14895		Almond	14804
				West Almond	--
A03	Hornell	14843		Alfred	
A04	Olean	14760		Station	14803
A05	Corning	14830		Black Creek	14714
A06	Batavia	14020		Belvidere	--
A07	Auburn	13021		North Cuba	--
	Geneva	14456		Phillips	
	Newark	14513		Creek	--
	Canan-daigua	14424		Belmont	14813
				Friendship	14739
A08	Ithaca	14850		Cuba	14727
	Cortland	13045		Nile	--
A09	Allegany County			Scio	14880
	Wiscoy	14789		Andover	14806
	Rossburg	14776		Elm Valley	--
	Center-ville	14029		West Clarksville	14786
	Hume	14745		Obi	--
	Swain	14884		Richburg	14774
	Fillmore	14735		Stannards	--
	Garwoods	--		Allentown	14707
	Cana-seraga	14822		Bolivar	14715
				Hallsport	--
	Short Tract	--		Whitesville	14897
	Fairview	--		Shongo	--
	Houghton	14744		Alma	14708
	Birdsall	14713		Little Genesee	14754
	Rushford	14777		Ceres	14721
	Caneadea	14717	A10	Steuben County	
	Bishop-ville	--		Wayland	14572
	Oramel	14765		North Cohocton	14868
	Aristotle	--		Ingleside	--
	Belfast	14711		Atlanta	14808
	Rawson	--		Perkins-ville	14529
	Angelica	14709			

Zone or Sector	Location	Zip Code	Zone or Sector	Location	Zip Code
A10	(continued)		A10	(continued)	
	Patchin-ville	--		West Cameron	--
	Prattsburg	14873		Risingville	--
	Pulteney	14874		Thurston	--
	Cohocton	14826		Cameron	14819
	South Pulteney	--		South Canisteo	--
	Catawba	--		Coopers Plains	14827
	Keuka	--			
	South Dansville	--		Cameron Mills	14820
	Urbana	--		Painted Post	14870
	Wallace	14890			
	Wheeler	--		Gibson	--
	Hammonds-port	14840		Greenwood	14839
				Jasper	14855
	Burns	--		Rathbone	14875
	Haskin-ville	--		South Corning	14830
	Avoca	14809		Erwins	--
	Arkport	14807		Addison	14801
	Stephens Mills	--		Rexville	14877
				Presho	--
	Mitchells-ville	--		Woodhull	14898
	Rheime	--		Caton	--
	Kanona	14856		Freeman	--
	Howard	--		Troups-burg	14885
	North Urbana	--		Lindley	14858
	Towles-ville	--	A11	Livingston County, Major Towns	
	Bath	14810		Dansville	14437
	Sonora	--		Nunda	14517
	Bradford	14815		Mount Morris	14510
	Savona	14879			
	Canisteo	14823		Geneseo	14454
	Adrian	--		Avon	14414
	Hornby	--	A12	Warsaw	14569
	Campbell	14821		Perry	14530
	Hartsville	--		Arcade	14009

Other Zip Codes for New York State and the United States

Zone or Sector	Location	Zip Code	Zone or Sector	Location	Zip Code
	New York State				
20	Military	090	3	Utica (M-Z)	134
		to 098	4	Utica	135
21	New York	100	55	Watertown	136
2	Staten Island	103	6	Binghamton	
3	Bronx	104		(A-L)	137
4	Westchester		7	Binghamton	
	County	105		(M-Z)	138
25	White Plains	106	8	Binghamton	139
6	Yonkers	107	59	Buffalo (A-L)	140
7	New Rochelle	108	60	Buffalo (M-Z)	141
8	Suffern	109	1	Buffalo	142
9	Long Island		2	Niagara	
	Terminal	110		Falls	143
30	Long Island City	111	3	Rochester	
1	Brooklyn	112		(A-L)	144
2	Flushing	113	4	Rochester	
3	Jamaica	114		(M-Z)	145
4	Mineola	115	65	Rochester	146
35	Far Rockaway	116	6	Jamestown	147
6	Hicksville	{ 117	7	Elmira	148
7		118	8	Elmira	149
8	Riverhead	119			
9	Albany (A-L)	120			
40	Albany (M-Z)	121		Out of State	
1	Albany	122			
2	Schenectady	123	70	Maine*	0
3	Kingston	124	1	Pennsylvania*	15-19
4	Poughkeepsie	{ 125	2	Maryland*	2
5		126	3	Georgia*	3
6	Monticello	127	4	Ohio*	4
7	Glens Falls	128	5	Minnesota*	5
8	Plattsburgh	129	6	Kansas*	6
9	Syracuse (A-L)	130	7	Texas*	7
50	Syracuse (M-Z)	131	8	Colorado*	8
1	Syracuse	132	9	California*-	
2	Utica (A-L)	133		Alaska*	9

*The zip code number indicated includes other states in this zip code area.

E

ADDITIONAL
RESPONSES
TO
STAFF
QUESTIONNAIRES

Percent of College Staff Indicating Problem as Primary for the College Community

College Community Problem	Alfred Tech.		Auburn		Cortland		Cazenovia		Alfred University		Total
	Prof.	Auxil.	Prof.	Auxil.	Prof.	Auxil.	Prof.	Auxil.	Prof.	Auxil.	
Housing	64.1	64.7	25.9	21.4	13.4	24.1	21.9	4.1	62.2	71.4	41.0
Sewage	0.8	5.8	2.4	0.0	5.9	0.0	4.8	12.5	6.6	2.8	3.7
Students	0.8	2.9	0.0	7.1	4.4	17.2	2.4	0.0	0.0	0.0	2.4
Faculty	0.8	0.0	0.0	0.0	4.4	0.0	9.7	0.0	0.0	0.0	1.6
Racial	0.0	0.0	1.2	0.0	0.0	0.0	0.0	0.0	0.0	0.0	0.2
Zoning	8.5	0.0	3.7	0.0	7.4	6.9	12.2	16.6	6.6	0.0	6.5
Government	2.5	0.0	9.8	0.0	2.9	0.0	9.7	0.0	0.0	0.0	3.7
Entertainment	1.7	2.9	6.1	7.1	8.9	0.0	7.3	8.3	2.2	2.8	4.5
Poverty	0.0	0.0	2.4	0.0	8.9	3.4	0.0	0.0	0.0	0.0	1.8
Water	0.0	0.0	2.4	0.0	4.4	0.0	0.0	0.0	0.0	0.0	1.0
Community Spirit	0.8	0.0	3.7	7.1	0.0	0.0	0.0	0.0	8.8	8.5	1.0
High taxes	7.6	8.8	13.5	35.7	8.9	31.0	7.3	37.5	2.2	2.8	12.7
Tax source	5.1	0.0	1.2	0.0	1.4	0.0	0.0	0.0	0.0	0.0	2.0
Garbage	0.0	0.0	0.0	0.0	0.0	3.4	0.0	0.0	2.2	0.0	0.2
School	1.7	0.0	4.9	0.0	5.9	0.0	12.2	8.3	0.0	0.0	3.7
Police	0.0	0.0	0.0	0.0	0.0	0.0	0.0	0.0	0.0	0.0	0.0
Cultural	0.0	2.9	6.1	7.1	7.4	3.4	4.8	0.0	0.0	0.0	3.0
Industrial-shops	2.5	0.0	14.8	7.1	10.4	0.0	0.0	0.0	6.6	2.8	5.5
Transportation	1.7	0.0	0.0	0.0	1.4	6.9	4.8	12.5	0.0	2.8	2.2
Parking-other	0.8	11.7	1.2	0.0	2.9	3.4	2.4	0.0	2.2	5.7	2.6
Total	100.0	100.0	100.0	100.0	100.0	100.0	100.0	100.0	100.0	100.0	100.0
N	117	34	81	14	67	29	41	24	45	35	487

Note: College community problems as listed in the above table are housing, sewage disposal; student-townspeople relations; faculty-community relations; racial relations; zoning and land use planning; quality of local government; entertainment, recreation; poverty, unemployment, welfare; water supply and pollution; community spirit, social relations; high taxes; tax sources; garbage disposal; school system; police, fire protection; cultural activities; industrial development; shopping facilities; transportation; parking; other.

TABLE E.2

Spouse Employment, as Indicated by College Staff, in Percent

	Alfred Tech.		Cortland		Alfred University		Cazenovia		Auburn		Total
	Prof.	Auxil.	Prof.	Auxil.	Prof.	Auxil.	Prof.	Auxil.	Prof.	Auxil.	
Employed	48.6	72.4	43.6	61.9	38.1	62.9	69.7	100.0	48.4	100.0	55.2
Not employed	51.4	27.5	56.3	38.1	61.9	37.0	30.3	0.0	51.5	0.0	44.8
Total	100.0	100.0	100.0	100.0	100.0	100.0	100.0	100.0	100.0	100.0	100.0
N	107	29	55	21	42	27	33	18	64	8	404

Note: Details may not add up to totals because of rounding.

TABLE E.3

Community Attitude Toward the College, as Indicated by College Staff

Community Attitude	Alfred Tech.		Cortland		Alfred University		Cazenovia		Auburn		Total
	Prof.	Auxil.	Prof.	Auxil.	Prof.	Auxil.	Prof.	Auxil.	Prof.	Auxil.	
Very favorable	13.9	35.2	13.2	30.0	28.2	42.8	4.4	16.0	42.6	46.6	24.6
Fairly favorable	70.4	47.0	48.5	43.3	52.1	51.4	40.0	52.0	51.2	40.0	53.3
Neutral	9.5	14.7	22.0	13.3	13.0	2.8	8.8	24.0	4.8	0.0	11.3
Fairly unfavorable	6.0	0.0	14.7	13.3	6.5	2.8	44.4	8.0	1.2	13.3	10.1
Very unfavorable	0.0	2.9	1.4	0.0	0.0	0.0	2.2	0.0	0.0	0.0	0.6
Total	100.0	100.0	100.0	100.0	100.0	100.0	100.0	100.0	100.0	100.0	100.0
N	115	34	68	30	46	35	45	25	82	15	495

Note: Details may not add up to totals because of rounding.

TABLE-F.1

Student Preferences on College Location Relative to Commutation Possibility, in Percent

Commutation Possibility	Alfred Tech.	Cortland	Alfred University	Cazenovia	Auburn	Total
Favored	23.8	15.7	19.0	21.3	61.5	26.6
Not favored	76.2	84.3	81.1	78.7	38.5	73.4
Total	100.0	100.0	100.0	100.0	100.0	100.0
N	151	121	95	47	78	492

<u>Note</u>: The question was asked as follows: "All things considered, what is best for your goals? One, a college like this <u>within</u> commuting distance of your home, or two, a college like this <u>outside</u> commuting distance of your home?" Details may not add up to totals because of rounding.

TABLE F.2

Students' Second Reason for Attending a Particular College, in Percent

Reason	Alfred Tech.	Cortland	Alfred University	Cazenovia	Auburn	Total
Reputation	13.5	14.7	10.8	14.9	10.1	12.8
Commutation	6.8	3.5	3.2	2.1	16.5	6.4
Near home	12.2	6.0	9.7	6.4	7.6	8.9
Low cost	12.8	26.7	8.6	0.0	34.2	17.6
Away from home	14.9	18.1	15.1	12.8	5.1	13.9
Parent	7.4	2.6	11.8	14.9	5.1	7.5
Counselor	15.5	7.8	15.1	6.4	0.0	10.1
Other	16.8	20.6	25.8	42.6	21.5	22.8
Total	100.0	100.0	100.0	100.0	100.0	100.0
N	148	116	93	47	79	483

Note: The following question was asked: "Underline your two major reasons for attending this college, then enter 1 and 2 (in order of importance) below: (1) reputation of the college and curriculum, (2) within commuting distance, (3) can't commute, but fairly near home, (4) low cost, (5) location away from home, (6) athletic program, (7) advice of high school counselor, (8) parents or relatives, (9) counselor at college, (10) social reasons, (11) I like this area and climate, (12) other [specify]." Parts 6, 9, 10, 11, and 12 were combined in the above table.

TABLE F.3

Employers of College Students, in Percent

Employer	Alfred Tech.	Cortland	Alfred University	Cazenovia	Auburn	Total
College	15.7	10.7	21.1	22.9	7.7	14.9
Firm in town	0.0	6.6	2.1	2.1	25.6	6.3
Firm out of town	8.5	2.5	4.2	0.0	11.5	5.9
Self-employed and odd jobs	5.2	6.6	11.6	6.3	10.3	7.6
Unemployed	70.6	73.8	61.1	68.8	44.9	65.3
Total	100.0	100.0	100.0	100.0	100.0	100.0
N	153	122	95	48	78	

Note: The following question was asked: "While attending college are you: (check one) (1) employed by the college, (2) employed by a noncollege firm in the college town, (3) employed by a noncollege firm outside the college town, (4) self-employed in specific work (typing, etc.) for various people, (5) work at odd jobs for various people (handyman, etc.), or (6) unemployed." Parts 4 and 5 were combined in the above table.

TABLE G.1

Average Annual Salary of Staff at the State
University of New York, Alfred Agricultural and
Technical College, 1968, in Dollars

Faculty	10,668
Administration	11,030
Technical staff	6,665
Stenographers	4,948
Typists and clerical	4,452
Maintenance staff	5,598

Source: State University of New York, Alfred
Agricultural and Technical College, Office of the
Assistant to the President (letter), 1968.

TABLE G.2

New Residential and Commercial Construction,
Alfred Village, 1961-67, in Dollars

Year	Actual Valuation	Year	Actual Valuation
1961	92,600	1965	306,100
1962	90,800	1966	43,600
1963	144,700	1967	107,700
1964	109,700		

Note: Equalization rates for 1961-65 were at
34 percent; for 1965-67, at 80 percent.

Source: Herman Sicker, Mayor of Alfred Village, letter to Cornell University, dated September
17, 1968 (in files of the village).

TABLE G.3

New Residential and Commercial Construction,
City of Cortland, 1960-65, in Dollars

Year	Residential	Commercial	Total
1960	427,000	358,000	785,000
1961	491,000	143,000	634,000
1962	329,000	219,000	548,000
1963	668,000	330,000	998,000
1964	372,000	642,000	1,014,000
1965	267,000	803,000	1,070,000

Source: Data based on building permits on record in the City Clerk's office.

TABLE G.4

Average Annual Salary of Staff at the
State University of New York,
College at Cortland, 1967-68, in Dollars

Faculty-administrative	11,700
Secretarial-clerical	5,270
Maintenance and operation	5,580

Source: State University of New York, College at Cortland, Finance Office, 1968.

BOOKS

Bauer, Raymond A., ed., _et al_. _Social Indicators_.
   Cambridge: Massachusetts Institute of Technology Press, 1966.

Becker, Gary S. _Human Capital_. New York: Columbia
   University Press, 1964.

Bourne, Dorothy D., and James R. Bourne. _Thirty
   Years of Change in Puerto Rico, A Case Study of
   Ten Selected Rural Areas_. New York: Frederick
   A. Praeger, 1966.

Chapin, F. Stuart, Jr. _Urban Land Use Planning_. Urbana, Ill.: University of Illinois Press, 1965.

_____, and Shirley F. Weiss, eds. _Urban Growth
   Dynamics: In a Regional Cluster of Cities_.
   New York: John Wiley and Sons, Inc., 1962.

Christaller, Walter. _Central Places in Southern
   Germany_. Translated by Carlisle W. Baskin.
   Englewood Cliffs, N.J.: Prentice Hall, 1966.

Clark, Burton R. _Educating the Expert Society_. San
   Francisco: Chandler Publishing Company, 1962.

Dahl, Robert A. _Who Governs? Democracy and Power
   in an American City_. New Haven: Yale University Press, 1961.

Dickinson, Robert E. _City, Region, and Regionalism_.
   New York: Oxford University Press, 1947.

Dror, Yehezkel. _Public Policymaking Reexamined_.
   San Francisco: Chandler Publishing Company,
   1968.

Eckstein, Otto. Water Resource Development: The
    Economics of Project Evaluation. Cambridge,
    Mass.: Harvard University Press, 1958.

Fowler, Irving A. Local Industrial Structures, Eco-
    nomic Power, and Community Welfare, Thirty
    Small New York State Cities, 1930-1950. Totowa,
    N.J.: Bedminster Press, 1964.

Friedmann, John. Regional Development Policy, A
    Case Study of Venezuela. Cambridge: Massachu-
    setts Institute of Technology Press, 1966.

Friedmann, John R. P. The Spatial Structure of Eco-
    nomic Development in the Tennessee Valley, A
    Study in Regional Planning. Chicago: Univer-
    sity of Chicago Press, 1955.

Goldsen, Rose K., Morris Rosenberg, Robin M. Williams,
    Jr., and Edward A. Suchman. What College Stu-
    dents Think. Princeton, N.J.: Van Nostrand
    Company, Inc., 1960.

Green, Raymond J. The Impact of the Central Business
    District on the Municipal Budget. Washington,
    D.C.: Urban Land Institute, 1962.

Halsey, A. H., Jean Floud, and C. Arnold Anderson,
    eds. Education, Economy, and Society. New
    York: Free Press of Glencoe, 1962.

Harbison, Frederick, and Charles A. Myers. Educa-
    tion, Manpower, and Economic Growth, Strategies
    in Human Resource Development. New York:
    McGraw Hill, 1964.

Haveman, Robert H. Water Resource Investment and
    the Public Interest. Nashville, Tenn.: Vander-
    bilt University Press, 1965.

Holmes, Lowell D. Anthropology, An Introduction.
    New York: Ronald Press Company, 1965.

Hoover, Edgar M. The Location of Economic Activity.
    New York: McGraw Hill, 1963.

Isard, Walter. <u>Methods of Regional Analysis: An</u>
    <u>Introduction to Regional Science</u>. Cambridge:
    Massachusetts Institute of Technology Press,
    1960.

Jacob, Philip E. <u>Changing Values in College: An Ex-</u>
    <u>ploratory Study of the Impact of College Teach-</u>
    <u>ing</u>. New York: Harper, 1957.

Johnson, Harry M. <u>Sociology, A Systematic Introduc-</u>
    <u>tion</u>. New York: Harcourt, Brace, and World,
    Inc., 1960.

Kneller, George F. <u>Education and Economic Thought</u>.
    New York: John Wiley and Sons, Inc., 1968.

Losch, August. <u>The Economics of Location</u>. New
    Haven, Conn.: Yale University Press, 1954.

Machlup, Fritz. <u>The Production and Distribution of</u>
    <u>Knowledge in the United States</u>. Princeton,
    N.J.: Princeton University Press, 1962.

McKean, Roland N. <u>Efficiency in Government Through</u>
    <u>Systems Analysis</u>. New York: John Wiley and
    Sons, Inc., 1958.

Miller, Delbert C. <u>Handbook of Research Design and</u>
    <u>Social Measurement</u>. New York: David McKay
    Company, Inc., 1964.

Moore, John R. <u>The Economic Impact of TVA</u>. Knox-
    ville: University of Tennessee Press, 1967.

Moore, Wilbert E. <u>The Impact of Industry</u>. "Moderni-
    zation of Traditional Societies Series." Engle-
    wood Cliffs, N.J.: Prentice Hall, Inc., 1965.

Novick, David. <u>Program Budgeting, Program Analysis</u>
    <u>and the Federal Budget</u>. A Rand Corporation
    Study. Washington, D.C.: U.S. Government
    Printing Office, 1965.

Parnes, Herbert S. <u>Forecasting Educational Needs</u>
    <u>for Educational and Social Development</u>. Paris:

Organization for Economic Cooperation and Development, 1962.

Parsons, Talcott. "General Theory in Sociology." Sociology Today, Problems and Prospects. Robert K. Merton, Leonard Broom, and Leonard S. Cottrell, Jr., eds. New York: Harper and Row, 1959.

Rossi, Peter H., and Robert A. Dentler. The Politics of Urban Renewal. New York: Free Press of Glencoe, 1961.

Shevsky, Eshref, and Wendell Bell. Social Area Analysis. Stanford, Calif.: Stanford University Press, 1955.

Thompson, John H., ed. Geography of New York State. Syracuse: Syracuse University Press, 1966.

Thompson, Wilbur R. A Preface to Urban Economics. Baltimore: Johns Hopkins Press, 1968.

Vidich, A. J., and J. Bensman. Small Town in Mass Society. Princeton, N.J.: Princeton University Press, 1958.

Warren, Roland L. Studying Your Community. New York: Free Press, 1965.

Weber, Adna N. The Growth of Cities in the Nineteenth Century. Ithaca, N.Y.: Cornell University Press, 1963.

Yamamoto, Kaoru, comp. The College Student and His Culture: An Analysis. Boston: Houghton Mifflin, 1968.

GOVERNMENTAL PUBLICATIONS
AND RESEARCH REPORTS

American Academy of Political and Social Science. Political Intelligence for America's Future. ("The Annals," Vol. CCCXXCVIII.) Philadelphia:

American Academy of Political and Social Science, March, 1970.

Appalachian Regional Commission. <u>A Regional Investment Plan for the Appalachian Region of New York State</u>. Albany: Appalachian Regional Commission, State of New York, 1967.

Armacost, Peter H. "The Student and His Public Image, The Dean Speaks Out." Bulletin No. 2. Champaign, Ill.: National Association of Student Personnel Administrators, April, 1967.

Blair, Lachlan. "College and Community, A Study of Interaction in Chicago." Chicago: Department of Urban Planning, University of Illinois, 1967. (Mimeographed.)

Boston University Metrocenter. "The Urban University and the Urban Community, Problems of Town and Gown." Seminar No. 4. Boston: Boston University, 1966.

Breese, Gerald, comp. <u>The Impact of Large Installations on Nearby Areas</u>. Prepared by the Bureau of Urban Research, Princeton University. Port Hueneme, Calif.: U.S. Naval Civil Engineering Laboratory, 1965.

Brick, Michael. <u>The Need for Higher Education Facilities in the Mohawk Valley</u>. New York: Teachers College, Columbia University, 1965.

Bureau of Statistical Services, State Education Department. <u>Annual Educational Summary, New York State, 1964-65</u>. Albany: State Education Department, 1966.

Clavel, Pierre. "The Genesis of the Planning Process: Experts and Citizen Boards." Unpublished Ph.D. dissertation, Cornell University, 1966.

Committee for Economic Development. <u>Community Economic Development Efforts, Five Case Studies</u>. New York: Frederick A. Praeger, 1966.

Crain, Clark N. A Prediction Model for Population
    Impact by Military Installations, Parts I and
    II. Operations Analysis Standby Unit, Univer-
    sity of Denver. Springfield, Va.: U.S. Depart-
    ment of Commerce, Clearinghouse for Federal
    Scientific and Technical Information, Sills
    Building, 1959.

Doody, Frances S. The Immediate Economic Impact of
    Higher Education in New England. Boston: Bu-
    reau of Business Research, Boston University,
    1961.

Gerard, Roy. Impact I, Economic Impact of Le Moyne
    College on the Syracuse, New York Community.
    Syracuse: Le Moyne College, 1962.

Goldsmith, William Woodbridge. "The Impact of the
    Tourism and Travel Industry on a Developing Re-
    gional Economy: The Puerto Rican Case." Unpub-
    lished Ph.D. dissertation, Cornell University,
    Department of City and Regional Planning, 1966.

Graduate School of Public Affairs, State University
    of New York. Metropolitan and Area Problems:
    News and Digest. Vol. VII, No. 5. Albany:
    State University of New York, 1964.

Hirsch, Werner Z. Decision Tools for Education.
    Los Angeles: Institute of Government and Public
    Affairs, 1964.

_____, Elbert W. Segelhorst, and Morton J. Marcus.
    Spillover of Public Education Costs and Benefits.
    Los Angeles: University of California, Institute
    of Government and Public Affairs, 1964.

Hogan, Lloyd L. Measurement of the Ability of Local
    Governments to Finance Local Public Services.
    Albany: Bureau of Educational Finance Research,
    State Education Department, University of the
    State of New York, 1967.

Jones, Barclay G., and Jon T. Lang. Studies in Re-
    gional Development: Population, Activities,

and Incomes in Chenango, Delaware, and Otsego
Counties. Ithaca: Cornell University, New
York State College of Agriculture, 1965.

_____, Richard L. Ragatz, and Phaichitr Uathavikul.
Regional Analysis for Economic Development: A
Demonstration Study of Schoharie County.
Ithaca, N.Y.: Cornell University Center for
Housing and Environmental Studies, Division of
Urban Studies, 1964.

Larson, Gustav E. Can Our Small Towns Survive?
Washington, D.C.: U.S. Department of Agriculture, Resource Development Aid, July, 1960.

Lee, Douglass B., Jr. Analysis and Description of
Residential Segregation: An Application of
Centrographic Techniques to the Study of the
Spatial Distribution of Ethnic Groups in Cities.
Ithaca, N.Y.: Cornell University, Center for
Housing and Environmental Studies, Division of
Urban Studies, 1968.

_____. "Urban Models and Household Disaggrega-
tion, An Empirical Problem in Urban Research."
Unpublished Ph.D. dissertation, Cornell University, Department of City and Regional Planning,
1968.

Lichfield, Nathaniel. Cost-Benefit Analysis in Urban
Redevelopment. Berkeley: University of California, Institute of Business and Economic Research, 1962.

Lindsey, Fred D. What New Industrial Jobs Mean to a
Community. Washington, D.C.: Economic Research
Department, Chamber of Commerce of the United
States, 1965.

Moore, Vincent J. Buffalo-Amherst Urban Impact Study
Design. Albany: New York State Office of
Planning Coordination, 1968.

National Zip Code Directory. Washington, D.C.: Zip
Code Publishing Company, 1967.

New York State Department of Commerce. Business Fact Book, 1967-68. Albany: Part I, Business and Manufacturing, Syracuse Area, 1968; Part II, Population and Housing, 1963.

New York State Division of the Budget. "Community Colleges, Budget Analysis 1965-1966." Unpublished report. Albany: State University of New York, 1966.

_____. "The Executive Budget, Fiscal Year April 1, 1968 to March 31, 1969." Submitted by Nelson A. Rockefeller, Governor. Albany: New York State Division of the Budget, 1968.

Parsons, Kermit C. "The Potential Demand for Higher Education in the Chemung Valley Region to 1985." A Report to the Executive Committee of the Chemung Valley Study of Higher Education. Ithaca, N.Y.: 1968. (Mimeographed.)

Perloff, Harvey S., and Vera W. Dodds. "How a Region Grows, Area Development in the U.S. Economy." Supplementary Paper No. 17. New York: Committee for Economic Development, 1963.

Peterson, Richard E. The Scope of Organized Student Protest in 1964-65. Princeton, N.J.: Educational Testing Service, 1966.

Rondinelli, Dennis A. "Establishing a Community College: The Public Decision Process, A Case Study." Unpublished paper, City and Regional Planning Department, Cornell University, 1966.

Singletary, Otis A., ed. American Universities and Colleges. Tenth edition. Washington, D.C.: American Council on Education, 1968.

Skinner, Albert T. "Auburn Community College, Report of the President for the Year July 1, 1965 to June 30, 1966." Auburn, N.Y.: Board of Education of the Auburn City School District, 1966.

Starbuck, William H.   "Evaluation and Prospectus:
    School of Business Administration, Clarion State
    College." Ithaca, N.Y.: Cornell University,
    1968. (Mimeographed.)

State Education Department, Bureau of Statistical
    Services. Annual Educational Summary. Albany:
    University of the State of New York, 1965.

_____, Division of Higher Education. Going to
    College in New York State. Albany: University
    of the State of New York, 1965.

State of New York. Report of the Temporary Commission
    on the Need for a State University. Albany:
    Williams Press, Inc., 1948.

_____. The Executive Budget, Volume 1, 1949-50,
    1959-60, and 1968-69. Albany: State of New
    York, 1949, 1959, and 1968.

State University of New York, College at Cortland.
    General Catalog, 1968-69. Cortland: State Uni-
    versity of New York, 1968.

_____. The Master Plan. Albany: State University
    of New York, 1960.

_____. The Regents Tentative Statewide Plan for
    the Expansion and Development of Higher Educa-
    tion, 1964. Albany: State Education Depart-
    ment, 1965.

Thompson, Ronald B. Enrollment Projections for Higher
    Education 1961-1978. American Association of
    Collegiate Registrars and Admissions Officers.
    Washington D.C.: American Council on Education,
    1961.

Tiebout, Charles M. The Community Economic Base
    Study. New York: Committee for Economic Devel-
    opment, 1962.

Uathavikul, Phaichitr. "Decision Theory and Regional
    Economic Growth: A Model of Resource Utilization

in the Context of Regional Opportunity Loss."
Unpublished Ph.D. dissertation, Cornell University, Department of City and Regional Planning,
1966.

U.S. Bureau of the Census. U.S. Census of Popula-
tion: 1960. Volume I. Characteristics of the
Population, Part 34, New York. Washington, D.C.:
U.S. Government Printing Office, 1963.

U.S. Department of Health, Education, and Welfare.
Toward a Social Report. Washington, D.C.: U.S.
Government Printing Office, 1969.

U.S. Office of Education. Total Enrollment in Institutions, 1959-60. Washington, D.C.: U.S. Government Printing Office, 1960.

Vernon, Raymond. The Changing Economic Function of
the Central City. New York: Committee for
Economic Development, 1959.

Weisbrod, Burton A. External Benefits of Public Edu-
cation. Princeton, N.J.: Industrial Relations
Section, Princeton University, Research Report
Series No. 105, 1964.

Wells, Ralph G., ed. The Economic Value of Educational Institutions to New England. New England
Council Education Study. Boston: Bureau of
Business Research, Boston University, College
of Business Administration, 1951.

                        ARTICLES

American Association of University Professors. "The
Economic Status of the Profession," AAUP Bulletin, XLVII, 2 (1961).

Becker, Gary S. "Underinvestment in College Education," The American Economic Review, L (May,
1960).

Bonner, Ernest R.   "The Economic Impact of a University on Its Local Community," _Journal of the American Institute of Planners_, XXXIV (September, 1968).

Brunner, Edmund de S., and T. Lynn Smith.   "Village Growth and Decline, 1930-1940," _Rural Sociology_, IX (1944).

Dost, Jeanne.   "Reassessment of the School Location Problem: A Multifunctional Role for the School in the Urban Environment," _Annals of Regional Science_, II, 2 (December, 1968).

Esser, George H., Jr.   "Urban Growth and Municipal Services," _Popular Government_ (November, 1956, and April, 1957).

Fischer, John.   "Survival U: Prospectus for a Really Relevant University," "The Easy Chair," _Harper's Magazine_ (September, 1969).

Friedmann, John.   "The Strategy of Deliberate Urbanization," _Journal of the American Institute of Planners_, XXXIV, 6 (November, 1968).

Hurtt, Spencer M.   "The Impact of Institutional Growth on Urban Land Use," _Urban Land_ (January, 1968).

Huxtable, Ada Louise.   "The State Office Building Dilemma," _The New York Times_, Section 2, Architecture, November 2, 1969.

Kariel, Herbert G.   "Student Enrollment and Spatial Interaction," _Annals of Regional Science_, II, 2 (December, 1968).

Kraushaar, John L.   "How Much of an Asset Is a College?" _College and University Business_, XXXVI, 2 (February, 1964).

Maass, Arthur.   "Benefit-Cost Analysis: Its Relevance to Public Investment Decisions," _Quarterly Journal of Economics_, XXC, 2 (May, 1966).

McConnell, Harold. "Spatial Variability of College
    Enrollment as a Function of Migration Potential,"
    The Professional Geographer, XVII (1965).

Miller, Delbert C. "Town and Gown: The Power Struc-
    ture of a University Town," American Journal of
    Sociology, LXVIII, 4 (January, 1963).

Mischaikow, Michael K., and Thaddeus H. Spratlen.
    "A Regional Impact Model for Measuring the
    Flow-of-Funds and Income Effect Generated by
    Institutions of Higher Learning," Annals of Re-
    gional Science, I (December, 1967).

Parsons, Kermit C. "Universities and Cities: The
    Terms of Truce Between Them," Journal of Higher
    Education, XXXIV (April, 1963).

Schultz, Theodore. "Investment in Human Capital,"
    The American Economic Review, LI (March, 1961).

Stewart, John R. "The 'Gravitation,' or Geographical
    Power of a College," Bulletin of the American
    Association of University Professors, XXVII
    (1941).

"The Campus Boom: A New College a Week," Newsweek
    (February 20, 1967).

"The Troubled American, A Special Report on the
    White Majority," Newsweek (October 6, 1969).

Wellin, Paul. "A Guttman Scale for Measuring Women's
    Neighborliness," The American Journal of Soci-
    ology, LIX (1953).

Winstead, Warren J. "The Economic Impact of a New
    University upon Its Community," Investment
    Dealers Digest (November 17, 1967).

Zelinsky, Wilbur. "Changes in Geographical Patterns
    of Rural Population in the United States, 1790-
    1960," The Geographic Review, LII (1962).

NEWSPAPERS

Alfred Reporter, December, 1969.

Ithaca Journal, January 4-March 6, 1969; April 9,
      1969.

The New York Times, January 21, 1968; March 23, 1969;
      November 16, 1969.

OTHER SOURCES

Center for Air Photo Studies, Cornell University.
      Ithaca, N.Y.: New York State Land Use Study.
      July, 1968. Files of the Center.

Johnston, Orville. "Staff Salary Study." State
      University of New York, Alfred Agricultural and
      Technical College. Office of the Assistant to
      the President. September 17, 1968. Files of
      the college.

"Map of New York State." Humble Oil and Refining
      Company. Convent Station, N.J.: General Draft-
      ing Company, Inc., 1967.

Sicker, Herman. Mayor of Alfred Village. Letter to
      Cornell University. September 17, 1968. "Con-
      struction in the Village of Alfred, 1961-67."
      Files of the village.

U.S. Geological Survey. Washington, D.C. Map of
      Alfred, New York, 1964.

RESOURCE
PERSONS
FOR
MULTICOLLEGE
SURVEY

Bagley, Clarence H. Director of Institutional Plan-
    ning. State University of New York, Cortland,
    N.Y.

Baisler, A.W. President. Jamestown Community Col-
    lege, Jamestown, N.Y.

Brown, Foster S. President. St. Lawrence University,
    Canton, N.Y.

Buxton, Chester L. President. Paul Smiths College
    of Arts and Sciences, Paul Smiths, N.Y.

Clifford, P. C. Director of Research. State Univer-
    sity of New York Agricultural and Technical Col-
    lege at Delhi, Delhi, N.Y.

Eckel, Rhea M. President. Cazenovia College, Caze-
    novia, N.Y.

Eisenhart, Charles R. President. Adirondack Commu-
    ity College, Glens Falls, N.Y.

Eskow, Seymour. President. Rockland Community Col-
    lege, Suffern, N.Y.

French, Albert E. President. State University of
    New York, Agricultural and Technical College at
    Canton, Canton, N.Y.

Garber, Herbert. Director of Institutional Studies.
    State University. of New York, Oswego, N.Y.

Gray, Irma E. Assistant to the President. Ulster
    County Community College, Stone Ridge, N.Y.

─────────────

    Note: Community colleges listed are part of
the State University of New York.

301

Gregg, William L. President. Fulton-Montgomery Community College, Johnstown, N.Y.

Grego, Richard F. President. Sullivan County Community College, South Fallsburg, N.Y.

Gutmann, Frank E. Director of Business Operations. Clarkson College of Technology, Potsdam, N.Y.

Hallam, Kenneth. Director of Institutional Research. State University of New York, New Paltz, N.Y.

Holland, Albert E. President. Hobart and William Smith Colleges, Geneva, N.Y.

Jenner, Walter. Research Assistant. Office of Institutional Research. State University of New York, Plattsburgh, N.Y.

Johnston, Orville. Assistant to the President. State University of New York, Alfred Agricultural and Technical College, Alfred, N.Y.

Klinger, Wallace R. Acting President. Hartwick College, Oneonta, N.Y.

Lester, Virginia L. Director of Educational Research. Skidmore College, Saratoga Springs, N.Y.

Martens, Freda R. H. Director of Institutional Research. Dutchess Community College, Poughkeepsie, N.Y.

McLaughlin, Jean. Director of Personnel. Vassar College, Poughkeepsie, N.Y.

McLaughlin, R. President. Herkimer County Community College, Ilion, N.Y.

McNally, James L. Director of Institutional Research. State University of New York, Geneseo, N.Y.

McVean, James E. President. Jefferson Community College, Watertown, N.Y.

Miller, A. Jerome. Registrar. St. Bonaventure University, St. Bonaventure, N.Y.

Nasca, Donald. Director of Research. State University of New York, Brockport, N.Y.

Netzer, Royal F. President. State University of New York, Oneonta, N.Y.

Newsom, Walter. Director of Institutional Research. Ithaca College, Ithaca, N.Y.

Novak, Robert T. President. State University of New York, Orange County Community College, Middletown, N.Y.

Paine, S. W. President. Houghton College, Houghton, N.Y.

Randall, Clarence B. Vice President for Business Affairs. St. Lawrence University, Canton, N.Y.

Schultz, Charles H. Assistant to the President. Alfred University, Alfred, N.Y.

Schultze, L. W. Director of Institutional Studies. State University of New York, Fredonia, N.Y.

Simpson, Alan. President. Vassar College, Poughkeepsie, N.Y.

Skinner, Albert T. President. Auburn Community College, Auburn, N.Y.

Smith, R. G. Special Assistant to the President. Colgate University, Hamilton, N.Y.

Smith, Stanton B. Assistant to the President. State University of New York, Agricultural and Technical College, Canton, N.Y.

Walsh, Garnar. Director of Institutional Research. State University of New York, Potsdam, N.Y.

Wheeler, Marianne. Administrative Assistant to the
    President. Corning Community College, Corning,
    N.Y.

Whipple, Royson N. President. State University of
    New York, Agricultural and Technical College
    at Morrisville, Morrisville, N.Y.

Young, Eva L. Administrative Assistant to the Presi-
    dent. State University of New York, Genesee
    Community College, Batavia, N.Y.

Young, Kenneth E. President. State University of
    New York, Cortland College, Cortland, N.Y.

JULIAN MARTIN LAUB is a Principal Urban Planner in the New York State Department of Environmental Conservation. He received a B.A. in Engineering from New York University in 1951, an M.S from Alfred University in 1965 and a Ph.D. from Cornell University in 1970.

After working in industry for General Motors, and Eastern Engineering and Planning Consultants, Dr. Laub joined the faculty of the State University of New York, Agricultural and Technical College at Alfred. From 1959 to 1966 he taught architectural and environmental technology, and authored a book in this area. Dr. Laub entered the Department of City and Regional Planning at Cornell University in 1966, and while completing his doctorate in that field, he was engaged as a visiting professor in the College of Architecture, Art, and Planning and as a Research Associate in the Department of Rural Sociology.

Dr. Laub is a member of The American Institute of Planners, The New York State Society of Professional Engineers, and The American Academy of Political and Social Science.